MONAGHAN

The Irish Revolution, 1912–23
Monaghan

Terence Dooley

FOUR COURTS PRESS

Set in 10.5 on 12.5 point Ehrhardt for
FOUR COURTS PRESS LTD
7 Malpas Street, Dublin 8, Ireland
fourcourtspress.ie
and in North America for
FOUR COURTS PRESS
c/o ISBS, 920 N.E. 58th Street, Suite 300, Portland, OR 97213.

© Terence Dooley and Four Courts Press 2017

A catalogue record for this title
is available from the British Library.

ISBN 978–1–84682–616–0

All rights reserved. No part of this publication may be reproduced,
stored in or introduced into a retrieval system, or transmitted,
in any form or by any means (electronic, mechanical,
photocopying, recording or otherwise), without the
prior written permission of both the copyright
owner and the publisher of this book.

Printed in England
by TJ International, Padstow, Cornwall.

Contents

	LIST OF ILLUSTRATIONS	vii
	LIST OF ABBREVIATIONS	ix
	ACKNOWLEDGMENTS	xi
	The Irish Revolution, 1912–23 series	xiii
1	Frontier county: Monaghan in 1912	1
2	Home rulers and rebels, 1912–14	19
3	'It's a great war for the farmer'	32
4	'The Dublin Insurrection of 1916 came and went without a ripple'	45
5	'The Sinn Féin party is gaining strength in all parts', 1917–18	58
6	'Private vengeance exacted its toll over cover of civil turmoil', 1919–21	73
7	'The best interests of the county demand ratification of the Treaty': Civil War, 1922–3	101
8	'Is everything we love gone forever': the Big House, 1912–23	111
9	Revolution?	123
	NOTES	134
	SELECT BIBLIOGRAPHY	152
	INDEX	161

Illustrations

PLATES

1. Michael E. Knight, his father George Knight and brother, George Walter Knight.
2. Thomas Toal and his wife, Susan.
3. Thomas McGahon.
4. Edward Kelly.
5. Bernard O'Rourke.
6. Charles Laverty.
7. Household staff at Glaslough, taken at golden wedding anniversary celebration of Sir John and Lady Constance Leslie, 1905.
8. Sir John and Lady Constance Leslie and family, Glaslough, 1905.
9. Banner of Ballybay LOL No. 211.
10. Banner of Aghabog AOH.
11. Monaghan UVF officers at Knockballymore training camp, January 1914.
12. Monaghan Ulster Volunteer Nursing Corps, Newbliss, 28 July 1914.
13. Edward Carson at Newbliss House, 28 July 1914.
14. UVF demonstration, Newbliss, 28 July 1914.
15. 'Orange Proclamation': postcard issued in the aftermath of the Larne gun-running incident, 1914.
16. Monaghan UVF badge.
17. Monaghan senior football team, Ulster champions 1916.
18. General Owen O'Duffy.
19. James Vogan and other gamekeepers on Leslie estate at Glaslough.
20. Fr Lorcan Ó Ciaráin.
21. Smithboro Loyal Orange Lodge Brass Band, c.1920.
22. Funeral of Lt.-Col. Gerald Madden, 12 November 1915.
23. Monaghan RIC discovering a poitín still near Carrickmacross, c.1918.
24. Carrickmacross Comrades of the Great War, c.1920.
25. Unidentified IRA volunteer outside Carrickmacross RIC barracks, 1921.
26. Mary Nolan, president of south Monaghan Cumann na mBan.
27. General Dan Hogan.
28. Castleshane House.
29. William Black of Gola House, Ballyleck.
30. Funeral of William and Robert Fleming, St Maeldoid's Church of Ireland cemetery, Castleblayney, March, 1921.
31. Free State soldiers at the Ballybay crossroads, outside Carrickmacross, 1922.

32 Unidentified Monaghan IRA volunteers.
33 Patrick McCarville.

Credits

23, 24, 25, 26, 31, 32 Carrickmacross Workhouse; 29 Robert Devine; 7, 8, 19 Sammy Leslie; 1 George Knight; 22 Johnny Madden, Hilton Park; 2, 4, 9, 10–18, 21, 27, 30 Monaghan County Museum; 6 David Murray; 5 O'Rourke family; 28 Rosanna Watts.

MAPS

1	Places mentioned in the text	xiv
2	Monaghan's Protestant population	2
3	Parliamentary constituencies in 1910	4
4	Local government divisions	5
5	UVF companies in Monaghan	22
6	Distribution of the Crown forces	83

Abbreviations

AC	*Anglo-Celt*
AOH	Ancient Order of Hibernians
ASU	Active Service Unit
BMH	Bureau of Military History
Cd, Cmd	Command Paper (British parliamentary papers)
CI	County Inspector, RIC
CO	Colonial Office, TNA
DD	*Dundalk Democrat*
DÉ	Dáil Éireann
DI	District Inspector, RIC
DIB	*Dictionary of Irish biography*
DORA	Defence of the Realm Act(s)
DT	Department of the Taoiseach
GAA	Gaelic Athletic Association
GHQ	General Headquarters
GNR	Great Northern Railway
GOC	General Officer Commanding
GPO	General Post Office
Hansard	House of Commons debates
HO	Home Office
IFS	Irish Free State
IHS	*Irish Historical Studies*
IMA	Irish Military Archives
INF	Irish National Volunteers
IPP	Irish Parliamentary Party
IRA	Irish Republican Army
IRB	Irish Republican Brotherhood
ITGWU	Irish Transport and General Workers' Union
IV	Irish Volunteers
LOL	Loyal Orange Lodge
MCM	Monaghan County Museum
MP	Member of Parliament
MSP	Military Service Pension
NAI	National Archives of Ireland
NLI	National Library of Ireland
NMUA	North Monaghan Unionist Association
NS	*Northern Standard*
O/C	Officer Commanding

ÓFMLA	Tomás Ó Fiaich Memorial Library & Archive
PRONI	Public Record Office of Northern Ireland
RDC	Rural District Council
RIC	Royal Irish Constabulary
SF	Sinn Féin
TCD	Trinity College Dublin
TD	Teachta Dála, member of Dáil Éireann
TNA	The National Archives, London
UCDA	University College Dublin Archives
UDC	Urban District Council
UIL	United Ireland League
USC	Ulster Special Constabulary
UVF	Ulster Volunteer Force
WO	War Office, TNA
WS	Witness Statement to Bureau of Military History

Acknowledgments

Unless the clay is in the mouth the singer's singing is useless.[1]

It is thirty years since I first wrote about County Monaghan during the 1912 to 1923 period, then for an MA degree on the subject of unionist politics in the county; this research later spawned several publications. In the last few decades, there has been an explosion in the number and variety of primary sources that have become available for the period. Any historian should be prepared to reappraise their earlier work, where appropriate, when such a wealth of new material becomes available. This book attempts to do that and is written in the spirit of this series, both as a scholarly examination of the revolutionary period 1912–23 and with a much broader audience in mind. As the English historian, George M. Trevelyan, once wrote: 'If historians neglect to educate the public, if they fail to interest it intellectually in the past, then all their historical learning is useless except insofar as it educates themselves.'[2]

Revisiting sources and discovering new ones has been a hugely stimulating exercise. While I have accumulated many new debts, old ones have also to be acknowledged.

I would like to begin by thanking the archivists and custodians of records who provided me with access to records in their keeping: Blackrock College Archives; the British Library; Carrickmacross Workhouse and Heritage Centre (especially for permission to use images in their keeping); Clogher Historical Society; Clongowes Wood Archives; the Gallery of Photography Ireland; Louth County Library; Maynooth University Library; Monaghan County Library; Monaghan County Museum (especially for permission to use images in their keeping); the National Archives of Ireland; the National Archives, London; the National Library of Ireland; the Cardinal Tomás Ó Fiaich Memorial Library & Archive, Armagh; the Public Records Office of Northern Ireland; the Russell Library, St Patrick's College Maynooth; St Macartan's College, Monaghan; Trinity College Dublin; University College Dublin Archives.

I have so many individuals to thank that I am concerned I will offend by leaving someone out. If you have helped me in some way, no matter how small, and your name does not appear here, I offer you my apologies for the oversight: Art Agnew, Revd Robert Agnew, Sr Una Agnew, Patricia Barbour, Liam Bradley, Noel Breakey, Fidelma Byrne, Deirbhile Cahill, Dr Leigh-Ann Coffey, Anne Corley, Bill Cotter, Brian Crowley, Jacqueline Crowley, Robert Devine, Peter & Niamh Dooley (my 'halfway house'), Eugene Dunne, Bishop Joseph Duffy, Professor Patrick Duffy, Rita Edwards, Deborah Flack, David Gahan, Kevin Gartlan, Alan Hand, Mícheál Hoey, Michael Kelly, Mary F.

Kirley, George Knight, Trish Lambe, Catriona Lennon, Sammy Leslie, Theresa Loftus, Johnny Madden, Maoliosa Maguire, Grace Maloney, Dr Dónal McAnallen, Tony McCarthy, Áine & Leo McGlew, Peggy McMahon (Nolan), Theo McMahon, Caroline Mullan, Maeve Mullen, Catherine Murphy, David Murray, Dr Tom Nelson, Francie O'Donoghue, Professor Eunan O'Halpin, Dr Rory O'Hanlon, Kieran O'Harte, Ailbhe Rogers, Einion Thomas, Jack Tennison, Fiona Wall, Rosanna Watts.

I am most indebted to Professor Vincent Comerford, Dr Donal Hall, Larry McDermott, Dr Ciarán Reilly and Professor Christopher Ridgway for reading earlier drafts and offering sage advice and correcting errors. Needless to say, I alone am responsible for what appears in this final version.

I would like to extend my gratitude to Professor Mary Ann Lyons and Dr Daithí Ó Corráin for inviting me to contribute to this important series and offering continued support and advice. Their patience and professionalism has been greatly appreciated. My thanks to Dr Mike Brennan for producing the maps. As always, it has been a pleasure to work with Four Courts Press; special thanks, therefore, to Meghan Donaldson, Martin Fanning, Martin Healy and Anthony Tierney.

Essexford, where I grew up, recalls the meeting of Robert Devereaux, 2nd earl of Essex, and Hugh O'Neill at Aclint in 1599. Essex is said to have bivouacked with his forces by the ford that divides the parish of Killanny between the counties of Monaghan and Louth and by extension the provinces of Ulster and Leinster. To this day, a water pump stands there which has its body painted green by Louth County Council and its handle black by Monaghan County Council. What better symbol of the significance of borders! I would like to extend a very warm thank you to friends and neighbours in Killanny, both sides of the parish border, and a special thank you to my family members living there and further afield.

Finally, and by no means least: Annette and I have been blessed with two very wonderful children, Conor and Áine. That they share with me a deep attachment to Killanny and Monaghan is an added bonus! This book is dedicated to both of them with equal measures of love and affection.

The Irish Revolution, 1912–23 series

Since the turn of the century, a growing number of scholars have been actively researching this seminal period in modern Irish history. More recently, propelled by the increasing availability of new archival material, this endeavour has intensified. This series brings together for the first time the various strands of this exciting and fresh scholarship within a nuanced interpretative framework, making available concise, accessible, scholarly studies of the Irish Revolution experience at a local level to a wide audience.

The approach adopted is both thematic and chronological, addressing the key developments and major issues that occurred at a county level during the tumultuous 1912–23 period. Beginning with an overview of the social, economic and political milieu in the county in 1912, each volume assesses the strength of the home rule movement and unionism, as well as levels of labour and feminist activism. The genesis and organization of paramilitarism from 1913 are traced; responses to the outbreak of the First World War and its impact on politics at a county level are explored; and the significance of the 1916 Rising is assessed. The varying fortunes of constitutional and separatist nationalism are examined. The local experience of the War of Independence, reaction to the truce and the Anglo-Irish Treaty and the course and consequences of the Civil War are subject to detailed examination and analysis. The result is a compelling account of life in Ireland in this formative era.

Mary Ann Lyons *Daithí Ó Corráin*
Department of History *School of History & Geography*
Maynooth University *Dublin City University*

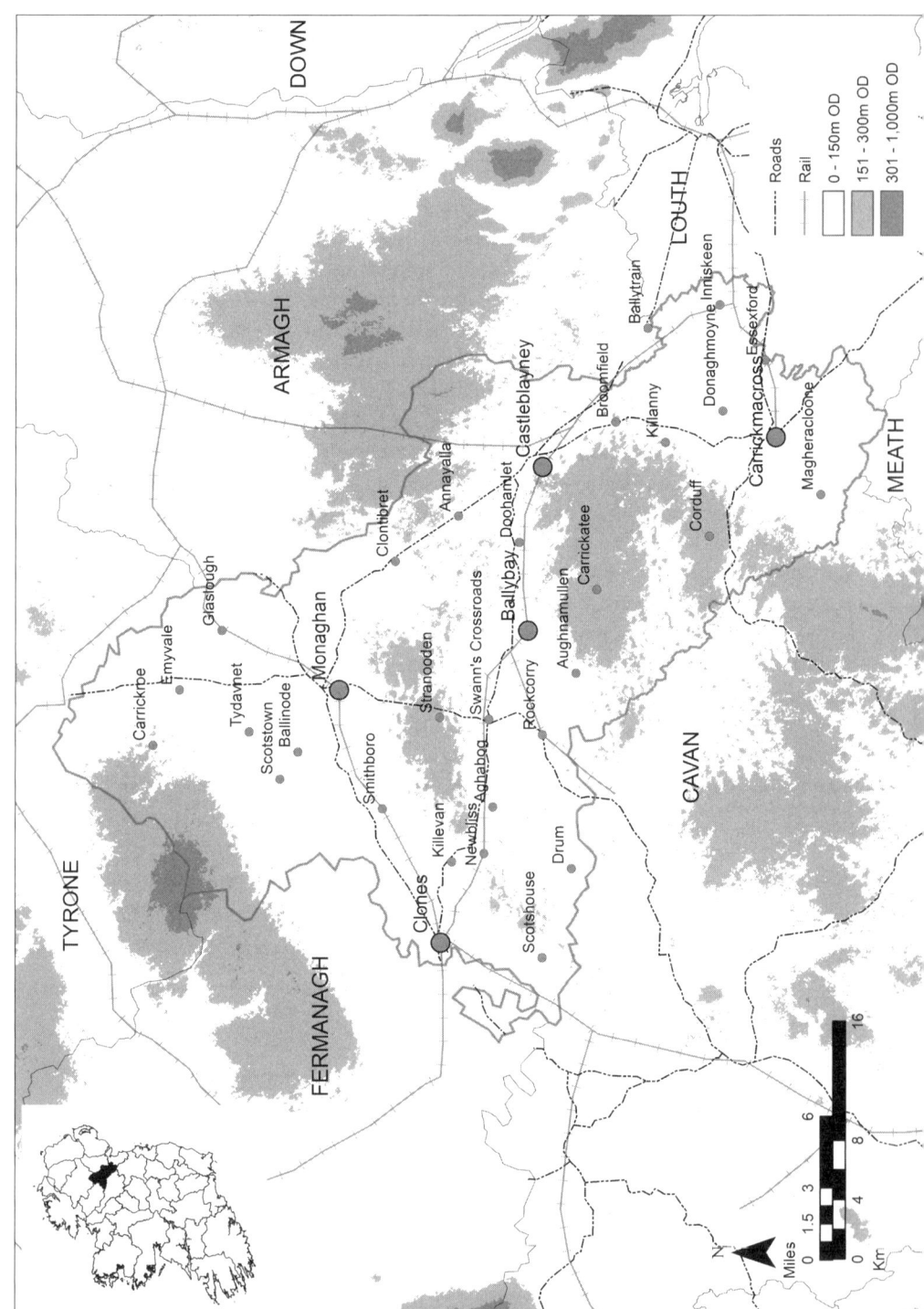

1 Places mentioned in the text

1 Frontier county: Monaghan in 1912

County Monaghan is landlocked, bordered by Tyrone to the north, Armagh and Louth to the east, Cavan and Meath to the south and Fermanagh to the west (see map 1). From its Leinster border, it spears its way into the heart of Ulster. For hundreds of years, it has been a borderland, a contested space that has left a mark on landscape and mindsets alike. From the sixteenth century, successive settlements transformed the physical landscape, created new social elites as well as complex religious and political constructs that shaped uprisings in 1641 and 1798. A bloodless social and political revolution from 1879 to 1909, from the beginning of the Land War to the passing of the last British land act for Ireland, witnessed once again the reorientation of landholding structures, and the transfer of political power at local and national levels. The historiography of the revolutionary decade of 1912–23 does not always take account of the long history approach but in a county such as Monaghan, where demographics influenced politics, everything that came before 1912 created the conditions for what happened in the decade that followed. Thus, a broad introduction to the longer historical context is helpful.

From the twelfth century, Monaghan was the gateway from the English Pale into Gaelic Ulster. The road north from one of the first points of entry at Essexford in the southernmost barony of Farney was known as *Bealach na Sasanach* (the road of the English). Until the late sixteenth century, Monaghan represented what Patrick Duffy has described as 'an island in a sea of active colonial enterprise, where residual Gaelic land-holding structures were comparatively unaltered'.[1] In 1575, Walter Devereaux, 1st earl of Essex, was granted Farney by Queen Elizabeth I, thus beginning the process whereby the old Gaelic ruling families had to give way to the new settlers. In the 1640s, predominantly Anglican landlords arrived with the Cromwellian settlement. This was followed later in the century by influxes of Presbyterians, some from previously planted regions of Ulster, and others fleeing famine in Scotland in the 1690s. Finally, in the eighteenth century the introduction of Presbyterian colonies by established landlords such as the Murray-Kers in Newbliss and the Leslies in Glaslough gave rise to areas now known as Scotch Corner and Scotshouse.[2] By 1911, fully one-quarter of Monaghan's total population of 71,455 was Protestant (see map 2): 8,725 Church of Ireland (12.2 per cent), 8,512 Presbyterians (11.9 per cent) and 860 others (mainly Methodists, 1.2 per cent).

The transfer of land (and by extension wealth and power), the displacement of native Catholics and the establishment of concentrated Protestant communities left lasting legacies of resentment which, at different times, man-

1

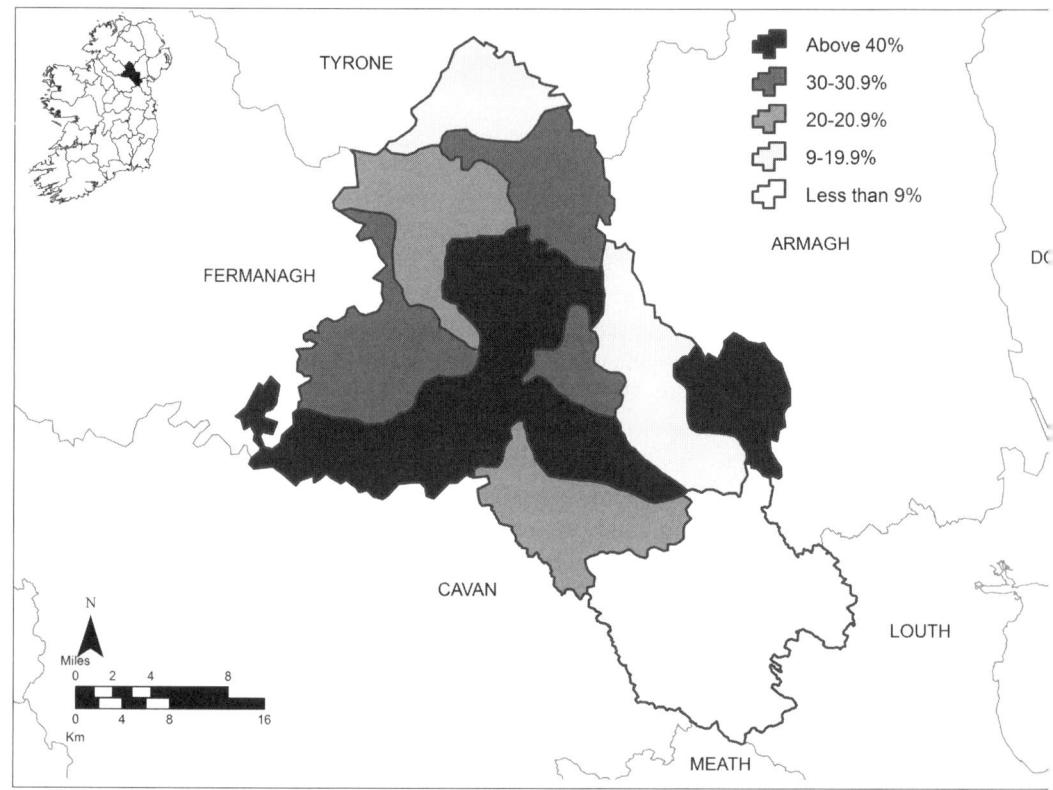

2 Monaghan's Protestant population

ifested in sectarian violence and, indeed, created a folk and literary culture of the dispossessed.[3] During the long nineteenth century in Monaghan, as Christopher McGimpsey has illustrated, 'local sectarian passions ... were kept inflamed by the great political questions' of the day.[4]

However, tensions were not simply between Catholics and Protestants. There had also been a long tradition of sectarian and economic struggle between Presbyterian tenant farmers and Church of Ireland landlords, in particular during the tenant right campaign of the post-Famine era. Thus, Catholics and Presbyterians who went to different places of worship on Sundays could come together on Mondays if they shared agrarian grievances. In the general election of 1880, so many Presbyterians voted against their Church of Ireland landlords when returning two Liberal candidates – John Givan and William Findlater – that the result sent shock waves throughout Conservative Ulster. In Monaghan, it encouraged gentry and aristocratic families such as the Leslies of Glaslough, the Rossmores of Monaghan, the Dartreys of Rockcorry, the Maddens of Clones and the Murray-Kers of Newbliss to reconfigure their political position. In the past the Dartreys had been Liberals and one of the Maddens had flirted with home rule in the 1870s but after the 1880 election Conservatism became the dominant ideology for all. Moreover, they looked towards the Orange Order (and its traditional Presbyterian working-class membership) as a bulwark against any further incursion on their power, in the process creating a broad Protestant alliance opposed to an expansionist Catholic Church that had become closely aligned itself with both the bourgeoning home rule and Land League movements (the latter also aligned to Fenianism). The emergence of a unionist movement in response to home rule and Parnellism in the 1880s provided landlords with the opportunity to re-establish a position of authority and leadership.

Developments during the early years of the Land War (1879–81) reinforced confessional divisions. In 1883, Lady Dartrey could only lament that 'the religious bitterness has become quite dreadful'.[5] Before the Monaghan by-election of that year, which resulted in the return of the nationalist Timothy Healy, the editor of the unionist *Northern Standard* was adamant that 'Into the present struggle the question of landlord and tenant does not enter ... The struggle now is between Protestantism and Roman Catholicism, between those who are attached to the Protestant constitution of Britain and rebels.'[6] At a unionist rally in Monaghan town, Lord Rossmore warned his audience that theirs was a fight against 'any attempt to place Ireland under a government of murderers, butchers, and socialistic rebels'.[7] He exposed Protestant fears of the expropriation of Protestant property; it was a fear that unionist leaders were to use in the future to reinforce rank-and-file support. For example, on the eve of the 1885 general election, the editor of the *Standard* provocatively warned his Protestant readers that nationalists wanted 'their neighbour's ox, their neighbour's ass, and every wood and field that is his, and they want it without any pay for it'. The editorial emphasized that home rule posed a particular threat to Ulster 'which by its own industry and loyalty' had become 'an object of prey which those plunderers think it is worth fighting for'.[8] Even at that stage, the editor clearly indicated that Ulster unionists were becoming separated from the more constitutional-minded southern unionists.

Sectarian sentiment was just as prevalent on the other side of the politico-religious divide. In January 1914, Thomas Toal, then in his fifteenth year as chairman of Monaghan County Council, told a nationalist gathering in Monaghan town that they should not allow Protestants 'to trample on them as they had done in the past' for 'he could remember the time his father would not get one perch of ground in the district where he lived, not while there was an Orangeman to take it'.[9] This type of inciteful rhetoric was characteristic of

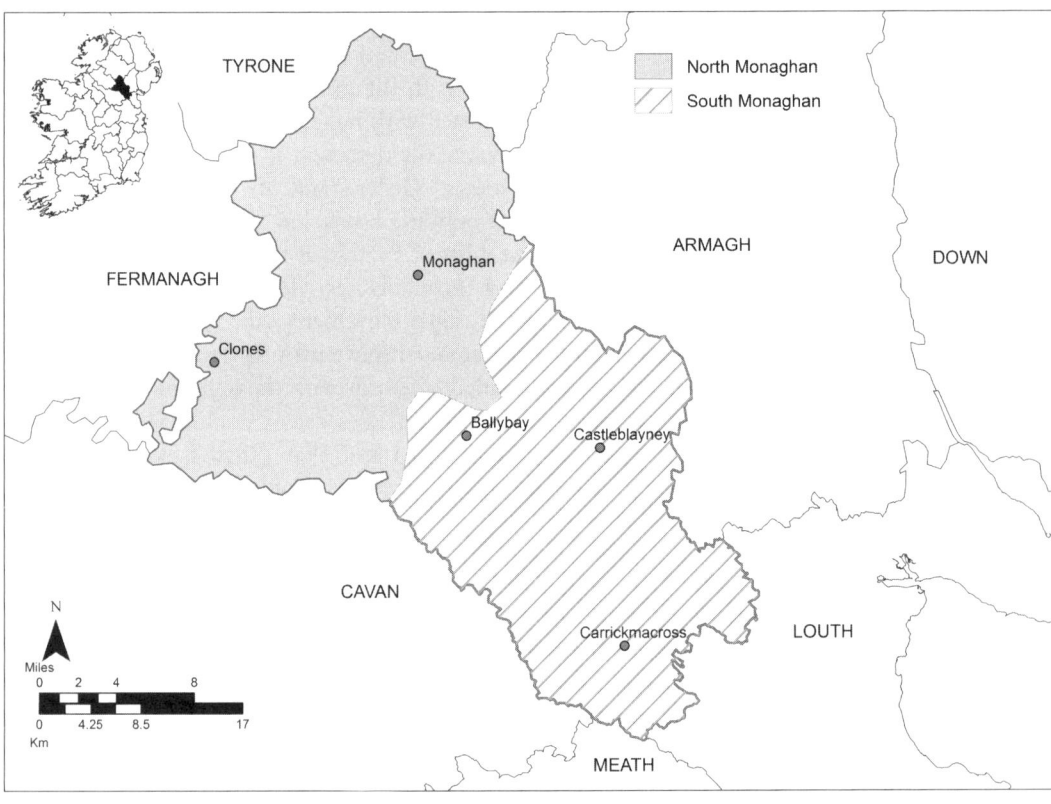

3 Parliamentary constituencies in 1910

Monaghan politics from the Land War era through the third home rule crisis of 1912–14. In 1913, Thomas McGahon, the ultra-Redmondite editor of the *Dundalk Democrat* (which was widely read in Monaghan), whose father had been born in Inniskeen, denounced 'the few Orange clergymen' and others of 'education and position' who 'by abuse and misrepresentation of the Catholic faith and its professors, influence the ignorant men who hasten to these harangues'.[10] This was somewhat hypocritical given that his own newspaper could equally be accused of fomenting sectarianism. Since the Famine, newspapers such as the nationalist *Democrat* (founded in 1849) had become important agents in the politicization of the masses. When the *Northern Standard* was founded a decade before in Monaghan town, its first edition announced that 'the principles of this journal ... shall be strictly conservative of the British connection ... in the capital of Irish Conservatism – the Protestant north' and Monaghan was deemed 'the frontier county' of that Protestant north.[11] As lit-

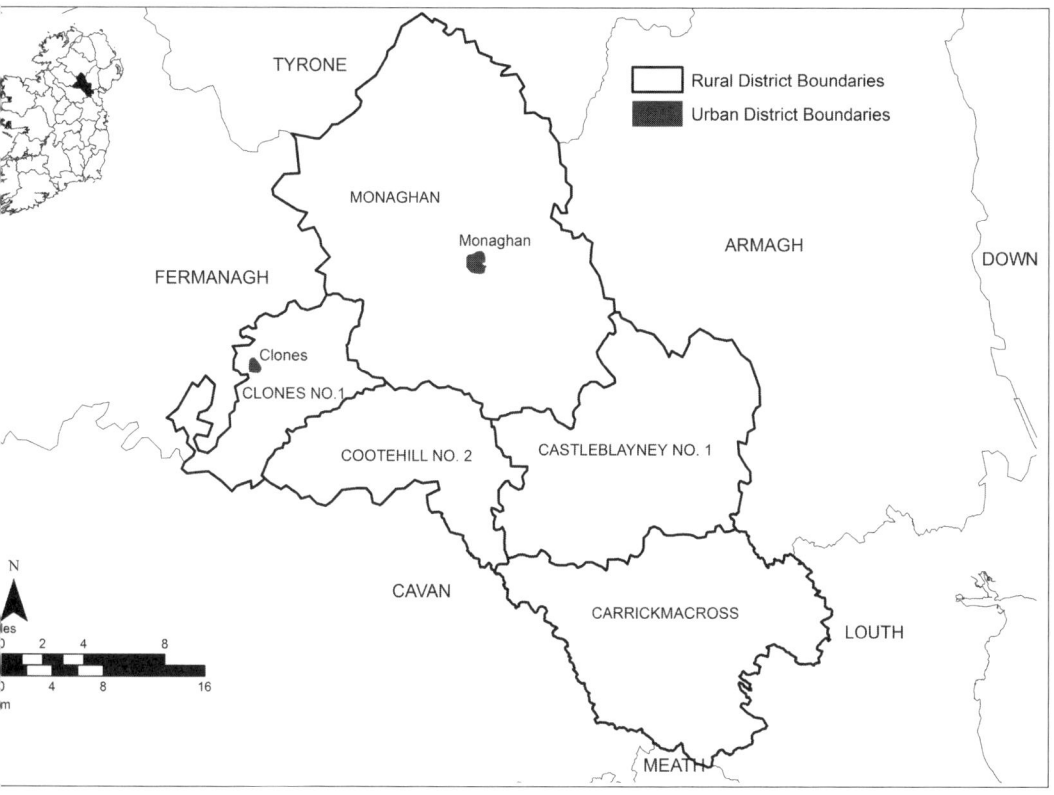

4 Local government divisions

eracy increased, the weekly arrival of these newspapers into towns, villages and rural areas became an event to look forward to, so people could read or hear about events from Killanny to Kimberley, and from Magheracloone to Khartoum.[12] The editorials and reportage in both the *Standard* and *Democrat* played to the newspapers' constituent audiences, and the rhetoric undoubtedly had an influence on those who read (or listened).

The wider Irish unionist movement, with the support of the British Conservative Party, was successful in preventing the enactment of the first two home rule bills in 1886 and 1893. The social and political reforms introduced to appease Ireland from the 1880s brought about a non-violent revolution that arguably transformed Irish life and society considerably more than the revolution of the 1912–23 period. The Franchise and Redistribution Acts of 1884–5 almost tripled the electorate in Monaghan (from 5,300 to 14,000), empowering more nationalists, especially small farmers who were amenable to nationalism. The acts created a North and South constituency in the county (see map 3) that split the unionist vote and made the return of a unionist in the future virtually impossible. In the parliamentary elections of 1886, 1892 and 1895, Sir John Leslie, H.W. Jackson, Major William Tennison and Peter Westenra (son of Lord Rossmore) unsuccessfully contested the two constituencies and from 1895 to 1910 nationalists were elected unopposed.

The revolution in local politics culminated in the Local Government (Ireland) Act of 1898. The recently enfranchised Catholics could now fight it out with their Protestant neighbours for control of the urban and rural district councils (see map 4) of Carrickmacross, Castleblayney, Monaghan, Clones and Cootehill no. 2 (which stretched from Cavan into the west of the county), and, the most prestigious prize of all, the county council. The act represented the first opportunity for Catholics democratically to revolutionize control of local government and so, in the first elections of 1899, Monaghan nationalists organized their campaign so effectively through the Catholic parish structure that only one unionist candidate – John Gray from Aghabog – was returned to the council. Four others were nominated *ex officio* by the grand jury: Peter Westenra, Edward Lucas, Robert Leslie and H.I. Tottenham. Unionist representation on the council was proportionate to their demographic strength, but ineffective in terms of policy-making decisions. In the past, the grand jury had practised patronage in a discriminatory fashion but after 1899 the county council successfully swung the balance in favour of nationalist tenders for council-financed projects and, indeed, in the allocation of salaried positions. In 1911, nationalists were awarded all thirty-seven salaried positions by the council. This led J.C.W. Madden of Hilton Park to complain the following year that 'the local government act has been used to keep us [unionists] out of every office of profit in the county ... Whenever a place is going to which a salary is attached then I say the principle acted upon is that no Unionist need apply.'[13] As early as 1895, Denis Carolan Rushe had written in his *Historical sketches of Monaghan*: 'We have passed through a great social revolution without almost feeling it, with the least bloodshed or suffering that ever marked a great change'.[14] Rushe, a solicitor in Monaghan town, became secretary of the first county council in 1899. His fellow nationalist councillors were of the Land War generation. They were strong farmers, businessmen and professionals whose families had prospered during the post-Famine decades, in large part because the dramatic 29 per cent population decline in Monaghan between 1841 and 1851 had cleared the way for better opportunities in terms of access to more land. They had determinedly hung on to that prosperity during the Land War so that by the end of the century they were in position to take control of local government.[15]

However, pragmatic political decision-making very often overrode sectarian practices. In a county dominated by agriculture, it was imperative that agricultural committees should be comprised of those with most to offer. Thus, Thomas Toal was instrumental in having Lord Rossmore appointed chairman of the Monaghan committee of agriculture and later recalled: 'he gave us very valuable assistance in carrying out all our [? duties] ... though he was at one time a very [? bitter] opponent of Home Rule'.[16] At the beginning of 1912, the committee comprised two Catholic priests, three Catholic nationalists and nine Protestant farmers (including former landlords, Colonel Edward Lucas Scudamore and Major E.J. Richardson). In 1920, one member noted that down the years 'there had not been a single incident to mar the harmony and good feeling existing amongst the members of the committee, though it was composed of men of different religious persuasions and holding different political views'.[17] In some respects, he summed up the complexities of local society and, in particular, the way in which the local political elites were able to compartmentalize their lives when it was necessary to separate civil duties from politics.

The most prominent politician during this entire period was Thomas Toal. His life story sheds light on the manifold changes that impacted emerging Catholic middle-class families such as his from the Land War era to independence; he was one of the 'vivid faces' of provincial Ireland about whom so little is yet known.[18] Toal was born on 24 March 1862, one of six sons of a prosperous farmer from Smithboro in north Monaghan.[19] In 1879, aged seventeen, he inherited a portion of the family farm. During the Land War that followed, Protestant businesses in the village of Smithboro came under financial pressure from a dwindling customer base as the local community became more polarized. Toal took advantage of the situation and opened a grocery and public house. In his memoirs he recalled:

> At this particular time the trade was in the hands of the Greacen and McCoy families who for a very long time done [*sic*] the whole trade of the district. Most people were heavily in debt to them in their books. Still our Catholic people rose to the occasion and made a great effort to have their accounts settled and transfer their trade to us, this being the first occasion for a Catholic of any standing to make an effort to capture a share of the trade of his own people.

He highlighted the fact that his brother, James, was a leading Land Leaguer: 'it gave him a big pull with the Catholics and Nationalists with the result from the start we got a good Catholic support'. Something not acknowledged in Toal's account was that until then, Protestant shopkeepers had kept families from destitution by allowing them to run up large amounts of credit. The economic position in Smithboro was more nuanced than Toal's retrospective sectarian stance allowed for. One must be mindful that his memoir was written post-independence when a degree of triumphalism in the literature, published and unpublished, coloured the recollections of those who considered themselves the victors. Toal remembered the opening of his first business as an opportunity to 'do credit to myself, my wife and family and to my religion and country'. He saw the fulfilment of his ambitions as both a patriotic and religious victory stemming from an era when the nation had been redefined in Catholic, Gaelic and nationalist terms.

Typifying the new elite, Toal was a devout Catholic. Two of his thirteen sons became priests; after Bernard's ordination at the national seminary, Maynooth, Toal wrote: 'I had always a great ambition to have some of my sons priests, thank God for the great privilege he has conferred on us'. His Catholicism informed his politics; he became an opponent of Parnell after the divorce scandal in 1890. When the Irish Parliamentary Party (IPP) was eventually reunited, he gave his wholehearted support to Redmond and this lasted until at least 1918.

When men like Toal emerged to prominence they used all of their newfound influence to enhance their positions. In the 1880s and 1890s, he diversified his commercial interests by branching into the jarvey trade, groceries, seeds, manures, coal and other hardware products. He purchased a number of farms and became a grazier. Where did these farms come from? From bachelor relations perhaps, or evicted neighbours who could no longer afford to pay their rents. He kept between 50 and 100 store cattle, selling at least three times a year. The cattle, he later claimed, 'paid me well. I got good profit for grazing and feeding.' Yet, as a leading member of the United Irish League (UIL), the largest political organization in Monaghan by 1912, he publicly advocated the breaking up of grazier farms for the relief of congestion among the small, uneconomic holders of the county. Political double standards were not unique to Toal.

By the turn of the century, Toal's business empire, in his own words, was 'enormous' and stretched as far as Belfast, then a thriving city that was very much the commercial focus of Monaghan businessmen, nationalist and unionist alike. During the third home rule crisis, northern unionists would typically contrast the industrialized north-east with the backward agricultural south to make a case for exclusion, but that ignored southern investment in the city and its importance and relevance to Monaghan businessmen such as Toal. Between 1900 and 1909, he could afford, as he put it, to lose £2,000 in creamery shares and £1,000 in the Great Southern & Western Railway without this significantly impacting his overall financial standing. He was now a major employer in north Monaghan and a hugely successful merchant on whom farmers over a large area were dependent for everything from groceries to agricultural seeds. Invariably, as a man of wealth and social standing (residing in an impressive neo-Georgian residence on the outskirts of Smithboro that incorporated all the trappings of the demi-gentry), political power followed. Dependency brought votes. In 1899, he became chairman of Monaghan County Council, a position he retained for over forty years. He used his wealth to become effectively a full-time local politician; otherwise, he could not have sat on as many committees and fulfilled as many obligations across the county on a weekly basis. He anticipated an important role for himself in a home rule Ireland.

From an early stage, Toal's closest friend and political ally was Denis Carolan Rushe. He had taught Toal the principle of strength in numbers and unity: 'if you had four sticks and tie them together, it would be very hard to break ... but separate them one by one you could very easy break them'. James C.R. Lardner, a relation of Rushe, took over the latter's practice when he became secretary to the council. Educated in Clongowes Wood College in Kildare on a scholarship provided under the Educational Endowments Act of 1885, Lardner was schooled in politics by Toal and Rushe and won the North Monaghan by-election in 1907. In Westminster, he immediately took up the cause of unpurchased and evicted tenants in Monaghan, and would later make significant contributions to the third home rule debate on 'nuts and bolts' issues concerning, for example, the old age pension, and the running of the Irish post office service.[20] He also delivered home rule speeches in Britain. Lardner held the North Monaghan seat until 1918.[21] The emergence of this triumvirate of Lardner, Toal and Rushe epitomized the middle-class Catholic elite who controlled provincial Ireland and signified the importance of connections in consolidating elitist political and social positions.

The main players in the southern constituency included Edward (Eddie) Kelly from Killanny, businessman, merchant, farmer and auctioneer; and Bernard O'Rourke from Inniskeen, mill owner, entrepreneur and farmer. Like Toal, their wealth provided them with the means to pursue their political ambitions. Toal, Kelly and O'Rourke all sat on the county council together and also chaired, at different times, their respective boards of poor law guardians, rural or urban district councils, branches of the UIL or Ancient Order of Hibernians (AOH), and, in 1914, companies of the Irish National Volunteers. They controlled county council sub-committees (O'Rourke, for example, sat on ten committees at one time). In 1910–12, in the lead up to the introduction of the third home rule bill, they worked tirelessly on the IPP's behalf, issuing declarations of 'implicit confidence in the party' and 'unabated and unbounded confidence' in John Redmond, the party leader.[22]

By 1912, these men of property – 'the largest rate payers in the district'[23] – comprised an influential socio-political nationalist clique who worked and socialized together, and kept friendly relations with the parish priest, the local auctioneer, solicitor and bank manager, and enhanced their social exclusivity through marriage. On stepping down as chairman of the Carrickmacross RDC in May 1916, Kelly claimed that 'political matters should not interfere with the personal friendship of the members'.[24] Like their unionist counterparts, they could compartmentalize their lives. In February 1912, all major nationalist politicians in the county including Lardner and Toal attended the funeral of Presbyterian businessman, Robert Greacon.[25] In Clones, Michael E. Knight, local solicitor and grand master of the Orange Lodge, represented Catholic and Protestant clients alike. When he founded the Clones Golf Club in 1912 he made it clear that politics should never to be discussed.[26] In the same year, the Nuremore Golf Club near Carrickmacross was founded by an interdenominational mix of the town and hinterland's social elite and Protestant and Catholic clergy. In the same area, the Shirleys of Lough Fea re-established the Carrickmacross Harriers Club with support from other gentry families such as the Withringtons, Boltons and Brownes but also from Catholic clergy, medical professionals, including Dr Bernard McCaul and Dr Peter McKenna, and Catholic businessmen and farmers such as Brian and Jack Shevlin. These were much the same 'swells' the *Democrat* listed as forming the Carrickmacross Lawn Tennis Club the following year.[27] Thus, in the county's socially prestigious tennis, hunt and golf clubs – by 1914, there were at least five demesne golf clubs at Glaslough, Dartrey, Rossmore, Hope Castle and Ballybay House – the Protestant gentry, prominent businessmen and professionals mingled easily with their Catholic counterparts. Peadar Livingstone made the point in his orthodox nationalist interpretation of Monaghan's history that

> Unionists always considered themselves to be superior people. They had been superior since the Plantations and they were determined to hold on to that superiority. The other inhabitants of the island, in their view, were an inferior sort of race, not to be trusted with any responsibility. They were simply the Paddy McMahons and the Hughie Duffys while the Unionists were known as the Mr Boyds and Mr Wilsons.[28]

The point could just as easily have been made that there were nationalists who were known as the Mr Toals, Mr Lardners and Mr O'Rourkes. Monaghan was no different to elsewhere; as Ernie O'Malley observed: 'In the towns the tuppence-ha'penny looked down on tuppence, and throughout the country the grades in social difference were as numerous as the layers of an onion'.[29]

The nationalist elites had come to believe that constitutional politics was the respectable way forward. They had no difficulties continuing to participate in the politics of a country that would remain an integral part of the British Empire under home rule.[30] As R.V. Comerford has observed, this 'was in line with a widespread, if by no means universal, acceptance in Europe that bourgeoning nationalities should continue to exist within the composite polities'.[31] Most of these men, according to Thomas McGahon, had come to a stage in their lives when they no longer regarded England as 'the enemy'.[32]

By the turn of the century the complexities of Monaghan politics and society were reflected in the proliferation of political and cultural organizations in the county. In 1898, the UIL had been founded by William O'Brien to agitate for the break-up of the large western ranches and their redistribution among smallholders. In 1900, it played a significant role in the unification of the fractious IPP under John Redmond and it subsequently took on the mantle of a constituency organization. In 1907, there were thirty UIL clubs in County Monaghan with a total membership of over 6,600, twice the national average. Fearghal McGarry rightly contends that the strong membership suggested the added dimension of sectarian politics in Monaghan.[33] However, it was also the case that it stemmed from the slow procedure of the 1903 Land Act. In the south of the county, where the Shirley family procrastinated over the sale of their 20,000-acre estate, the UIL was particularly active. Some local nationalists saw a benefit in this; Revd Daniel O'Connor of Donaghmoyne, the grand old man of Monaghan constitutional politics, wrote to John Dillon, deputy leader of the IPP, of his fear that 'once the land question has been settled the bulk of the people will take little interest even in the great national issue, Home Rule'.[34] There were claims that 'those who had bought their farms were indifferent or hostile to the nationalist cause'.[35]

The land question did not simply disappear with the transfer of ownership; there also remained in Monaghan a serious congestion problem, that is a proliferation of small uneconomic farms. By 1913, almost 8,000 out of just over 20,000 holdings in the county were less than fifteen acres in size and, therefore, uneconomic.[36] The Ranch War, organized by the UIL for the redistribution of grazier lands, may have primarily affected large areas of the midlands in the 1906–10 period,[37] but it had also impacted counties such as Monaghan where 'ranches' were later defined by one county councillor as a holding over fifty acres in size.[38] Moreover, while the Ranch War as an organized campaign had ended around 1910, localized demands for the redistribution of lands had not and would not for some considerable time. In the summer of 1912, Corduff UIL had proclaimed that 'till the land was safe for the people there could be no forward movement, for the land was the foundation from which all industry and all permanent prosperity sprung'.[39] In February 1913, it was said that there were hundreds of applicants for land under the redistribution of the Wilson estate at Latton.[40] Thus, the UIL in Monaghan remained an essential mechanism for the redress of agrarian grievances.[41] It held an annual north and south convention, established its own courts to enquire into local agrarian disputes and repeatedly called for the break-up of large holdings.[42] These calls, as seen in the case of Toal, were characteristic of the political double standards voiced by the local political elites. As Alvin Jackson contends, 'graziers sat on public platforms denouncing the very system from which they were profiting'.[43]

The other prominent nationalist organization, the Ancient Order of Hibernians, was, like the Orange Order, denominationally exclusive and most prominent in strongly Catholic areas bordering on south Armagh and in the mixed religious parishes of mid-Monaghan including Aghabog and Killevan.[44] Its members were expected to adhere stringently to the teachings of the Catholic Church; for example, members of Killanny AOH were instructed to receive Holy Communion on St Patrick's Day 1916 and to take the total abstinence pledge.[45] A few weeks later, those who did not were instructed through the *Democrat* to do so on Easter Sunday, 23 April.[46] The AOH saw itself as a moral enforcer; around Carrickmacross in 1912–13 it established a vigilance committee to stamp out the spread of 'evil literature and immoral postcards'.[47] In line with the Catholic Church, the AOH was strongly opposed to socialism; the Killanny AOH passed a resolution in November 1913 condemning the 'attacks made on our clergy by James Larkin'.[48] However, it would be erroneous to assume that the AOH had the full support of the Catholic clergy and hierarchy. In February 1914, Bishop Patrick McKenna of Clogher was informed by Canon Patrick McKeown (who had just spent seven years in Monaghan): 'a few of the priests, especially the younger priests, might be prepared to show practical sympathy [towards the AOH], a small number regards the Hibernians as anti-Christ. Between these two extremes is a very large number who have no quarrel with the Hibernians, but who are not prepared to join them.'[49] McKenna himself was wary of the AOH but equally cognisant of its influence. In the neighbouring diocese of Armagh, Cardinal Logue did not denounce the political side of the AOH but 'objected strongly to the culture of drink and dance halls on which he believed the order was based'.[50]

The AOH grew during the summer of 1912 when its *raison d'être* was the administration of sickness and unemployment benefits to its members under the terms of the National Insurance Act of 1911. It had traditionally operated as a benevolent society providing sickness benefits, grants for burials, and finding jobs for its members. At its height in 1916, there were 46 divisions with 2,170 members in Monaghan.[51] This was impressive in comparison to Michael Wheatley's findings for the five counties of Leitrim, Longford, Roscommon, Sligo and Westmeath that had an average of just over 25 divisions.[52] Other than numbers, very little is known of the AOH, including its composition. Local notes appeared in the *Democrat* on a weekly basis but they offered only information on future meetings and forthcoming social events; everything else was shrouded in secrecy. On 13 February 1916, two members of Killanny AOH 'were severely cautioned for talking of the business of the Order outside' and one member was expelled.[53] However, there were also very public displays of

AOH strength: divisions had their own bands, held parades, built halls and their members wore sashes and carried illuminated banners. Its colourful parades, with all the trappings of pageantry, added to local and nationalist celebrations, especially on St Patrick's Day, while its other activities such as bazaars, concerts, dances and theatricals provided popular social outlets and were a source of fund-raising. At the end of September 1916, Corduff AOH announced its forthcoming winter programme that was anticipated as 'a happy means to dispel the monotonous gloom of winter in a rural district.'[54]

The AOH also had a political side. Like the UIL, it worked towards home rule and for the benefit of the IPP. In Monaghan, there was often an overlap of membership between the two organizations. For example, Eddie Kelly was chairman of both the Killanny UIL branch and AOH division. In Inniskeen, during the third home rule crisis, Bernard O'Rourke convened joint meetings of the UIL and AOH to stamp out the 'remains of factionalism' that had been a blight on south Monaghan politics since the 1910 general election, and to ensure that prospective candidates had home rule at heart.[55] A decade later, AOH antagonism towards Sinn Féin (SF) would lead to bitter and violent acrimony in the county.

The rise of cultural nationalism has been seen as a major catalyst in the drive towards Irish independence. The most prominent organizations, the Gaelic Athletic Association (GAA, founded 1884) and the Gaelic League (1893), had mixed success in Monaghan in their early years. The GAA got off to a vibrant start after its foundation but by 1912 it was floundering. A report in the *Democrat* that year claimed: 'People are asking if Gaelic football is a thing of the past in Farney ... The sight of a camán is as rare as the proverbial white crow. Wake up Farney ere the games of our forefathers are listed in the great store of our long faded glories.'[56] In January 1913, six clubs in the vicinity of Monaghan town were disbanded.[57] However, the Monaghan GAA was reinvigorated by Newbliss-born Patrick Whelan, who was president of the Ulster Council from 1909 to 1918,[58] and fellow Monaghan man, Owen O'Duffy, secretary of the Ulster Council after 1912.[59] In 1914, Monaghan won the Ulster double of senior football and hurling championships for the only time in their history. By July 1916, there were fourteen GAA clubs with an estimated 406 members.[60] The relationship between the GAA and politics at that stage is by no means clear cut. At a meeting of the Monaghan GAA board in June 1916, O'Duffy refuted claims that 'the GAA is anti-British and is a political organization, that football matches are used for political meetings as well'.[61] However, he may have been acting coyly, as a very strong relationship between the GAA and republicanism evolved over the coming years under his influence.

Protestants in Monaghan remained at a distance from the GAA. They could play cricket with Catholics but the GAA was too closely associated with nationalism. Moroever, sabbatarians had little time for the organization further north in the province, and sabbatarianism remained an issue for Protestants who wished to play GAA in Monaghan long into the future.[62] Nor did Protestants generally see any cultural or social value in the Gaelic League and few joined. Post-independence, Hugh Hunter, for example, told the Irish Boundary Commission that Irish 'will be of no service to our families when they grow up', while John Gillespie, a Castleblayney solicitor, argued it 'would never become a useful language for people in commerce or in the professions'.[63] From a Monaghan perspective, where politics was driven by politico-religious divides, it was perhaps unfortunate that the Gaelic League was founded the same year as the second home rule crisis. Like the Land League, it became too closely associated with the home rule movement and Catholic teaching. In December 1909, Bishop McKenna stated that 'everyone of them who took part in the movement for the revival of the Irish language became also a good Catholic, because the associations of the past were the associations of their faith'.[64]

Although the Gaelic League got off to a promising start among Monaghan nationalists, like the GAA it began to stall within a decade, kept alive only in pockets by enthusiasts such as Henry Morris in Donaghmoyne (and wider Farney) and Fr Lorcan Ó Ciaráin in Rockcorry, notably the two areas where SF was to come to early prominence. Its support base was too narrow, attracting only the clergy, professionals (particularly teachers) and the intelligentsia. Morris was aware of the anomalous position of the Irish language: 'while many of those who are most anxious for its preservation are ignorant of it or know it but imperfectly, those who have it as a birthright and know it well don't prize it'.[65] Peadar Livingstone later concluded that the lower classes had little enthusiasm for learning a language that was 'nearly done away with', for it was not going to be their gateway to social improvement.[66] There was, indeed, a certain social snobbery involved in Gaelic League membership, suggested by Owen O'Duffy's reminiscence that

> Gaelic League classes in those days meant not only learning the language but practising Irish patriotism. We all vowed to encourage Irish, and nobody would risk the scorn of his classmates by turning up in clothes made outside Ireland instead of in good Irish tweeds, by riding a bicycle other than a Pierce or a Lucania.[67]

Similarly, learning the Irish language held little appeal for the nationalist upper classes, many of whom looked towards the empire to find positions for their children in the British civil service. The upper class 'shoneen' was denounced in the *Democrat* for treating Irish as the 'vulgar' language of the peasant.[68]

While the RIC did not record the number of clubs in 1912, they enumerated only three branches of the Gaelic League with forty-five members in

January 1916.⁶⁹ It seems that in Monaghan, rather than the Gaelic League giving impetus to the independence movement, it was the other way around. After the 1916 Rising, the League received a boost when the likes of Patrick Whelan and Owen O'Duffy became more actively involved and their influence helped bring on board Toal and Rushe. Just a fortnight before the Easter Rising, Whelan called the Gaelic League, 'the greatest movement in Ireland at the present time ... because it represented in every district the spirit and backbone of the nation. For many years past the old Irish spirit had been fading from the homes of the people.'⁷⁰ In retrospect, O'Duffy saw in the Irish language 'an essential preliminary to the rebuilding of national pride and the clearing of the national honour from the stain of conquest'.⁷¹ O'Duffy would later claim that there was a strong crossover between membership of the League and the GAA and that they 'formed the backbone of the Volunteers when they came to Monaghan'.⁷² This was more a case of patriotic nostalgia than reality.

Monaghan unionists had their own distinctive diversity of social and cultural movements, as evidenced in the weekly columns of the *Standard*. The most vibrant of these was the Orange Order, the foundation of which dated back to the late eighteenth century. It was mainly confined to the North Monaghan parliamentary constituency where unionists were most densely concentrated; by 1912, it had come to represent all Protestant denominations and classes in the county from small Presbyterian farmers to aristocratic Anglican families, including the Maddens, Leslies, Dartreys and Rossmores.⁷³ Their day of celebration and pageantry remained 12 July, which attracted thousands of members each year, but local Orange lodges also regularly organized soirées, picnics and concerts. Unionist clubs had come into existence in 1893 but had fallen into abeyance after the defeat of the second home rule bill that year. They were resurrected again in 1910–11 when the threat returned. Like the AOH and UIL, there were social dimensions to unionist club activities; they were not just forums for political debate and discussion. The working classes, particularly in the towns, also played soccer (what Gaels generally termed 'the game of the foreigner'), organized through the Monaghan and District League. There were cricket greens in Monaghan, Clones, Ballybay and Newbliss (and, of course, this was also a favourite sport of Catholics before the GAA ban). Among the upper echelons of aristocratic and gentry society, Big Houses hosted shooting parties on demesnes to which families invited the local clergy, professionals and stationed army officers (at least up until the barracks of the 5th Battalion of the Royal Irish Fusiliers was closed in Monaghan town in July 1908).⁷⁴ Regular guests also included local RIC officers from the twenty-one barracks in the county, especially the county inspector, Ernest Phillip Tyacke.⁷⁵

It was the aristocracy and gentry who experienced most revolutionary change over the extended period from 1879 (see chapter 8). Cumulatively, a succession of crises from the beginning of the Land War in 1879 meant that within a decade or so most landlords came to realize that their economic position had become untenable. John Madden of Hilton Park told the Cowper Commission in 1887: 'If I could get what I consider to be the value of my property and get rid of my house and demesne, on the improvement of which I spend thousands of pounds, if I could get that back I would shake the dust off my feet and leave the country and be glad to do so, because I think prosperity in this country is quite out of the question'.[76] Moreover, the nationalist rhetoric of the Land War era had occasioned a very public attack on landlords. Shane Leslie of Glaslough, in his own inimitable fashion, captured the fearful apprehensions caused by such rhetoric in the 1880s:

> The mountainy men would descend on the village and gardens and divide up the beautiful grounds in which we played. Mr Gladstone, who was more wicked than any bad man in the Bible, had promised to give all our woods, house and demesne to the Catholics who already had them divided up and were playing dice for them in the public house.[77]

In the end, the transfer of lands – around 80 per cent of the county's holdings had been completed by 1912 – was peaceful and most of the county's great families remained in residence: the Maddens stayed on at Hilton Park, the Leslies at Glaslough, the Rossmores at Rossmore Park, the Dartreys in their Rockcorry neo-Elizabethan pile, and the Lucas Scudamores at Castleshane. They were by no means destitute; the generous terms of the Wyndham Land Act (1903) had given them a lifeline. But while they continued to provide estate employment, they did not invest their capital sums in local industry or infrastructure; that was to prove a mistake in the long term. Instead, their investments went outside Ireland to other areas of the empire where railways were expanding and precious metals and minerals were being mined. In the years after 1903, the Leslie investment portfolio 'bulged' with the most fanciful stocks and shares on the advice of Sir Ernest Cassel, the investment guru of his time.[78] Plates 7 and 8 showing the servants at Glaslough and the golden wedding anniversary celebration of Sir John and Lady Constance provide visual evidence of the continued grandeur that characterized the *belle époque*. Moreover, the Leslies did not sell their 1,500-acre demesne at Glaslough; neither did the Rossmores who retained an 800-acre demesne on the outskirts of Monaghan town, nor the Maddens who kept around 1,000 acres in Clones, and the Dartreys 1,000 acres at Rockcorry.

Outside the demesne walls, there remained among Catholics the niggling resentment that most Protestants were better off than them. The evidence, at least in terms of farm size, backed this up. In 1911, the highest concentration of Protestants was coterminous with areas that previously had large landed estates, in particular Muckno (Castleblayney), centred on the Hope estate, Ematris on the Dartrey estate, Donagh on the Leslie estate, and Clones on the Madden estate. Sixty per cent of all holdings in excess of 100 acres in the county were located in these regions. A more detailed case study of fifty-two townlands in the two rural parishes of Ematris and Aghabog shows that of the 151 farms, almost 64 per cent were less than twenty acres in size, and Catholics and Protestants held equal numbers of these. However, as farm size increased the number of Catholic-owned farms decreased: Protestants owned 63 per cent of all farms between twenty-one and fifty acres and, perhaps more significantly, all of the seven farms over fifty-one acres in size were Protestant owned.[79]

As Thomas Toal's memoir suggested, there was a traditional resentment that in the towns of Carrickmacross, Castleblayney, Ballybay, Clones and Monaghan, unionist merchants, businessmen and professionals were disproportionately represented in trade and commerce. In the overwhelmingly Catholic and nationalist town of Carrickmacross there were thriving Protestant unionist businesses including, on Main Street alone, William Galbraith (chemist), Robert Stratton (grocer), J.G. Howell (watchmaker/jeweller), Emily Raeburn (merchant), Isabella Eakin (draper), John Elphinstone (grocer and publican), and Thomas Hanna (grocer and druggist). There were undoubtedly those who traditionally would not 'darken the door' of a shop or public house owned by a member of a different denomination but until the revolutionary period the general case seems to have been that economic good sense prevailed in the face of sectarian considerations. However, the third home rule crisis brought resentment of economic inequality to the fore, and was exploited by politicians: when J.C.R. Lardner stood in the market square of Monaghan town in January 1910 and asked his nationalist audience to look around and to judge for themselves who were the most prosperous merchants, doctors, lawyers and undertakers 'in a county where the ratio between Catholics and Protestants was 3:1', the sectarian undercurrents were not difficult to detect.[80]

Lardner delivered his speech about a week before the January 1910 general election. Following a vigorous campaign, 95 per cent of unionists eligible to vote in the North Monaghan constituency turned out in support of Michael E. Knight, the first unionist to contest a parliamentary seat in Monaghan for fifteen years. Although Knight had little hope of wresting the seat from Lardner, the turnout was intended as a message to their co-religionists elsewhere in the province that Monaghan Protestants were no less opposed to home rule than they were. When the government introduced a bill later that year that aimed to remove the House of Lords' absolute veto, Knight condemned it as an abomination 'originated by English socialists and backed up by the disloyal party in Ireland against an essential part of our Protestant constitution [that is] fraught with much despair'.[81] When the bill received royal assent the following August, the passing of home rule seemed inevitable and so at the monster unionist rally at Craigavon on 23 September 1911, Knight emphatically proclaimed that Monaghan unionists were ready 'to adopt all necessary measures for the preservation of our remaining rights'.[82] Two days later, the Ulster Unionist Council, by now the directing body of the anti-home rule movement, and dominated by Belfast commercial and professional interests, agreed upon a policy to resist the establishment of a Dublin parliament, and appointed a committee to submit a constitution for a provisional Ulster government that would stage a *coup d'état* if the third home rule bill was passed. It also planned another elaborate mass demonstration for 28 September 1912, the main aim of which was to have unionists throughout the province sign a Solemn League and Covenant.

For Monaghan unionists of all denominations and classes, 1912 was thus a watershed. During the previous two home rule crises of 1885 and 1893, they knew they had the support of Conservative elements in Ireland and Britain and the safety of the House of Lords' veto to prevent the passing of home rule into law. The Parliament Act of 1911 removed that safety net. The third home rule bill offered Ireland only a narrow measure of autonomy. It did not equate to full independence. Rather, it provided for the establishment of a legislature with severely restricted powers, free to operate only within the constraints of the mother parliament's watchful eye at Westminster. However, as far as Monaghan unionists were concerned, it contained inadequate safeguards and thus they were convinced that their position, and their civil and religious liberties, could only be safeguarded within the union. From 1912, Monaghan unionists decided to take a determined stand to prevent any further encroachment. The nationalist majority could not stand idly by; the proposed Dublin parliament might have only limited powers within the wider imperial structures, but for the nationalist middle classes it represented the culmination of generations of political struggle.

2 Home rulers and rebels, 1912–14

> Being convinced in our consciences that Home Rule would be disastrous to the material well-being of Ulster, as well as the whole of Ireland, subversive to our civil and religious freedom, destructive of our citizenship and perilous to the unity of the Empire, we ... do hereby pledge ourselves ... to stand by one another in defending for ourselves and our children our cherished position of equal citizenship in the United Kingdom, and in using all means which may be found necessary to defeat the present conspiracy to set up a Home Rule parliament in Ireland.

These words were the distilled pledge of the Ulster Solemn League and Covenant signed by 5,360 Monaghan men over sixteen years of age on 28 September 1912, designated Ulster Day, in what was an impressive feat of organization by the unionist movement throughout the county. Some 5,119 women also signed a parallel Declaration. Signatures for both were collected in churches, parochial halls and Orange lodges. Mrs Brownlow collected 148 signatures house-to-house around Carrickmacross, a staunchly nationalist area, where unionists may not have wanted to congregate as publicly for the purpose as they did further north in the county.[1]

As is clear from the quotation, the Covenant was a very public act of defiance, some might even argue treason, pledging the signatories to use 'all means', which included physical force, to oppose home rule.[2] It reiterated arguments from the past, expressing unionist fears of living under a Dublin nationalist parliament that would ruin the economy of Ulster, destroy their civil and religious liberties, and endanger the unity of the empire. But it also magnified those fears by including reference to future threats that might be faced by the children of the signatories growing up in a society impoverished materially and culturally. The scriptures read in the various churches in Monaghan were carefully chosen to emphasize that God was on the side of the covenanters: from the Book of Chronicles (20:15), men and women were assured 'not to be afraid for it is not your battle, it is God's' and from Psalm 86:7: 'In the day of my trouble I will call upon thee; for thou wilt answer me'.[3] The Covenant, therefore, took on the guise of a crusade where religion and politics were entwined. No public display of this magnitude had been seen in Monaghan since 1883 when the Orangemen of the county and of neighbouring Fermanagh had gathered in their thousands at Roslea, County Fermanagh, to counter a home rule celebration following Timothy Healy's by-election victory.[4] The difference, however, was that Ulster Day was not spontaneous.

No one has yet undertaken the mammoth task of authenticating the Monaghan signatories but, if taken at face value, those who signed the Covenant and the Declaration comprised almost 60 per cent of the *entire* Protestant population of Monaghan.[5] Little wonder then that a few months later Edward Carson, the Dublin-born leader of the Ulster unionists, should praise the efforts of Monaghan unionists for mobilizing in such numbers, despite the fact that they 'had greater difficulties and greater dangers to overcome'.[6]

The difficulties and dangers related to their minority status in Monaghan and the sectarian nature of local society that had given rise to sporadic acts of sectarian violence since the beginning of the third home rule crisis. This included damage to property such as Orange halls and Protestant church windows, the appearance of public graffiti, verbal abuse and physical intimidation. On 12 July 1912 an Orange band returning from the celebrations was attacked by nationalists in Castleblayney, with shouts of: 'This is the last Twelfth the rotten Orange flag will float through [Castle]Blayney'.[7] The Orangemen in the parade retaliated by firing a number of revolver shots at their unarmed assailants, thus prompting the editor of the *Democrat*, Thomas McGahon, to write:

> The exasperation of the Catholic population is easily accounted for, given the fact that [Castleblayney] is a Catholic town and that the police did not arrest those Orangemen who fired several shots. The Catholics are always so tolerant about these 12 July marches which proves that this time they must have been provoked.[8]

History refutes McGahon's claim: nationalists around Castleblayney had rarely been tolerant of the Twelfth but in 1912 tensions were particularly high.[9] The county inspector was circumspect: 'In consequence of the collision between the parties ... sectarian animosity has been somewhat embittered in Castleblayney'.[10] The nationalist protestors were buoyed by the fact that the third home rule bill had been introduced in parliament on 11 April. For two years, John Redmond, leader of the IPP, had supported Herbert Asquith's Liberal government on the back of Asquith's guarantee that home rule for Ireland would be a major priority. When, under the Parliament Act of 1911, Asquith's government curbed the power of the House of Lords to veto bills sent up from the Commons, the passage of home rule could only be delayed for two years after the introduction of the bill. As throughout Ulster, this became the motivation for unionist organization in Monaghan. Moreover, there was an added concern because an aborted amendment to the bill proposed by a Liberal backbencher, Agar Robartes, proposed that the four mainly Protestant counties of Antrim, Down, Derry and Armagh should be excluded from its terms. Redmond was opposed to this and Sir Edward Carson, the

Ulster unionist leader, said he would not give up Fermanagh and Tyrone, where the religious divide was fairly equal.[11] Ominously, Carson did not mention Monaghan, Cavan or Donegal. However, leading Monaghan unionists such as Gerald Madden refused to believe that Carson would betray them by succumbing to 'the pernicious suggestion' of partition; it would be 'a base betrayal' of the Covenant.[12] A few months later, the editor of the *Northern Standard* considered it unthinkable that 'such a splendid body of Loyalists should be deserted and left to the tender mercy of the antagonists'.[13] While Agar Robartes' proposal came to nothing, the first tentative steps towards partition had, nonetheless, been taken.

A month after Ulster Day, it was reported that of the fourteen unionist clubs in the county, members at Glaslough, Clones, Newbliss, Drum and Castleblayney were drilling without arms. CI Ernest Tyacke noted: 'Such ostentatious display [of drilling] on the part of the Newbliss and Drum clubs is beginning to excite feelings of resentment amongst the Nationalist neighbours who, however, are restrained by their clergy and by other influential members of their party from active opposition'.[14] At this stage, the county's leading nationalists may not have felt they had to react to provocation as home rule was within their grasp but historically they or the clergy or the police had never been completely successful in restraining the working classes for whom sectarian activity was often a form of nebulous social recreation.

The drilling of unionist clubs was a prelude to the formal establishment of the Ulster Volunteer Force (UVF) in Monaghan, a unionist militia designed to support the pledge to resist the implementation of home rule by force if necessary that was established in January 1913 when the home rule bill was rejected by the House of Lords. By August, there were two battalions in the county: the 1st, with headquarters in Monaghan town, was comprised of members from Clontibret, Glaslough, Ballinode, Monaghan, Smithboro and Shanroe, while the 2nd Battalion comprised men from Drum, Clones, Ballybay, Dartrey and Newbliss (see map 5). By March 1914, there were 2,070 UVF members in Monaghan (almost 34 per cent of eligible males), compared with three battalions of 3,406 men in Cavan and seven battalions comprised of 7,378 in Armagh.[15]

From the beginning, the UVF in Monaghan was organized through the Orange lodges and operated in areas where unionist clubs had previously existed. Instruction was carried out primarily under the direction of the county gentry: Richard Dawson, earl of Dartrey; Colonel John Leslie of Glaslough; Colonel J.C.W. Madden of Hilton Park and Major E.J. Richardson of Poplar Vale. The same pattern occurred in neighbouring County Tyrone.[16] When Gerald Madden took control of the northern battalion, he wrote to his brother, J.C.W., that 'our whole credit and honour is at stake in this movement, we said we would fight and I do hope that there will be no climb down in Belfast or

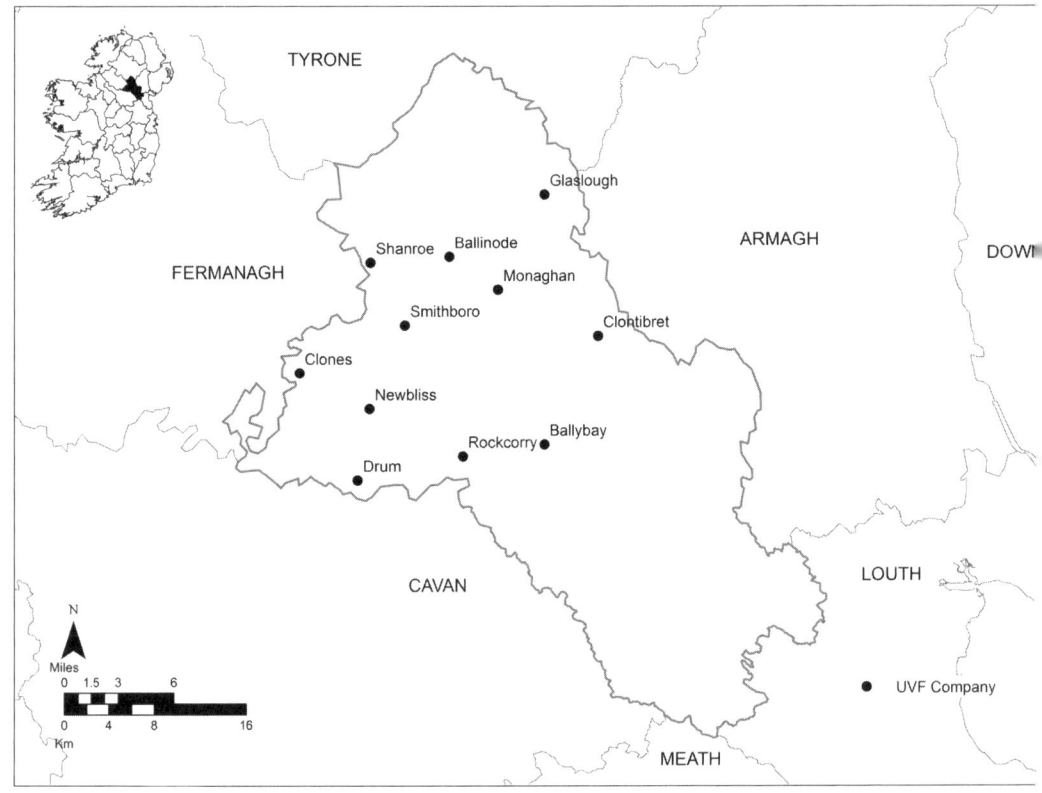

5 UVF companies in Monaghan

by the English Unionist Party'.[17] Gerald's private correspondence reveals that sectarianism was not exclusive to the working classes; in June 1913 he wrote to his brother: 'I am sorry you had difficulty with the Roman Catholics about the presentation of colours, it just shows how they would treat Protestants or British troops if they got their way', and concluded, 'They shan't get the upper hand if we can prevent it, and I believe if we only stand firm we shall smash this beastly government'.[18] Unionist antipathy to the British Liberal government (1905–15) was clearly evident.

In the early stages the gentry provided a limited number of arms, including air rifles.[19] They also allowed the use of their demesnes for drilling purposes. In December 1913, skirmishing took place at Glaslough, Poplar Vale and Mount Louise. In April 1914, the *Belfast Newsletter* reported on a 'fairly large crowd of spectators' who watched training exercises at Glaslough: 'The place chosen for the operations was ideal as timber cutting had been in progress and the fallen trees and hilly ground provided splendid cover for the attacking force'.[20] When carrying out manoeuvres such as these, the gentry did not take kindly to being spied upon by the police and so in February 1914 J.C.W. Madden warned CI Tyacke that he would 'forcibly remove any police sergeant or constable entering my place in the future'.[21] His message recalled the traditional deference expected by the gentry from the police.

Professionals such as solicitors Michael E. Knight, William Martin, George Ross and Herbert McWilliam, and clergymen, including Revd C.M. Stack, were also prominent. Knight came from an Anglican family that had its roots in Monaghan stretching back to 1678, when his ancestors purchased a small estate of around 150 acres from an officer in Cromwell's army.[22] Rather than landed gentry, the family produced generations of professionals who entered law or medicine or the church. Michael was born in 1869 and in time took up residence in the family home on the Diamond in Clones, where he practised as a solicitor. His grandson recalls: 'He was a leading Orangeman [grand master of the Monaghan Orange Lodge from 1904 to 1960] and Freemason and was devoted to the care and maintenance of his Church, always holding a senior position in the select vestry. For decades he was diocesan registrar looking after all the legal business of the Church of Ireland diocese of Clogher (on a voluntary basis).'[23] He was also a founding member of the local Church of Ireland secondary school in Clones, as well as founder of Clones golf and soccer clubs.[24] He immersed himself in local politics, and was a member of Monaghan County Council from its inception. He worked assiduously on numerous county committees dedicating his energies to the promotion of the county's agricultural economy, wider infrastructure and social reforms. He was highly respected by his fellow councillors including nationalists such as Toal and Rushe but his continued loyalism compromised his standing with them, especially in the 1912–23 period. He stood as a unionist candidate in three general elections, January and December 1910 and 1918. When Gerald Madden went to war in 1914, Knight took his position as commander of the northern battalion of the Monaghan UVF.

Anglican and Presbyterian clergy resented any encroachment on their religious and civil liberties, and denounced the 1911 *Ne Temere* decree that forbade mixed marriages unless the children of such unions were reared in the Catholic faith. Revd C.M. Stack was enthusiastic enough to organize a twenty-three man UVF company in the very nationalist parish of Magheracloone, where only three residents had signed the Covenant.[25]

The role of the county's leading Protestant businessmen is more difficult to determine. They did not figure as prominently in county or local leadership circles, at least not to the same extent as in neighbouring Tyrone, for example.[26] Public prominence in this respect would have been detrimental to their commercial interests. However, it has been suggested that they provided strong financial assistance.[27] While the shopkeepers held back, their assistants as well as clerks, railway workers, mail car drivers, artisans, manual workers and, in rural areas, farmers and their sons joined the rank and file in significant numbers.[28] Although no element of compulsion is inferred, landlords almost certainly brought their house and demesne staff into the force. At Glaslough, James Vogan, head gamekeeper, and a recognized marksman, was ideally placed to teach family and local members of the UVF how to shoot. Another drill instructor was Robert Totten, a former private in the Royal Irish Fusiliers, who had been regimental orderly to Sir John Leslie when he was in command of the regiment, and in 1912 worked for Leslie as his private groom.

By early spring 1914, the wider Ulster UVF movement was showing the serious nature of its intent. In February, J.C.W. Madden received a 'secret' circular from General Hacket Pain, commander-in-chief of the UVF, that set out the province's mobilization scheme 'in case of urgent necessity'. The rank and file were to be made aware that conflict was a possibility and that they had to be ready with arms and ammunition, food, tools for trenching, maps and so on.[29] Just two months later, on 24 April 1914, a huge shipment of arms was landed at Larne, Bangor and Donaghadee. The motor car corps conveyed the arms to secret dumps. Two weeks later, Madden received a memorandum from Hacket Pain notifying him that the rifles were to be 'earmarked for the most efficient men' and that the time had 'come when the main body of the armed men in each area according to local conditions, should be prepared to move in any direction in the service of the Cause'.[30] On 8 May 'large quantities' of arms and ammunition were brought via Armagh to the Leslie residence at Glaslough before distribution throughout Monaghan during the nights which followed. Recalling events over thirty years later, F.H. Crawford, the mastermind behind the Larne gun-running, writing to James Craig, was fulsome in his praise of 'the real heroes', the men who risked their lives delivering the guns 'in the very heart of the most hostile districts of Nationalism, in counties such as Monaghan'.[31]

There was no interference from the police in Monaghan despite the fact that the importation of arms was illegal. CI Tyacke claimed that as the cars arrived into the county between midnight and 6 a.m. it was too dark to identify the registration plates of the vehicles involved. Furthermore, he could not be certain if arms were taken to Dartrey because 'there [were] so many gates to the demesne that the police could not watch them all'.[32] It was a rather pathetic excuse from an officer who, while undoubtedly diligent, was an establishment figure who pandered to the local gentry and aristocracy. The RIC's inaction drew an immediate response from the editor of the *Democrat*, incensed by the fact that the Royal Proclamation of 4 December 1913 that prohibited the importation of arms had been deliberately flaunted.[33] Under a banner headline pronouncing 'Treason', McGahon declared:

> Any person even slightly acquainted with the history of Ireland during the latter half of the nineteenth century, must be struck by the remarkable contrast between the inaction and apparent cowardice – if not treasonable participation in outrage – of the authorities in Ulster last week and the whole-heartedness with which the forces of the law were brought to bear on nationalists in the past.[34]

The Monaghan UVF were now in possession of almost 1,700 rifles stored mainly in landlords' houses and demesnes at Glaslough, Dartrey, Poplar Vale, Ballyleck, Greenmount, Hilton Park and Beech Hill.[35] The remainder were kept in Orange halls throughout the north of the county and even in Protestant national schools and clergymen's homes. At the 12 July celebrations at Ballybay in 1914, less than three months after Larne, Michael E. Knight told his fellow-Orangemen that they were rapidly approaching a time 'when it might become necessary for them to translate their words into deeds' and when that time came, they in Monaghan 'would not be found wanting'.[36] The rhetoric on the day was openly belligerent. Revd William Armstrong asserted that 'County Monaghan will never submit to a Dublin parliament. Ulster Protestants will never be slaves', while J.C.W. Madden claimed: 'We seek no quarrel with the United Irish League or Hibernians but if we have to fight we will do so'.[37]

In July 1913, the editor of the *Standard* had opined that young men had not spent 'their hours of leisure for many months in drilling, route marching and acquiring military discipline just for fun'.[38] By the end of July 1914 the Monaghan UVF was well organized, well armed, drilled (but levels of competency as soldiers have to be questioned), with a motor car corps and women drivers, a basic intelligence service (including sympathetic telephone exchange operators) and an ambulance service. Up to this point the role of women in the UVF and the wider unionist organization was considerable. In May 1911, the countess of Dartrey who 'shared the views of her noble husband on this very important and vital matter' of opposition to home rule formed a Monaghan Women's Unionist Association, affiliated to the recently formed wider Ulster Women's Unionist Council.[39] The association concentrated on fundraising activities; for example, in November 1913 a concert in Monaghan town raised 'the princely sum' of £130 for the UVF Indemnity Fund set up the previous January.[40] Scores of young Protestant women joined the UVF nursing corps, prepared to treat the wounded in the event of an outbreak of hostilities when, 'their brothers and fathers would require their care through their nursing qualities.'[41] At the same time country houses, including Glaslough, Newbliss, Hope Castle and Dartrey Castle, were being prepared as field hospitals by their female chatelaines, women such as Miss Murray-Ker, a significant landlord in her own right, the countess of Dartrey, motivated by her financial independence, and Leonie Leslie, motivated by her American roots.[42] Writing in April

1914, the Monaghan CI believed that relations between nationalists and unionists were set to deteriorate.⁴³ The UVF was preparing to defy the authorities in Ireland but were they equally prepared to kill their nationalist neighbours in pursuit of their objective to defeat home rule?

The arrival of a large consignment of arms to Dartrey Castle in Rockcorry may have been 'missed' by the police, but it was not missed by local nationalists. There, the parish priest was Fr Lorcan Ó Ciaráin, one of a number of radical Catholic clergymen in the county. Ó Ciaráin was a farmer's son from Drumsnat in north Monaghan, close to Thomas Toal's village of Smithboro. After his education at St Macartan's College, he entered St Patrick's College Maynooth in the early 1880s, when he became politicized, his nationalism having first been stimulated by Land League politics in his native area.

In the national seminary, he was a classmate of Fr Eugene O'Growney, an Irish language enthusiast, and they both worked together to revive the Irish language among their fellow students: 'We made a solemn resolution', Ó Ciaráin later recalled, 'to spend the recreations and walks only with Irish speaking students'. Ó Ciaráin believed that 'Irishmen should work to make Ireland Irish and free – not a province, no matter how prosperous – and that they should never aim at anything lower, even if it took many generations to attain.'⁴⁴ By 1887, both he and O'Growney were reading Michael Cusack's *Celtic People*, the newspaper of the GAA. Ó Ciaráin introduced O'Growney to Madden's *United Irishmen*, Tone's *Memoirs*, 'and practically everything in book form of the Young Ireland literature'. In return, O'Growney introduced him to the works of O'Curry, O'Donovan and Petrie. Both men were founding fathers of the Gaelic League in 1893 and Ó Ciaráin went on to become, in the words of a contemporary, a 'tireless and indefatigable leader of the language movement in Monaghan'.⁴⁵

Ó Ciaráin also became an early supporter of SF; indeed, he has even been credited in one account with naming the organization in 1905.⁴⁶ He was certainly a close friend of Arthur Griffith.⁴⁷ (Griffith's family had lived in Scotshouse, not very far from where Ó Ciaráin had been reared, though no evidence was found of them having been in contact as they grew up.) When Irish Volunteer (IV) organizer J.J. 'Ginger' O'Connell visited the Rockcorry area in 1914 he noted:

> I met the Rev. Lorcan Ó Ciaráin, PP – 'the poorest parish priest in Ireland' as he described himself. But it was in money only that the reverend gentleman was poor, for in national spirit and energy as well as the qualities of a priest he was rich enough and to spare. Fr Ó Ciaráin had organized and kept going and got armed a Volunteer corps, and had besides trained every male parishioner – and some of the females – to be crack shots: he was a fine marksman himself.⁴⁸

Ó Ciaráin claimed his parish was so poor because it was made up of servant boys and girls, the minions, as he saw them, of the local Big House, Dartrey Castle.[49] He had a long history of discord with the earl of Dartrey over agrarian as well as local political matters that came to a head following the Larne gun-running, the arming of the UVF on his doorstep, and the prominent role of Dartrey in that organization. Ó Ciaráin formed a nationalist committee that composed a circular, in both Irish and English, for distribution among all of his Catholic parishioners. Declaring that it was 'surely time that we, who have always lived in obedience to the law, should be allowed to arm that we may defend our lives', the committee sought donations from supporters at home and abroad to arm the Ematris (sometimes Rockcorry) IV.[50] John McGahey's later claim that the Ematris Volunteers were well armed thanks to Fr Ó Ciaráin suggests that the initiative was successful.[51]

The Ematris company was the first of the IV to be founded in Monaghan, following the establishment of the national movement at the Rotunda in Dublin on 25 November 1913 by Eoin MacNeill. This meeting was attended by a number of Monaghan men, including Dr Conn Ward who became Monaghan IRA intelligence officer during the War of Independence.[52] The IV were founded in defence of home rule and in response to the UVF and so it quickly appealed to north Monaghan nationalists in areas where the UVF was strongest. In January 1914, at a Volunteer rally in Monaghan town, Thomas Toal told his audience that he was delighted to head the movement 'in support of Ireland and the united Irish Parliamentary Party'.[53] There were at least fifteen priests present, as well as Patrick Whelan, president of the Ulster Council of the GAA; Owen O'Duffy, Whelan's right-hand man; James Lardner MP, and Denis Carolan Rushe, secretary of the county council, who told the crowd that 'Any person who was not willing to join the Volunteer force was certainly a coward'.[54]

The political climate was different in south Monaghan where up to April 1914 the UIL and the AOH were strongly opposed to the IV in the belief that the movement would undermine all the constitutional efforts made in the past to secure home rule. In March Michael Daly, a UIL officer on the south Monaghan executive, told a gathering at Carrickmacross that they 'were not starting a Volunteer force. The north of the county might do as it chose, but they would stand by the men and the means that had won for them so far.'[55] This reflected long-standing political tensions between the two Monaghan constituencies; the south, for example, had never managed to have a councillor successfully appointed as chairman of the county council, a position up to then monopolized by Toal. Imitation, Daly claimed, was the sincerest form of flattery and to start a counter movement to the UVF was merely 'playing into the hands of the Carsonites'.[56] After the Larne gun-running episode in April 1914, and the revelation at the beginning of May that an amending bill would accompany the home rule bill, attitudes changed. Eddie Kelly recalled: 'But when the Irish people and the Irish party found that the English government were allowing the Carsonites of the north to arm their forces and to frighten the nationalists in Ulster, they decided that the Volunteer movement should spread over the whole county'.[57] In May, the national secretary of the AOH instructed local clubs to draft Hibernians into the Volunteers.[58] At the inauguration ceremony of the IV in Magheracloone that month, Fr Thomas Maguire emphasized that they were to be used as 'a protection and means of defence against the hotbloods of the North'.[59] Maguire's rhetoric offered little comfort to the small unionist minority in south Monaghan: 'No, we will not persecute the isolated Protestants amongst us, but we will gather our armed forces together and proceed northwards and teach those bigoted planters that they are not to be ungodly tyrants and that they will not hold a corner of Ireland as a portion of England, to maintain her foothold and her garrison.'[60] Maguire called on the Volunteers 'to prepare to sacrifice our blood on the altar of holy Ireland'.[61] It was a type of rhetoric that was popular throughout Europe prior to the outbreak of the First World War and would be espoused in Ireland by Patrick Pearse; such oratory could, as the *Democrat* noted, whip audiences into a frenzy.[62]

The existence of two politico-religious paramilitary style organizations further polarized local communities and had a detrimental impact on local businesses. In May 1914, the CI reported that 'businessmen and employers generally take a gloomy view of the outlook', and feared that 'an outbreak may occur at any time which will cause violent sectarian animosity which will be deep seated and long standing and will do very great injury to trade'.[63] The RIC district inspector in Clones claimed that

> the crisis has injured the trade of all sides – one man whom I know well told me that his Protestant customers send for orders by post rather than come into his shop. Another man, a Unionist engaged in the leather trade, also told me that his RC country customers have dwindled away so much that his turn over has fallen in 3 months by nearly £100.[64]

As news of the arming of the UVF spread through the press the number of IV rose from a few hundred in March to over 5,000 by June divided into thirty-seven companies.[65] In July, the CI complained that 'a large number of the followers of the National Volunteers are of a class that cannot be disciplined or controlled and these may at any time cause serious disturbance'.[66] At no stage did he make a similar comment regarding the UVF, even though the class composition of its rank and file was similar.

In February 1914, John Redmond wrote to Joseph Devlin, the Ulster-based president of the AOH, and enquired about the serious nature of unionist opposition to home rule. Devlin replied that 'We have exceptional sources of information in regard to the Ulster Volunteer movement and we are convinced that its danger is grossly exaggerated'.[67] However, Asquith and his chancellor of the exchequer, David Lloyd George, were concerned about the threat of armed insurrection and called on Redmond to seek compromise in order to avoid bloodshed in Ulster. The result was the 'county option' scheme proposed by Lloyd George in February-March 1914, whereby any Ulster county could opt out of home rule for a period of six years by means of a plebiscite. Reactions on both sides of the political divide in Monaghan were predictable. William Swann, editor of the *Standard*, deemed the proposal to be of such 'a contemptuous nature' that it 'did not merit discussion in any Unionist journal'.[68] On 16 February, Monaghan Unionist Club resolved that 'no suggestion of settlement which does not provide for the total exclusion of Ulster will be accepted by us, and that we are still determined to remain true to our Covenant, and if necessary to go to the greatest extremes to carry out its provisions and the protection of our civil and religious liberties.'[69] Nationalists were no more conciliatory, although Bishop McKenna of Clogher and Cardinal Logue both agreed that 'county option' was the best that could be achieved under the circumstances.[70]

In spite of opposition, Asquith proceeded with the bill believing that the prospects of a six-year delay would weaken the sense of urgency amongst Ulster unionists. In the meantime, the government prepared to make a show of force by strengthening the Crown forces in Ulster. In a reactionary move, sixty cavalry officers in the Curragh resigned their commissions rather than be party to coercing Ulster unionists into accepting home rule. The subsequent history of the so-called 'Curragh Mutiny' need not be recounted here but its consequences were of importance in Monaghan. The government's plan was condemned by Monaghan unionists as 'an attempted *coup d'état* by force of arms'.[71] The 'mutiny' focused minds on the very real possibility of partition and drew attention to the army's partisanship.[72] Nationalists in Monaghan and Cavan read the incident as another blatant attempt by Carson to manipulate opposition to home rule: 'It was nothing else than enlisting the assistance of the officers of the British army in the political campaign with which Carsonism is identified'.[73] The only comment made by CI Tyacke was that 'the preparation for future conflict made by the Ulster Volunteers is aggravating the Nationalists into counter-preparations and the feeling between the parties is likely to become more bitter whilst the crisis continues'.[74] On the eve of the third reading of the home rule bill in May, Monaghan Orange Lodge made known its determination that 'we shall never submit to the County Monaghan being put under a Dublin parliament, and any such proposal will meet our strenuous resistance, if necessary by force'.[75]

On 25 May 1914, the third reading of the home rule bill was carried in the House of Commons. In June, the Government of Ireland (Amendment) Bill was introduced into the Lords that made provision for a mechanism that would allow for partition; instead of county option the whole province could opt out after six years. This drastic amendment was unacceptable to the majority of the Commons. It was now up to Asquith's government to try to narrow the gap between what the Commons had offered and what the Lords demanded. As a means to this end, the king summoned a conference at Buckingham Palace on 21 July 1914, bringing Redmond, Carson, Asquith and Conservative leader, Andrew Bonar Law, face to face. Prior to the conference, the UUC had held a secret session at which Carson spoke of the gravity of the situation: 'Nothing remained for them in Ulster but to carry out the policy they had resolved on long ago and to make good the Covenant'.[76] During the conference, Carson received a telegram: 'Fellow covenanters in Monaghan expect you to stand firm, better fight than to break Covenant.'[77] The area to be excluded proved to be insuperable but the IPP flirted dangerously with the exclusion proposals, with Redmond seemingly favouring county option as a method of determining the area of Ulster to be excluded from home rule.[78] Nationalists in Monaghan became increasingly worried. The editor of the *Democrat* suggested that

> The action of King George in summoning a conference to consider the impossible task of reconciling Irish nationalist claims with Orange prejudices and pretensions proves once more how little any Englishman understands Ireland or the Irish problem. Irish nationalists cannot compromise on the question of Irish nationality.[79]

The editorial was not a direct attack upon Redmond or the IPP, but there were signs that confidence in the leadership had diminished significantly.

The conference broke down on 24 July without agreement. Two days later, on 26 July, came the nationalist reply to Larne when Erskine Childers, an English-born convert to Irish nationalism, landed a consignment of arms for the IV at Howth. British soldiers, who unsuccessfully attempted to seize the arms, were jeered and taunted as they returned to their barracks. On Bachelor's Walk in Dublin city centre, the soldiers opened fire on the crowd, killing three people and wounding thirty-eight others. Contrasting this incident with Larne, the editor of the *Democrat* accused Dublin Castle of housing 'a nest of reactionary politicians disguised as officials who are prepared to trample on popular rights throughout the national province of Ireland, while conniving at and encouraging the illegal and traitorous conduct of their brother Tories and Orange dupes in Ulster'.[80]

Reaction in Monaghan to the Bachelor's Walk incident was immediate. The following day, the Farney battalion of the Volunteers, estimated at 900 men, was mobilized and told by another radical priest, Fr John Meenan of Carrickmacross, that political tensions had been made 'all the more acute by the hideous happenings of yesterday when defenceless creatures were shot down in the streets of Dublin', while a local reporter claimed that 'it would be impossible to describe adequately the deep feelings of resentment and indignation which found a place in the hearts of every man and woman in the vast crowd'.[81] It looked likely that the recreational Volunteers would soon have to decide whether they had the stomach to fight instead of merely parading.

Whether hostilities would have reached breaking point at a local level or beyond is now for counter-factualists to debate. Britain's involvement in a European war a few days later focused attentions elsewhere. Asquith's Liberal government placed the home rule bill on the statute book but postponed its implementation until the war's end; likewise, the question of partition was temporarily shelved. At the end of August 1914, CI Tyacke reported:

> The declaration of war by Britain against Germany and Austria has completely changed the political situation. Much of the bitterness between Unionists and Nationalists which has existed during the past 12 months has been obliterated by the sudden and great danger to the empire which both parties fully realize and there is a better feeling all round and a general rallying to the cause of the empire.[82]

The outbreak of war did not obliterate years of bitterness over night and whether nationalists were contemplating the dangers to the empire was a matter of some speculation, but the war certainly did become a temporary diversion from local politics and sectarianism. For a brief period, both sets of volunteers continued to drill, though 'not with the same keeeness', and Tyacke was confident that 'all danger of collision' had disappeared.[83]

3 'It's a great war for the farmer'

> ... father had left his bench and was talking excitedly to a crowd of men in the kitchen. He was telling them of Germany and Austria and Serbia ...
> 'The Germans will bate the world,' one of the listeners said.
> 'There'll be a price for our stuff,' another said.[1]

As historians have now amply illustrated, the First World War, for so long neglected in the historiography of twentieth-century Ireland, was, in fact, one of the major watersheds in the country's history. Between 1914 and 1918, western society and politics were transformed by events associated with the most cataclysmic event of the modern era. It is hardly surprising that the consequences would reach into every corner of Europe, and, indeed, touch every county, if not parish, in Ireland. Moreover, in the middle of the war, the 1916 Rising would reshape the history of modern Ireland; the national and the global combined to produce a very different country by 1918. This chapter examines how the First World War affected Monaghan in social and economic terms. The discussion of political developments of the period is reserved for the two chapters which follow.

The assassination of Archduke Franz Ferdinand received only a brief mention in the *Democrat* of 4 July 1914. Seen in the context of Bosnian antipathy to Austrian rule, it was described as 'the latest shocking tragedy' to befall the Habsburg family.[2] It was expected to be 'a short and decisive war', with minimal impact on Monaghan or Ireland as a whole.[3] On 3 August 1914, Redmond told the House of Commons that British troops could be withdrawn from Ireland and the country would be 'defended from foreign invasion by her armed sons, and for this purpose armed Nationalist Catholics in the South will be only too glad to join arms with the armed Protestant Ulstermen in the North'.[4] His speech was taken by Thomas McGahon as evidence of 'a new Ireland', one that, because of the certainty of home rule, was:

> calm, self-reliant, prepared to defend her shores and her rights, seeking to injure or offend none, but resolved to have and to keep that which is hers; confident in her strength, in the justices of her cause and the protection of the Almighty Power that eventually decides the destinies of nations.[5]

There was a certain triumphal tone in McGahon's editorial, an exuding of a new confidence emanating from the inevitable passing of home rule, and a drawing together of faith and fatherland, where identity and nationhood were linked with religion. With news beginning to filter through of the gentry and aristocracy offering to support and train the IV, McGahon felt, 'This surely brings us nearer that cordial unity of class and creed which is so desirable in Ireland'.[6] Further north in the county, Charles Laverty, a Castleblayney solicitor, told a UIL meeting: 'The democracies were being brought together, and would be brought still closer by the operation of home rule. They would become as Canada, Australia, South Africa and other self-governing parts of the British Empire, loyal and contented.'[7] This was another typical reflection of how Redmondites perceived Ireland's future within the empire. The police noted a sharp decline in politico-religious tensions and reported 'no opposition or counter demonstrations by the Unionist party'.[8] However, individual unionists remained truculent. When a tenant named Keown erected 'a home rule arch' in celebration on his Magheracloone farm, the landlord, Mrs Brownlow (the woman responsible for collecting signatures to the Covenant from door to door in Farney), had him served with an eviction notice. The chairman of the south Monaghan executive of the UIL warned: 'Mrs Brownlow will be sorry in the end that she acted in so high-handed a manner. The days of petty tyranny are past.'[9] It was no coincidence that the Brownlow estate became one of the most disturbed from April 1915 when a protracted and toxic dispute broke out there over the tenancy of three farms.[10] The secretary of the UIL made another telling remark: 'It's the wrong time to show such a spirit if they [unionists] want our sympathy for the empire'.[11]

Redmond then made another speech at Woodenbridge in County Wicklow on 20 September in which he urged Volunteers to go 'wherever the firing-line extends, in defence of right, of freedom and of religion in this war'.[12] The request did not resonate with the IV in Monaghan; Tyacke, like his fellow CIs in other counties, reported that 'with scarcely an exception' they hung back from recruitment, willing to fight for Ireland but not England and he concluded: 'There is no doubt that a large number of the Irish Volunteers have stopped drilling lest it should lead to their being sent to "the front"'.[13] Joseph McKenna had joined the IV in 1914 and later recalled how that 'phase petered out after the outbreak of the First World War in 1914 when a Captain White came and addressed our company and advised all to join the British army in the fight against the Germans'.[14]

Woodenbridge split the Volunteers. A majority sided with Redmond and became known as the Irish National Volunteers (INVs). A minority of about 10 per cent, McKenna among them, seceded and retained the name Irish Volunteers. In November, the police reported a company of IV in Newbliss, about seventy strong, under the command of Patrick Whelan.[15] At the same time, in neighbouring Aughnamullen West and the village of Rockcorry, 'Sinn Féin influence' was said to have been at work under Fr Bernard Maguire and

Fr Lorcan Ó Ciaráin (with the assistance of the schoolmaster and mistress at Corravaccan) who from the outbreak of the war were circulating anti-recruiting leaflets.[16] Ó Ciaráin's Ematris Volunteers had also split from Redmond. From the moment the split occurred in Monaghan, the police conflated the Irish Volunteers with 'Sinn Féin' and used the latter term to describe those immediately dismissed by the nationalist press as 'sham extremists', 'cranks and notoriety-hunters' who compounded the 'political disease' of factionalism that had affected Monaghan nationalist politics in the past.[17] Ó Ciaráin achieved notoriety for his anti-recruitment campaign. In September 1914, he delivered his most vitriolic anti-recruitment speech at Corravaccan chapel in Rockcorry:

> If there was anyone foolish enough to enlist he hoped he would be sent to the front as soon as possible and that Ireland would not be at any loss; that the only loss Ireland would sustain would be the loss of the bones to make bone manure, and that France or Belgium, wherever the bones lay, would be so much the richer and that if they were not shot he hoped they would return in such a physically unfit condition that they would not be able to marry which would be a blessing as they would not be able to continue their species.[18]

From the outset, recruitment in Monaghan, on both sides of the politico-religious divide, was slow. In August, CI Tyacke claimed that the UVF were showing no signs of enthusiasm to enlist, claiming that 'only one or two have so far expressed their readiness to go to the front', and this he put down to them waiting for directions from Sir Edward Carson.[19] As for the INV, they showed 'no disposition for service as soldiers, they state that they are waiting for home rule to pass before taking any steps and that then they will volunteer for the defence of Ireland'. Tyacke concluded: 'Scarcely any of them are armed or disciplined or properly drilled and they would be a poor fighting force without a course of military training'.[20]

The slow response came as a surprise to the aristocracy and gentry who had led the UVF and who expected the rank and file to join the army enthusiastically. On 11 September 1914, fifty-two members of the Monaghan UVF from across the north of the county enlisted at the Madden and Johnston Memorial Orange Hall in Monaghan town and were feted there before being paraded to the railway station.[21] This verified Tyacke's claim that they were waiting for directions from Carson; this was after the formation of the 36th Ulster Division in September, which seems to have been significant to the Monaghan UVF members in search of some form of identity in the British army. In time, the *Standard* would report that 'many Covenanters are upholding the cause of right and freedom on the European battlefields'.[22] The terminology was significant; it was another reminder to Ulster unionists, at a time when partition was being mooted, that Monaghan men were doing their share under the sacred commitment given a few years before. The *Standard* made sure to point out that brothers Thomas and Noble Jackson of Tanderageebrock were 'enthusiastic members' of the UVF and 'valued members' of Crosses loyal Orange lodge; William Mullan had 'rendered splendid service to the Unionist cause in the capacity of drill sergeant' of the UVF and was a member of Feragh LOL and Royal Black Preceptory; Alex Sproule of Monaghan town UVF came from a long line of family soldiers: his grandfather and three granduncles had fought at Waterloo.[23]

However, the fifty-two who enlisted in September represented only 2 per cent of the total UVF membership in the county and notably signalled the beginning of the end of recruitment in any significant numbers. Timothy Bowman has made the point that by October 'the most enthusiastic had recruited' throughout Ulster.[24] If the police reports and official recruitment statistics are accurate then this would certainly seem to have been the case in Monaghan. Between 15 December 1914 and 15 December 1915, a total of 319 recruits joined from Monaghan of which 213 were Catholics and 106 were Protestants, representing the lowest figure in Ulster. Cavan, for example, contributed 313 Catholics and 140 Protestants, while neighbouring Louth contributed 497 Catholics and 53 Protestants.[25] There followed a period when recruitment drives produced few results, even in unionist areas, a pattern not uncommon in neighbouring counties such as Tyrone.[26] In 1915–16, drives in Monaghan town, Carrickmacross, Castleblayney, Ballybay and Rockcorry failed to attract anyone. The *Democrat* took pleasure in ridiculing a recruitment drive in the Orange hall in Rockcorry that reputedly attracted 140 UVF men from the villages of Drum and Newbliss but which failed to secure a single soldier.[27] In January 1915, the editor of the *Standard* expressed his profound regret that the UVF had left themselves open to the charge that they were only good at playing soldiers in Orange halls where there was no danger from German bullets.[28] The shaming tactics adopted by M.E. Knight, who told a recruitment drive in Clones that those who went to the front voluntarily would be treated as 'gentlemen', while those who stayed at home would be looked upon with contempt, had no impact.[29] Between August 1915 and September 1916, only 100 joined the army in Monaghan compared to 200 in Cavan and 179 in Donegal.[30] By October 1917, the police reported that 'recruiting for the army is practically at a standstill'.[31]

With the failure of the government to enforce compulsory military service in Ireland in 1918, a new voluntary recruiting scheme was initiated by Lord Lieutenant J.D.P. French whereby the country was divided into ten areas in order to achieve a quota of 50,000 men by 1 October. Monaghan and Armagh constituted one area with a quota of 2,500 men. By 5 September

1918, of the 242 recruits from the Monaghan–Armagh area, only 22 were from Monaghan.

However, it has to be admitted that the available statistics present something of a conundrum, as do police complaints and contemporary criticisms. Earlier, the point was made that between 15 December 1914 and 15 December 1915, 550 men from Louth joined the army. Yet, Donal Hall, in his exhaustive effort to map the number of participants in the war from that county, gives a total figure of almost 3,000.[32] Similarly, and of more relevance to this study, Kevin Cullen has identified and named 539 men killed who had been born in Monaghan.[33] If the generally accepted average of one in five being killed is applied to this figure, then around 2,500 Monaghan natives may have served. Granted, Monaghan-born does not mean they were living in Monaghan at the time of the outbreak of war and a study of the regiments in which they were fighting illustrates this: Highland Light Infantry (14), Royal Scottish Fusiliers (8), Royal Scots (6) and forty-one identified in Canadian and Anzac forces. But if we take the number killed who were serving in Irish regiments, it totals around 300, the point being that many more Monaghan men enlisted than the statistics reveal.

As was to be expected, the contribution of the aristocracy and gentry, those with long military tradition of service to the army and navy and the empire as a whole, was significant. Norman Leslie was heir to the family estate at Glaslough since his father, Sir John, an avowed unionist and Orangeman, had broken the entail to disinherit his eldest son, Shane (christened John), because he had converted to Catholicism and nationalism. Norman – who had his own weaknesses, being something of a rake and womanizer – was a professional soldier and a serving officer when war broke out. He wrote to a female friend shortly before he left for the front:

> Try not to worry too much about the war anyhow. Units, individuals cannot count. Remember we are writing a new page of history. Future generations cannot be allowed to read the decline of the British Empire and attribute it to us. We live our little lives and die. To some are given chances of proving themselves men, and to others no chance comes. Whatever our individual faults, virtues or qualities may be, it matters not, for when we are up against big things, let us forget individuals and let us act as one great British unit, mixed and fearless. Some will live and many will die, but count the loss not. It is better by far to go out with honour than survive with shame.[34]

Characterized by imperial patriotism, chivalry, valour and romanticism, Leslie's beliefs fairly typified what young members of the gentry wrote before they encountered the horrors of trench warfare. Very few of the county's gentry or aristocratic families were not represented at the front and, indeed, very few escaped bereavement at some stage or another. Norman Leslie was one of the first killed, meeting his death at Armentières in October 1914.[35] The earl of Dartrey's son-in-law, Charles Pennant, was killed in 1915. Colonel Gerald Madden of Hilton Park (former commander of the north Monaghan UVF), F.K. Leslie of Glenburne, and two sons of J.T. Black of Ballyleck (and Gola) were all killed in 1915–16.

Those members of the landed families who did not go to war contributed as best they could on the home front. The women busied themselves on all types of committees engaged in charitable works and the comfort of the returning wounded, the preparation of parcels of food, cigarettes and blankets to be sent to the front, and fundraising for ambulances. Lady Dartrey was 'foremost in the good work' and president of the county's Soldiers and Sailors Help Society.[36] Two rooms of the Lucas Scudamore home at Castleshane were turned into a war hospital supply depot preparing prosthetic limbs and other medical requirements.[37] Lord and Lady Dartrey, Colonel John Leslie, Miss Murray-Ker and Colonel Lucas Scudamore were active on recruitment drives, while it was said of Colonel Richardson that 'he never spares himself when hard work is to be done in the interests of the Ulster Division'.[38] Michael E. Knight and others initiated collections in aid of the UVF Patriotic Fund after the Somme to ensure 'those of their number who may be maimed and broken do not suffer from want when they return home'.[39]

While the gentry found it difficult to comprehend what they perceived to be apathy amongst the farming classes, nationalists generally did not criticize and more frequently offered excuses as to why farmers' sons should stay at home. In October 1915, the county council passed a motion, which admittedly had a political agenda as it was objecting to the introduction of compulsory military service to Ireland, that stated: 'any further diminishing of the male population would render it impossible to carry on tillage and leave the country altogether dependent on foreign produce'.[40] Not long previously, one Monaghan unionist farmer found it incumbent upon himself to defend his class when he wrote to the *Standard* in June 1915 pointing out that pressure was already coming to bear on tillage farmers in the county for the want of labour. Monaghan, he argued, could not afford to lose any more of the agricultural workforce.[41] However, the gentry were less convinced. In December 1915, Colonel Lucas Scudamore complained that 'no set of people in the world ... had more done for them by the government than the farmers of Ireland and no set of people had done less for their country.'[42] Lucas Scudamore was not the only person to advert to economic prosperity as the damper on patriotic duty. From an early stage, CI Tyacke considered that young men from rural areas were being held back from enlisting by 'selfishness and want of patriotism', inspired by the 'comfortable conditions' resulting from the 'exceptionally good prices' on offer for farm produce. He remarked that it was unlikely that they would voluntarily 'relinquish their comfortable pursuits for the most arduous and dangerous life of the trenches'.[43] In Clare, David Fitzpatrick found that 'Protestants who had struggled grimly to maintain a respectable livelihood before the war, suddenly found their income rising'.[44] There were, of course, considerably more Protestants in Monaghan.

Perhaps there is also a case to be made in defence of Protestant farmers that the growth of agrarian agitation during the war years, fuelled by land hunger, acted as a further disincentive for their sons to enlist.[45] It was a case made by ardent southern unionist, J.M. Wilson (brother of Field Marshal Sir Henry Wilson), who did a tour of Ulster during the war years and argued that unionists felt 'a natural dislike to leave their homes unprotected as long as their nationalist neighbours abstain from recruiting'.[46] In Monaghan, Sir John Leslie made a similar point claiming he was aware of the fear among unionist farmers that if they were sent from Ireland, the county would be in danger from people, 'whose political opinions were not quite the same as theirs'.[47] When they joined the UVF they knew they would be at home every night to defend their property as well as their civil and religious liberties; it was a completely different matter to have to defend the empire far from Monaghan.

On the nationalist side, there were other factors that discouraged recruiting. Many of the county's Catholic clergy, besides Fr Ó Ciaráin, were generally not in favour of Irishmen joining the British army.[48] The IV, or 'Sinn Féiners' as Tyacke labelled them, organized anti-recruitment demonstrations throughout the county, but particularly in the south and central areas. In November 1914, anti-recruiting leaflets were circulated by the school master and mistress at Corravaccan school and posted at Rockcorry chapel.[49] As we shall see in the next chapter, such anti-recruitment activity often had an intimidating effect. Moreover, anti-recruiters soon had excellent propaganda as news of the slaughter at places such as the Somme came through, or letters from the front revealed the true horrors of trench warfare, or the returning wounded provided the horrific physical evidence to dispel any romantic notion attached to soldiering. After the Somme, E.N. Ensor pleaded for additional recruits through the columns of the *Standard* in August 1916: '[Courage] did not fail you on the 1st July, surely, surely you won't desert us in our hour of need'.[50] However, it seems that the 'glorious achievement' of the Somme sounded the death knell for recruitment among unionists as well as nationalists in Monaghan. In his September 1916 report, Tyacke noted: 'Recruiting is still bad throughout this county and is not likely to improve'.[51] Young men were simply no longer prepared to go voluntarily to their slaughter.

While recruitment figures may have been disappointing to Lucas Scudamore, he may have later regretted belittling the monumental sacrifices made by some families: for example, of the four sons of Samuel Steenson of

Glaslough, two were killed in action and one died of pneumonia at the front. Of the seven sons of Thomas Crawford of Newbliss who served, three were decorated for gallantry. An examination of the pages of the *Standard* for the last six months of 1916 clearly illustrates the devastating impact that the Somme alone had on so many Protestant families. The editorial of 1 August 1916, after news of dozens of Monaghan dead and scores of wounded and missing had reached home, proudly proclaimed: 'the glorious deeds of heroism of the Ulster Division in the great advance ... had filled with pride the people of the whole province.' One report told how 'Newbliss had indeed paid a heavy toll'; at least three men from the small village had been killed, one had died of wounds and three more were wounded or missing in action. Among those killed was Private Joseph Burke. On the very same day his brother, John, was badly injured in a gas attack, while their father, also John, died suddenly at home. Their neighbour, William Clarke, received news of the death of his son; another son had previously been wounded suppressing the 1916 rebellion in Dublin.

Another neighbour, Private James Dunn, the eldest son of William Dunn, serving in the Bedfordshire Regiment, was also killed. He had served his apprenticeship as a gardener on the Dartrey demesne in Rockcorry before moving to work for Earl Brownlow at Berkhampstead. While there, Lord Kitchener paid a visit and on hearing this, Dunn 'sought out and personally offered his services to his Lordship and his country'.[52] Shortly afterwards Revd W.M. Wilson of the Methodist Manse in Monaghan town received news of his son from a comrade: 'The last I saw of him was in crossing "No Man's Land" when he was shouting encouragement to his men and steadying them to face the shell-fire we were subjected to'.[53] Two sons of Henry Davis of Clones were killed. Lance-Corporal Mark Wallace of Killygoan was killed shortly after leaving the trench. His brother, Jack, had survived Gallipoli and was then serving in India. Private James Wilson of Corbrack House in Ballybay was killed and his brother, John, was reported missing. Private James Kennedy's family received news from Lieutenant T.F. Given: 'He was found by a search party belonging to another regiment, badly wounded, and was brought into the trenches, but, I am sorry to say, died soon afterwards. His body was buried ... in a cemetery just behind the line which we had been holding for some time previous to the 1st July.'[54]

The waiting and uncertainty for families, particularly during the horror of the Somme, was deeply stressful, so much so that M.E. Knight published a letter in the *Standard* on 20 July 1916 to caution against rumours: 'Considerable anxiety and doubt prevails among the relatives and friends of many of our gallant soldiers of the Ulster division from this county engaged in the recent fighting, no reliable news as to many of them has been received'. Reports in the *Standard* week after week listing death after death, or even the arrival home of scores of severely wounded young men (of whom so little is known) had a numbing effect; many of these would never see or walk or work again. There was also the additional concern over the psychological impact of war, characterized as 'shell shock'. The first such recorded Monaghan casualty was Sergeant T.H. Willis of Clones sent home from the Somme in July 1916. During that summer, Monaghan asylum reported significant increases in the number of 'criminal lunatics' admitted, but, in fact, these were soldiers suffering from shell shock; the authorities had to label them 'criminal lunatics' in order for the asylum to receive capitation.[55]

Of course, Catholic families suffered the same heartbreak although, notably, the *Democrat* never gave the comprehensive coverage to 'war heroes' accorded them in the *Standard*, or encased its headlines in black lines of mourning. The *Democrat* undoubtedly supported Redmond's stance on the war, while at the same time continuing its criticism of Ulster unionism's anti-home rule position with particular reference to the threat of partition. Moreover, its pages exposed the complex nature of local nationalist attitudes to the war, revealing that local society was much more complex in this respect than the tradition bequeathed to later generations. In December 1915, a letter appeared in the *Democrat* from two young privates serving in France. It is always dangerous to presume these matters but it is probable they were both Catholic nationalists because they wrote of how much they enjoyed 'the Gaelic notes' every week and finished their letter with 'Go on the Geraldines' (a reference to a local GAA club). They wanted to let everyone in Louth and south Monaghan know that 'All are happy and in the best of health and *anxious to strike a blow for the dear homeland* [author's italics]'.[56] Thus, as far as they were concerned, they were fighting for Ireland, even if their fight was on the Continent and in a British army uniform. Around the same time, telegrams were arriving in homes around Farney: James Casey of Magheross, a member of 5th Battalion, Royal Irish Fusiliers, had just been killed at Rocky Peak; a few weeks before, Charles Dunn of Inniskeen, a sergeant in the Royal Scots, died of wounds received at Loos; in May, Edward Finnegan of Drimmahill had died on the *Lusitania*. In early July 1916, three months after the 1916 Rising, the nationalist Carrickmacross UDC passed a resolution of sympathy to Revd T.S. Watson whose son had 'died in defence of his country as many thousands of brave Irishmen had done'.[57]

In November 1916, news reached Monaghan that Private Thomas Hughes, a Catholic from Broomfield, serving in the 6th Connaught Rangers, had been awarded the Victoria Cross. On 3 September, Hughes had been wounded during the Somme offensive. Despite his injuries he single-handedly captured an enemy machine-gun position, killing two gunners and capturing three or four prisoners. The nationalist-dominated Castleblayney board of poor law guardians agreed to present him with an address to welcome him home, there being unanimous agreement that 'Co Monaghan should not alone feel proud of him – Ireland should be delighted with the record of this young hero.'[58] When Hughes was demobilized in 1919, he returned home to a small farm outside Castleblayney. Three years previously he might have expected to return to a hero's welcome; instead, he returned to a very different Ireland to the one he had left.[59]

Some of the young Catholics who enlisted had previously gotten a taste for militarism from their Volunteer days. Private Thomas McKearney from Castleblayney, for example, was killed in March 1916; he had been in the INV and it was said that he had 'never missed drill practice'.[60] For others there was an element of adventure without the anticipation of the type of horror they were to experience (as undoubtedly was the case for their Protestant neighbours). Some, like the two young Dundalk privates, went out of patriotic duty to Ireland and in defence of small nations. In the early months, the local newspapers provided dramatic and graphic accounts of alleged German atrocities. When news of the sack of Louvain reached Monaghan, Charles Laverty, the last Redmondite to contest a Monaghan general election in 1910, condemned German atrocities on a town 'dear to the Irish heart that lifted up the Irish in Penal Days'.[61] Such pronouncements may have been enough to encourage some to enlist. However, the main reason was most likely economic; soldiering offered a wage and more importantly 'separation money' for the families of many who had few better options available to them. What is more certain is that considerably more Monaghan families, nationalist and unionist alike, were affected by the First World War than by the 1916 Rising or the War of Independence. And this was a fact not adverted to after 1922.

The war undoubtedly reinvigorated the local agricultural economy, but while there were those who prospered, there were many others left behind and over time this led to increased social tensions. Patrick Kavanagh, poet-novelist, born in Inniskeen in 1904, published a memoir in which he recalled that every Sunday during the war on his way home from Mass, he heard people enthuse: 'It's a great war for the farmer'. He recalled that: 'The price of farm produce soared. Everybody was in great good humour. They had money in every pocket … All hopes were centred in a long war and no one was disappointed.'[62] The evidence substantiated Kavanagh's claims. War broke out at an opportune time for farmers, just before the harvest. In July 1914, the last market in Carrickmacross before the outbreak of war, hay was sold for 36d. per hundredweight and eggs for 10d. per dozen. Almost four years later at the March 1918 market, hay was sold for 69d. per hundredweight; eggs for 34d. per dozen.[63] Little wonder Kavanagh wrote: 'Our parents paid more attention to the fowls than they paid to us children. The hens were laying golden eggs.' Even local children benefited, getting 5s. a stone from the sale of blackberries.[64]

CI Tyacke saw evidence of the new prosperity all around him: his reports in the early months of the war were full of comments such as 'the price of farm produce is higher than usual'; 'the prices of stock and farm produce are very high and farmers are "coining money"'; 'The farmers are realizing exceptionally good prices for their farm produce and are in comfortable circumstances.'[65] At the beginning of 1916 in Killanny, Withrington auctioneers sold a small farm of seven statute acres at the 'record price of £600' and a report on the sale expressed astonishment that 'there is no dwelling house or farm buildings on the lands and this renders the price all the more remarkable'.[66] James Thompson sold a 30-acre farm for £1,035 with a yearly rental of £27, which equated to 38 years' purchase when the best prices available under the 1903 Land Act had been around 25 years.[67] The farmers of Killanny had also formed a Farm Implement Society, a form of co-operative that promoted the sharing of modern farm equipment, the purchase of which had been necessary to keep up with demands in tillage.[68] Conacre (land for letting on the eleven-month system) was in plentiful demand as landowners released untenanted land and moved to exploit the market.[69] Before the war ended, farmers were paying up to £22 an acre for conacre, at least five times more than they had paid before the conflict.[70]

Agricultural prosperity had a spin-off for the shopkeepers who during the Christmas period of 1914 'generally did better than they had expected'.[71] The desire of the shopkeepers to reap wartime profits was clearly evident in the local newspaper advertizing columns; with more money to spend, farmers and their families were encouraged to come and see the 'first show of tailor-made suits' and 'exclusive millinery to match'.[72]

The Catholic Church took a dim view of the wartime extravagances. In his Lenten Pastoral of 1916 published in the *Democrat*, Cardinal Michael Logue, archbishop of Armagh and primate of All Ireland, preached that society was 'preparing a heritage of woe and grinding poverty for generations still unborn', and urged people to become more thrifty:

> Hence to meet these conditions, which will certainly come with the end of the war, it is a matter of ordinary prudence to practice, henceforward, the most rigid economy, avoiding needless expenditure, cutting off superfluities, turning to the best account the short interval of prosperity which war prices have brought to many.[73]

The shopkeepers, it might be argued, took this to an extreme in their own interests when, the following Christmas, the merchants in towns and villages throughout Monaghan announced the ending of the custom of 'Christmas boxes', on the pretext that wartime prices had made them financially impracticable; it was more the case, in Yeats' words, of them 'adding the ha'pence to the pence'. This flagrant greed impacted upon the rural labouring classes and the small uneconomic holders that wartime prosperity left behind. As early as February 1915, CI Tyacke noted that 'the high price of coal and provisions is severe on the poorer classes'.[74] At the end of 1915, there were 105 inmates in Carrickmacross workhouse, an increase of ten from the previous year (some of whom were wounded soldiers, not a good advertisement for taking the king's shilling).[75] At the beginning of 1916, charity balls were held in the town in aid of the local poor relief fund; socially exclusive extravaganzas to feed the impoverished![76] Meanwhile, there was a huge increase in the 'number of people who could not afford to pay for treatment in Dublin hospitals'.[77] While the private sector – from merchants to large farmers – was prospering, those in the public sector felt aggrieved. In January 1916, school teachers (who notably later played a prominent role in the revolutionary movement) resolved at a meeting of a Monaghan branch of the Irish National Teachers' Organisation:

> That owing to the increased cost of living, consequent on the present European conflict and the rather miserable wage of the great majority of Irish national teachers we respectfully emphasize the urgent need of an increase to our salaries in the form of a 'war bonus' as has been granted to other public departments.[78]

What angered people then was no different to what would continue to animate them a century after the 1916 Rebellion.

The mainstay politicians stayed clear of anything that suggested socialist or, as it was frequently referred to, Bolshevist involvement. Thus, when a resolution protesting against increased taxes was sent from Dublin to Carrickmacross board of guardians, Thomas Martin declared: 'Let these fellows that want to raise dissension go and mind their own business'; James Shevlin pointed out that 'there are a lot of crack-haired fellows in Dublin that want to raise rebellion'; while Eddie Kelly said that 'he would be against the idea of mentioning the taxation question, because to his mind it would be a kind of supporting this anti-Redmond move, and anything that was anti-Redmond he would oppose to the last nail'.[79]

Among those raising dissension in Dublin was one of the country's leading socialists, with strong Monaghan connections, James Connolly, founder of the Irish Socialist Republican Party, Ulster organizer of the Irish Transport and General Workers' Union (ITGWU), leader of the Dublin workers in the 1913 lockout after Jim Larkin's imprisonment, and commandant of the Irish Citizen Army, whose parents, John Connolly and Mary McGinn, both came from the Newbliss area.[80] Despite being born in Edinburgh, Connolly recorded on his 1911 census return that he had been born in Monaghan.[81] No one has been able to establish his motive for this. There does not seem to be much evidence of his having visited Monaghan during his lifetime, except a report in the unionist *Standard* that he had visited for the 1798 centenary to commemorate a relative who had been hanged as a rebel; the inference was that rebellion was in his blood.[82] Connolly does not seem to have had any profile in Monaghan in 1916, and while there were not very many in the county propounding socialist ideologies at the time, there was still a groundswell of discontent that could feed into revolutionary activity in the future, as discussed in chapter 4.

***

During the early years of the war, there were those who entertained hopes that as unionists and nationalists fought side by side in the trenches it might somehow lead to a conciliatory attitude when the war ended. In January 1916, J.H. Campbell's speech to the Commons was reported in the nationalist *Democrat*:

> He for one believed that when Irishmen who were fighting side by side in the trenches, and in many cases going down into the valley and shadow of death together, that after the war was over a new atmosphere would be created, and in that atmosphere he hoped there would be found a solution of those most acute domestic differences, a solution which would have been consistent with the loyalty and patriotism of the Irish people on the one hand and their national aspirations on the other.[83]

The editor of the *Standard*, William Swann, was less optimistic on such matters. Back in September 1914 he had asserted: 'it looks as if Mr Redmond is splendidly capable of talking imperially but that his followers are only capable of acting parochially. "England's difficulty is Ireland's opportunity" used to be their motto, and there is yet a hankering who believe it so.'[84] His allusion to the Fenian maxim was ironic given what was to happen in Ireland at Easter 1916, just two months after Campbell had voiced his aspirations for Ireland.

4 'The Dublin Insurrection of 1916 came and went without a ripple'[1]

>Having organized and trained her manhood through her secret revolutionary organisation, the Irish Republican Brotherhood, and through her open military organisations, the Irish Volunteers and the Irish Citizen Army, having patiently perfected her discipline, having resolutely waited for the right moment to reveal itself, she now seizes that moment, and, supported by her exiled children in America and by gallant allies in Europe, but relying in the first on her own strength, she strikes in full confidence of victory.[2]

In November 1915, local solicitor Edward Phelan organized a meeting in O'Neill's Hotel on the main street of Carrickmacross to form a recruiting committee. This was the same hotel where the Monaghan Gaelic Athletic Association had been founded in 1887.[3] Phelan typified many of those who had continued to support John Redmond after the 1914 split: from a middle-class, small town, Catholic nationalist background – his family were drapers on the Main Street – he was well educated, successful, mixed in all the right social clubs and circles, had local government experience and was young enough to have aspirations towards an important future role in a home rule Ireland. Like the vast majority of his peers, he had no difficulties with the limited nature of independence that the Home Rule Act promised to Ireland. A parliament in Dublin was greatly anticipated and, in the meantime, he supported Redmond's stance that Ireland should provide young men for the British army to fight for the freedom of small nations, of which Ireland was but one. Around fifty people attended – doctors, other professionals and businessmen of all religious denominations (there was no reference to farmers from the rural areas). Phelan spoke of the necessity 'to deal with present military exigencies and home defence … It is the opinion of the vast majority of Irishmen that this war must be prosecuted to a successful conclusion on the Continent, otherwise our country may soon become a second Belgium.'[4]

Fifty years later, when men like Phelan came under scrutiny in an independent Irish Republic celebrating the golden anniversary of the 1916 Rising, they were accused of having forgotten their true national identity, of having accepted the home rule bill as 'a pitiful concession to the aspirations of a nation, a sad ending to the dreams of Parnell and no answer at all to the ambitions of the Fenians'.[5] Phelan's pre-Rising middle-class nationalist Ireland was condemned as 'a tiny microcosm of the vast imperialistic macrocosm that was Great Britain', where 'all things English were being accepted without question as superior', where Irishmen played English games, amused themselves in English music-halls, and took pride in Britain's victories.[6] Those who bought into this interpretation overlooked the fact that for the majority of people in Monaghan in early 1916, Britain's victories were important: for constitutional nationalists such as Phelan the speedy implementation of home rule depended upon victory in the European war; for unionists, their supreme sacrifice in helping to win the war could not be ignored and consequently home rule could not be forced on Ulster; and for both sides of the politico-religious divide victory would simply mean the safe return home of hundreds of young Monaghan men and women of all persuasions who volunteered in various capacities.

While the names of hundreds of Monaghan-born war dead were consigned for decades to oblivion, remembered only by their families, three young Carrickmacross men – James Ross (a cousin of Private Joseph Ross killed in Belgium in the summer of 1915),[7] Eugene Donnelly and John Quinn – lived on in local lore because they disrupted the recruitment meeting in O'Neill's Hotel and almost immediately became 'martyrs for a principle'.[8] Local Volunteer, P.V. Hoey, later claimed that these men and their actions provided 'the signal for the national revival in Farney'.[9]

In the lead up to the recruitment meeting, rumours had been gathering that 'the shopkeepers in [Carrickmacross] town were going to dismiss their assistants to compel them to join the army'.[10] Rumours such as these could have a disconcerting effect. Sergeant John Duffy decided to take no chances and acting on information that there was going to be trouble, placed a constable on the door of O'Neill's and mobilized the other policemen on duty. As members of the recruitment committee left the hotel, they were accosted by a hostile crowd who 'hooted and cheered derisively' and Phelan was hit over the head with a brick.[11] Some of the men in the crowd, who were members of a recently formed IV company, then lined up in drill formation. Headed by a local brass band, they marched up and down the street, deliberately stopping a number of times at the residences of Phelan, Dr Bernard McCaul and Dr Peter McKenna, where the band then played loudly and the hostile crowd booed and hooted.[12] This was an old form of intimidation used since the 1880s by the Land League and the National League; it broke no laws but had the desired effect of announcing to the wider public who they should shun.

Three young local labourers – the aforementioned Donnelly, Quinn and Ross – were singled out from the crowd by the police and arrested. They were subsequently tried at Carrickmacross petty sessions on the charge of unlawful assemblage 'with divers other evilly disposed persons and did there and then by sundry acts in the nature of yelling, booing and marching to the sound of music, did strike terror into and terrify the loyal subjects of our sovereign lord, the King'.[13] Sergeant Duffy gave evidence that he saw Ross playing the melodeon, Donnelly giving words of command to the Volunteers, and Quinn at the head of the column. No civilian witness was called; perhaps none was prepared to give evidence. P.J. Kerley, the defendants' solicitor, placed the onus of blame for what happened on the inaction of the RIC: 'As usual the police', he told the court, 'were not in the right place'. Kerley admitted the young men were members of the IV but, he argued, they were entitled to march and had broken no law in that respect.[14]

The case was adjourned because the four magistrates could not agree on a unanimous verdict. Two of them were resident magistrates, J.W.E. Dunsterville and G.H. Shannon, professional servants of the Dublin Castle administration. In all probability, acting on behalf of the Crown, Dunsterville and Shannon would have found the trio guilty. However, the other two were local magistrates, Alexander Fennell from Carrickmacross and Bernard O'Rourke from Inniskeen. Fennell's position is unclear but it is certain that O'Rourke opposed any conviction.

In 1912, when the third home rule bill had been introduced, O'Rourke was thirty-six years old and, like Edward Phelan, very much fitted into the mould of what Senia Pašeta has described as 'the last generation of young and enthusiastic home rulers, the men and women who were poised to inherit the free and sovereign Ireland which seemed at last to be within reach'.[15] At the unfurling of a new UIL banner in Inniskeen on St Patrick's Day 1914, O'Rourke told an estimated audience of 2,500 people, 'he hoped that before twelve months it would be borne to Dublin for the opening of the new Irish parliament'.[16] The likelihood is that he saw himself as a candidate in the first elections.

However, within two years of the unfurling of the UIL banner, O'Rourke's political ideology had been radically transformed. He traced it to Redmond's declaration of support for the British war effort, but he had also become frustrated by the long suspension of home rule that resulted in disaffection among many Redmondites.[17] Ultimately, the procrastination of the British government proved fatal for the IPP. O'Rourke's radicalization was also a response to the growing militancy of Ulster unionism, and the consequent chain of events it triggered, including the arming of the UVF, the Curragh 'Mutiny' and Redmond's acceptance of the principle of partition.[18]

Local events also acted as catalysts in O'Rourke's conversion. The first occurred in Inniskeen in late 1914. Laurence Keenan purchased a farm at Keenogue from the Land Commission, which had repossessed it from James Meegan because he had defaulted on the payment of his annuities. This was a particularly sensitive issue. First of all, the Land Commission was accused of having acted no better than the landlords in the past. Second, Keenan had taken over what was technically an evicted farm and since the Land War days anybody guilty of this was treated with the greatest odium by the local community. Keenan was soon subjected to widespread intimidation. He was shunned, people refused to serve him in the local shops, and at night groups of young men gathered around his home, banging saucepans, using broken bottles as trumpets and causing a din aimed at keeping him awake.[19]

In February 1915, the intimidation led to the arrest of twelve men from Inniskeen. Great sensation and anger was caused by the sudden death of Michael McCabe, father of one of the young men, the presumed victim of a heart attack brought on by the arrest of his son. The Inniskeen UIL passed a resolution condemning the high-handed and 'arbitrary' action of the police and Thomas McGahon declared that this was not the type of activity expected after the passing of home rule: 'If they were German spies they would have been treated with more consideration ... I protest against such inhuman proceedings and star-chamber inquiries.'[20] The arrests led to an upsurge in local UIL membership with forty-four new members enrolling that month. On St Patrick's Day, the local division of the AOH prepared to march down to Keenan's farm in protest, only to be obstructed by a large force of police drafted in from Carrickmacross and outlying areas. The tone of the report in the following week's *Democrat* was loaded with sarcasm: 'It was a pity to see such a body of fine stalwart constables wasting their time on a quiet countryside road where there was nothing to be done, and at a time when the services of good men are so badly needed at the front'.[21]

Eventually, James Meegan, the ringleader, was arrested for his continuous harassment of Keenan and a magistrate was taken from Monaghan town to try his case. This simply added fuel to the flames. The *Democrat* asked: 'Why respect the suspicious process of calling in the resident magistrate from Monaghan to adjudicate in this paltry business, instead of bringing the accused before one of the local magistrates?'[22] There were two in the village of Inniskeen, O'Rourke being one and Dan McNello, a local publican, the other. Meegan was released on bail pending another trial but the UIL then intervened and summoned both men before a specially convened land court. Such courts were, of course, nothing new in rural Ireland but it had been some time since one was held in south Monaghan. The court found in favour of Meegan and ordered Keenan to relinquish his claim to the farm on receipt of payment of its market value. Keenan obeyed the decree even though the court had no judicial powers; otherwise life would have remained intolerable.

This local agrarian incident was important because, first, it highlighted continued local social tensions in relation to land issues that were of more concern to the men of Inniskeen and surrounding parishes than global conflict in far-flung places such as Ypres or Gallipoli. Second, the incident undermined the British judicial system and diminished respect for the police. Charlie Duffy, subsequently an IRA veteran, who was about fifteen at the time of the Keenogue dispute, recalled that 'from 1915 on the people of

Iniskeen did not like the police'.[23] The action by the RIC and the use of an outside magistrate to adjudicate radicalized O'Rourke, and inspired him to reorganize the IV in Farney. He informed those gathered at the first meeting in March that 'if they wanted peace, the best way was to be prepared for war'.[24] The southern barony of Farney was the first area of County Monaghan to move away from the path of constitutional politics and O'Rourke the first of the county's prominent public figures to swing towards SF. This was not the movement that Arthur Griffith had in mind but rather one that, in no particular order, opposed recruitment to the British army, was disenchanted with the failure of Redmond to secure home rule, was more inclined towards complete separatism, opposed to the growing threats of partition, and buoyed up by anger towards the judicial and police systems.

By February 1915, Tyacke noted that SF was spreading 'rapidly' as 'the Roman Catholic clergy are strongly in favour of it'.[25] One of the most prominent was Fr Bernard Maguire, who had been under police surveillance since at least November 1914 when he preached that 'Mr Redmond was nothing more than a recruiting sergeant of the English Crown'.[26] Maguire had been born in Annaveagh, near Scotshouse on 28 February 1869, educated at St Macartan's Seminary in Monaghan town and St Patrick's College Maynooth, where he distinguished himself as an excellent scholar, and where he most likely crossed paths with Fr Lorcan Ó Ciaráin. After his ordination in 1892, he was sent as a professor to the Irish College of Salamanca in Spain. He served as rector there from 1898 to 1904, the most senior administrative position in probably the most famous of the European Irish colleges. While the Salamanca archive, now on deposit in Maynooth, has much personal correspondence from other rectors, none seems to exist for Maguire that might throw light on why he returned to Monaghan as a curate. It is possible that some form of punishment was involved; he was certainly known to have a drink problem. In 1915, he was promoted to parish priest of Iniskeen, having served as curate in the Clogher parishes of Muckno, Aghalurcher and Aughnamullen.

Fr Maguire became known as 'Salamanca Barney'. He 'cut a stylish figure, driving around the parish in his pony and trap ... well educated, well-travelled, supremely self-confident'.[27] And he quickly befriended the most powerful man in the parish, Bernard O'Rourke. It was a fusion of local elites with some significance for the future. By late 1915, both men were of one mind politically. It may have been O'Rourke and Maguire who invited Patrick Pearse to Carrickmacross on 23 November 1915, a fortnight after the anti-recruitment demonstration, to address a Manchester Martyrs' event commemorating three Fenians executed in 1867 for their role in an attempt to rescue a fellow Fenian from a prison van in Manchester. Or it may have been Proinnsias de Búrca [sometimes Frank Burke], a British excise service employee stationed in Carrickmacross, a formidable organizer of the Volunteers throughout Ulster who had joined the IRB when working in London. His son, Brian, attended St Enda's school and so he got to know Pearse quite well.[28] Patrick and his brother, Willie, were known by some in Carrickmacross; in 1904, when the brothers were running the family business, they were commissioned to carry out work at the St Louis Convent where Willie sculpted a statue of the Blessed Virgin.[29]

A few months prior to his visit to south Monaghan, Pearse's graveside panegyric at the funeral of O'Donovan Rossa had brought him to national attention. However, he was by no means a household name in Monaghan. Years later, Francis Tummons remembered going to Mass on the Sunday after the rebellion where the parish priest announced that Pearse had unconditionally surrendered in Dublin: 'While I've no doubt the majority of the congregation on that Sunday morning were aware a rebellion against British rule had been in progress during the previous week, few indeed knew who this man Pearse was or what he stood for'.[30]

Pearse got off the train at Inniskeen village – the line ran from Dublin to Dundalk and then on to Carrickmacross via the village – where he stayed with O'Rourke.[31] Like O'Rourke, Pearse had moved towards separatism in response to the events that had taken place around him. Initially, he had welcomed the home rule bill in 1912, but had also warned that if it were rejected, only rebellion remained as a final option. In 1913, when the UVF embraced the threat of physical force as political strategy, Pearse argued that nationalists should do the same.

After inspecting the local Inniskeen Volunteers, Pearse was taken from the village to Carrickmacross where he was met by a deputation of at least two parish priests and seven curates from the town and the surrounding areas of Corduff, Aughnamullen, Magheracloone, Killanny and Inniskeen. On introducing Pearse, Fr John Meenan (an avowed separatist who, as president of Carrickmacross Golf Club, mixed easily at a social level with his unionist neighbours) told the audience that they were there 'to commemorate the dead who died for Ireland, and in that connection it was fitting that they should examine their national conscience and see how far they had been faithful to the memories and traditions for which they had died'.[32] Death, sacrifice and martyrdom were largely the themes of the night. Pearse proclaimed that 'No more heroic generation of Irishmen had ever lived than the Fenian generation'. Loud applause told him he was hitting the right note. He went on:

> The freedom of Belgium and Serbia had been worthy of millions of drops of blood. If anything was worth shedding blood for it was freedom. If it was a good thing for Belgians and Serbians to die for their countries' freedom, then it must be a good thing for Irishmen to die for Ireland.[33]

'Prolonged applause' met his final crescendo that the work of nationalists 'must be carried on until the slave is set free and the tyrant falls'; according to the local newspaper the hall was in a state of uproarious agreement when Fr Maguire proposed a vote of thanks, seconded by Bernard O'Rourke: 'It was refreshing and inspiring in these times to listen to the true gospel of Irish nationality. They should all resolve to follow the advice and counsel of Mr Pearse.'[34]

Unfortunately, except for a handful of individuals, we do not know who was in the hall that evening as the RIC were prevented from entering by a guard of Irish Volunteers. Presumably, many of those present had taken part in the anti-recruitment demonstration a couple of weeks before. There were others who, it seems, were just curious, maybe about Pearse the man or perhaps about his ideologies. These included some prominent Redmondites, leading officers in the local UIL and AOH. Thomas Lennon, an officer in the Inniskeen UIL; Thomas Campbell, vice-chairman of Carrickmacross AOH; and J.F. O'Toole, secretary of the south Monaghan executive of the UIL, were all subsequently reprimanded for attending and had to apologize publicly at a south Monaghan UIL convention. Lennon assured the officers that he did not associate himself with anything discussed at the Pearse meeting; Campbell emphasized that he 'had no foreknowledge of the proceedings' and so did not know what he was attending; while O'Toole claimed he had been 'asked to the concert to sing and not being at the time aware of the nature of the meeting consented to go', which he regretted.[35]

A few weeks after Pearse's visit, in December 1915, the case of Donnelly, Ross and Quinn again came before the courts. As on the previous occasion, O'Rourke was one of the magistrates due to sit on the bench but he was a few minutes late in arriving at the courthouse by which time the other magistrates had sentenced the three to imprisonment. O'Rourke was incensed at what he deemed a deliberate attempt to manipulate the law to secure a conviction. In a letter to the *Democrat* he suggested that

> The public may easily see that the case was rushed before a second local magistrate would arrive. Is it any wonder that Irishmen have a contempt for the law as administered in this country where subterfuge and technicalities of this sort are introduced to ensure a conviction.[36]

The imprisonment of the men led to a demonstration in Carrickmacross when the IV and local bands marched the prisoners to the train station. Three months later, when the released men were being transported from Armagh gaol to Carrickmacross, the train happened to break down at Inniskeen station. It was hardly a coincidence that Bernard O'Rourke was the only person in the vicinity with a motor car prepared to convey the men to Carrickmacross where another large demonstration was planned to greet them. Fr Bernard Maguire was on the reception platform with 'The O'Rahilly', an ardent nationalist and journalist, who had been central to the Volunteers' gun-running in 1914–15. Maguire gave the opening speech and concluded: 'A day would come when those who were now opposed to them would be glad to creep into the movement [SF] by the back stairs ... As a man and a priest he was proud of the movement and he hoped as he strove to guide the people right in religious matters, he would do so in matters political.'[37] Perhaps revealingly, there is no report of the young men having spoken. They were as voiceless there as they were in local politics.

The vast majority of prominent nationalists in Monaghan, the men of property on the local government boards, did not agree with Maguire or O'Rourke's separatism. They were vehemently opposed to those whom they labelled the SF 'rabble', in their minds little more than socialistic revolutionaries.[38] However, as described in the previous chapter, coinciding with all these events, especially in south Monaghan, was a growing reaction among the classes left behind in the economic boom. In Carrickmacross, SF and the Irish Volunteers appealed to labourers such as Donnelly, Quinn and Ross whose socio-economic prospects had not improved. The stymied attempts of the labouring classes to gain a commensurate share in wartime profits, an increase in wages in line with inflation, or, in the case of the smallholders, access to more land, increased discontent. Thus, their involvement in their hundreds in the demonstrations in Carrickmacross may have been as much a demonstration against the existing socio-economic order and the government's abject failure to address their concerns as it was against recruitment. There is one revealing local example.

In 1926, Lieutenant Bernard J. Browne, a former Catholic draper and merchant on Main Street, Carrickmacross, and a veteran of the First World War, applied to the Irish Grants Committee for compensation for loss of business during the 1916–23 period. His file contains a letter from a former neighbour and fellow merchant, Thomas Conlon, boot and shoe merchant from Parnell Street, Carrickmacross. Browne had met him a short time before he made his application, their first meeting in many years. Conlon's sense of guilt is clearly evident in the letter. He explained that before the war he had always been happy to deal with Browne, 'pleased with the goods ... the value was good and the quality reliable' and admitted that he 'never met anyone who ever had a word to say against you personally'. However, he continued

> ... the reason I did not do any business with you since 1915 was because when I went to your shop in May 1916 to purchase a new suit there was a large crowd of rough looking country fellows around the shop and warned me along with a good number of apparently your customers who were anxious to get into your shop, to clear off, that

this Browne's shop was boycotted, as Browne joined the British army and let them, meaning the British government, support Browne's British Bastards, meaning as I took it your children ... I was very sorry for your wife and little children under such circumstances, but the rough and determined manner of those [sic] boycotting party who stated they were carrying out the instructions of Sinn Féin soon cleared away any prospective purchasers who were near your shop.

The letter reveals how in time of extremity people will generally consider their own circumstances before the plight of others. They are likely to shun confrontation, even while knowing that what they are witnessing is morally wrong, but fear, intimidation and caution will prevent them from arguing. The dates mentioned in the letter are notable: Conlon stopped doing business with Browne in 1915, the year of the anti-recruitment meeting and public demonstrations, and he was stopped from going into the shop in May 1916, the month of the execution of the rebels. Conlon told Browne: 'your joining the army at such a time, and you so popular locally, was considered a challenge to the Sinn Féin organization and no doubt they worked more determined to do your business all the harm possible and their method of boycott was their sure weapon'.[39] One cannot be sure if this was the only reason for boycotting Browne and, if there were others, they may never be revealed, but the opposition to Browne was not motivated by sectarianism, he was a Catholic and an employer of Catholic labour (all four employees in his household and business were Catholics).

In January 1916, James Connolly, in his capacity as commandant of the Irish Citizen Army, had been brought on to the secret IRB military council by Pearse and others as they finalized their plans for rebellion. The military fiasco that followed that Easter has been well documented. There were a few Monaghan people employed or studying in Dublin who were caught up in the event, most notably Peadar MacMahon from Coas near Lough Egish, a section commander in the 2nd Battalion, Dublin Brigade, and his sister, Sorcha, a member of the central committee of Cumann na mBan who carried mobilization orders and acted as a courier throughout the Rising.[40] But County Monaghan typified the rest of the country in terms of its lack of preparedness for a national uprising. There were still only two IV companies with an estimated 73 members by May 1916.[41] Of these, John McGahey of the Rockcorry Company claimed they continued to drill up to Easter Week but 'got no information that an impending resort to an armed rising was contemplated'.[42] Regarding the second company, on Good Friday a very small band of Volunteers, probably no more than twelve, congregated in the Foresters' Hall, Carrickmacross, with small rations and limited arms. When news of MacNeill's countermanding order came through they disbanded and went home.⁴³ Peter Kavanagh's comment on his native Inniskeen encapsulated the county as a whole: 'The Dublin Insurrection of 1916 came and went without a ripple in our household or in the district, for that matter.'⁴⁴

No Dublin newspapers arrived in Monaghan on Tuesday, but there were 'disquieting rumours' circulating throughout the county of a Dublin Rising. Then, on Wednesday, news of the shelling of Liberty Hall and the arrival of thousands of British troops was met with 'cheer after cheer' in Monaghan town. On Sunday in Carrickmacross, Revd Daniel O'Connor told his parishioners: 'I have good news for you today. The Sinn Féin rebellion has been crushed and its leaders will be executed'.⁴⁵ This reaction to the Rising begs the question: what had happened to the multitudes who had turned out for the anti-recruitment meeting and to welcome home Donnelly, Ross and Quinn a few months previously? The evidence from the witness statements (in both the Marron papers and the BMH) substantiates the lack of support from the wider public for the Rising. Francis Tummons recalled what happened at Mass on the Sunday after the rebellion: 'The older men shook their heads and expressed the opinion that the use of arms was a misguided action and doomed to failure from the start. Who dared to resort to arms when England was plunged in war with Germany? Some even thought this way.'⁴⁶

The response from the nationalist middle classes was as to be expected. Thomas McGahon expressed some sympathy in the *Democrat* for 'the misguided men who fought with the desperate bravery that so often distinguished Irishmen, a mad and hopeless fight in Dublin', but his true opinion was more evident in the headline, 'An act of madness'.⁴⁷ He reasoned that 'never was there in any era or in any epoch a less excusable outbreak', clearly distinguishing this rebellion from ones which had preceded it in 1798, 1848 and 1867 because they could be justified as 'a genuine uprising of a harassed peasantry against intolerable wrong' [1798]; 'an echo of the continental Liberalism which found expression in popular outbursts in every European country' [1848]; or 'a reaction against the corruption that reigned in the parliamentary representation of Ireland ... against the continued ascendancy of the landlord party, the oppression of the tenantry, and the enforced contribution by the Catholics to the support of the Church that was not theirs' [1867].⁴⁸ But, he argued, so many social and political reforms had been granted since the last quarter of the nineteenth century, culminating in the passing of home rule, that no rebellion could be justified. While, he contended, 'these men really believed they were patriots fighting for their country ... they were in reality dealing her a deadly blow'. Theirs was 'a madness so menacing of Irish hopes, so destructive of peace and order and property in Ireland that the bitterest enemy of our people could not have planned worse for this unhappy country'.⁴⁹ Meanwhile, Monaghan MP, James Lardner, was in Dublin to defend

James Quigley, the Monaghan-born county surveyor in Meath who had got caught up in the Ashbourne ambush of the RIC led by Thomas Ashe, probably more by accident than design.[50] Quigley's was to be the only rebellion-related court martial that resulted in an acquittal.[51]

Another report in the *Democrat*, headed 'Revolutionaries and socialists', described the widespread plundering in Dublin where 'every slum and court and tenement seemed to vomit forth the lawless element in the population on a wild career of loot and pillage'. This could not be allowed to engulf the rest of Ireland.[52] Carrickmacross board of guardians recorded their 'highest condemnation of the action precipitated by a number of hot-headed revolutionaries and socialists'; once again the juxtaposition of revolutionaries with socialists is significant. While calling for leniency for the 'poor dupes' who had followed, the chairman, Eddie Kelly, had no sympathy for the leaders:

> Everyone should approve of the action of the authorities in shooting the rebel leaders – because that is what they are only a handful of revolutionists. I say it knowing that the press is here and that it will be published – they were nothing but the cowards who flinched conscription when their tried and true leader John Redmond – declared that Ireland would be a strong arm to assist England in this war (hear, hear). We are all ashamed of them.[53]

Kelly concluded: 'it is hard lines on those men who have spent the last 30 years working for the country to see their efforts destroyed by a treacherous gang', in other words the Land War generation who had already successfully effected one revolution and did not now want to lose the gains they had made. He would not have felt his pronouncements were unpatriotic, nor did any of his fellow guardians or members of the county council on which he also sat charge him with the same. In fact, the county council under Toal's stewardship also 'greatly deplored ... the recent regrettable occurrences in Dublin which resulted in the loss of the lives of many of His Majesty's soldiers and civilians'.[54] There was no mention of the executed leaders. Kelly and Toal were well aware of the temper of the country as a whole and that they spoke for the majority of the ruling elites. Notably, no one in Monaghan seems to have been preaching the message of the 1916 Proclamation that guaranteed 'religious and civil liberty, equal rights and equal opportunities to all its citizens', and 'to pursue the happiness and prosperity of the whole nation and of all its parts, cherishing all of the children of the nation equally, and oblivious of the differences carefully fostered by an alien government, which have divided a minority from the majority in the past'.

Local unionist response to the Rising was similar to that of the constitutional nationalists. Church, politicians and local community leaders were utterly condemnatory but more nuanced. The *Standard* condemned the destruction of life and property, claiming heavy casualties on both sides, £2 million in property damages and highlighting the destruction of the GPO, 'one of the architectural features of the city.'[55] Thus, there was an added cultural dimension to condemnation; the rebels were seen as vandals. Using reportage from the *Belfast Newsletter*, the *Standard* told its readers of the rebels coming from their 'lairs', armed with 'deadly weapons'. An eye-witness reporter claimed that a 'proclamation' was posted on the door of the GPO announcing that 'English rule in Ireland is now at an end' and that 'this precious document was signed by some very august person whose name I was not able to get'.[56] This seems to be the only mention of the Proclamation in the local newspapers, or, indeed, in the later Monaghan witness statements. In other words, there was no contemporary local debate about its merits (or demerits) as a social and political document. The promulgation of social equality did not appeal to the capitalistic men of property and those who fought for independence could not later lay claim to have achieved the ideals of the Proclamation.

In the *Standard*, the rebels were characterized as little better than brigands, said to have commandeered mail trucks which they then filled with 'carcases of beef and mutton, chickens, sausages, hams, bread with butter and other edibles', reportedly paid for in £5 and £10 pound notes stolen from the post office.[57] There was continuous emphasis on the moral turpitude of the insurgents. The Dublin mob – 'always in evidence on occasions of this nature' – became 'riotously drunk' while 'elderly women [were] rolling along the streets, their skirts held up to carry the load of looted goods'.[58] The report was intended to cause shock and abhorrence, to emphasize to Monaghan unionists what they could expect in a home rule Ireland: Dublin had been devastated, the rebels were guilty of abominable atrocities, they had let loose the 'Dublin mob', and they had dishonoured those Irishmen fighting for Ireland at the front. The County Monaghan Grand Orange Lodge passed a resolution recording its 'abhorrence and detestation of the recent rebellion', reaffirming its loyalty to the Crown, and 'recognizing in the rebellion the fruits of misgovernment in Ireland by the Radical party'.[59]

It has been well documented by historians how in a short period of time condemnatory attitudes towards the rebels, at least from nationalists, gave way to sympathy. The scale and method of the executions (drawn out over a number of weeks, and especially the inhumane execution of the wounded Connolly, who was tied to a chair because his injuries prevented him standing before the firing squad), as well as the mass arrest of suspects under the Defence of the Realm Act (DORA), including eight suspects in the Carrickmacross area, had a reactionary impact.[60] In the last issue of the *Democrat* for 1916, the editor was in no doubt that 'while the Sinn Féin rebellion aroused no sympathetic feeling in the masses of the people, the methods of its suppression did'.[61] For those who later fought in the War of Independence, the Rising assumed iconic status as *the* event that marked the beginning of the struggle for independence.

The fallout from the 1916 Rising was undoubtedly important in changing political atitudes and increasing the swing towards SF; in the decades that followed, the political events of the period were memorialized. But in a rural county such as Monaghan due consideration should also be given to the influence of continuing social conditions during the First World War. With the odd exception, such as Liam Mellows in Galway, the leaders of 1916 were no more in tune with social conditions in rural Ireland than local wealth and governing elites were in sympathy with the plight of the lower classes. However, the Rising and the executions were the primary catalysts in a longer process of ongoing change.

The first two years of the war, 1914–16, had created a number of tensions in Monaghan. For those who prospered, it raised expectations and in the process provided fertile ground for future revolution if those expectations were to be threatened, as had happened during the Land War. On the other hand, the 1916 Rising raised the hopes of others who had failed to prosper that a future revolution would correct social inequality, as promised in the Proclamation. For those who became cognisant of wider developments across Europe, or those disenchanted with the old order, SF offered an alternative. And those who had been told that the European war was being fought for the rights of small nations began to wonder where their own country sat in the scheme of things. In March 1917, Thomas McGahon regretted that while 'England ... is fighting for the rights of small nationalities on the continent of Europe, she refuses the admitted rights of one small nationality to administer its own internal affairs according to the will of the people'.[62] Even his previously unshakeable belief in the IPP had been compromised by disappointment. The seven signatories of the 1916 Proclamation and nine others were executed, yet they were not the first Irish rebels of the 1912–23 period. The Proclamation was no more defiant than the Ulster Covenant; in fact, it was more inclusive and much less sectarian. It was galling for separatists, and, indeed, most nationalists, that no leader of the Ulster unionist movement had been charged with any offence, not even with the illegal importation of arms. There was a growing sense of disquiet among nationalists in Monaghan when the execution of the Easter rebels was compared to the elevation of Sir Edward Carson to the cabinet table twelve months before in May 1915. This sense of double standard meant that after Easter 1916 both nationalist and unionist politics in Monaghan entered a new phase of tension and mutual suspicion.

5 'The Sinn Féin party is gaining strength in all parts',[1] 1917–18

The IPP unsuccessfully tried to reinvigorate its relationship with the wider nationalist public after the Rising. Early in May 1916, a party manifesto appeared in the *Democrat* highlighting the party's achievements over the previous forty years: home rule, land reform, local self-government, the extension of the franchise, the building of thousands of labourers' cottages, the establishment of a national university.[2] While undoubtedly an impressive record in Ireland, its achievements looked less substantial in a European context, where there was clear evidence in the growth of democratic power, particularly with expanding electorates, and a series of shifts in political ideologies. The IPP was not vigorous enough in its offensive against the emergent SF. John Redmond did not make a public speech until October, and, regardless of his reasons for failing to do so, this was viewed by many of his supporters as poor judgment. Even Thomas McGahon was critical: 'Mr Redmond has been too long silent, while his and Ireland's enemies day after day poured poison into the people's ears'.[3] A few months later, Thomas Toal declared that 'they must have a go ahead constitutional movement ... Mr Redmond has been too weak.'[4] It was impossible for experienced politicians like Toal not to see the rising tide of SF; they had to decide which movement really would deliver their political aims and ambitions.[5]

On the morning of 11 May 1916, the day before the final execution of the Dublin leaders, Bernard O'Rourke was having breakfast at home with his wife, Clare, when DI Peter Roe from Carrickmacross and ten policemen barged in, bayonets fixed to their carbines.[6] The house was searched, some 'seditious literature' was found and O'Rourke was taken away on suspicion of involvement in SF.[7] His arrest seems also to have been related to Roe's antipathy towards O'Rourke, who had been publicly critical of the RIC during the Keenogue dispute. As O'Rourke's wife put it to a friend: 'People were very proud of him the time he spoke up against the police and the whole county agreed with what he said as to their brutality etc. This is the only thing they can now bring against him.'[8]

O'Rourke was one of around 3,300 men arrested nationwide in the direct aftermath of the rebellion; almost 1,500 were released within a fortnight and 1,800 were interned. On 19 May a nationalist conference was held in Carrickmacross that denounced the continued detention of so many innocent figures 'in view of the fact of their having had no share whatever in the recent rebellion', while Eddie Kelly seconded a motion vehemently protesting against the continuance of martial law and demanding its immediate withdrawal.[9]

Kelly's intervention was significant because he had previously so forcefully denounced the leaders of the Rising.

O'Rourke was taken to Richmond Barracks in Dublin where he found himself enthused by the 'sparkling, hopeful countenances' of the men who shared his block: 'There they were – men from 16 to 60, of all classes, many of them exhausted and worn out, some of them unwell but all in the best of heart. I felt immediately that I was going to be at home during my stay at Richmond.'[10] O'Rourke was struck by their religious ardour, the fact that they chose to speak in Irish, and that their native tongue seemed to him to complement their religious devotion.[11] He, thus, drew together an idealistic version of the characteristics that would define IRA volunteers in the future.

When H.H. Asquith, the British prime minister, visited Richmond Barracks in May 1916 he singled out O'Rourke for 'a long chat', remarking that 'he was sorry he had to be detained there', and took the opportunity to question him about the future prospects of home rule.[12] When O'Rourke was released a few days later, he gave the impression that his imprisonment had imbued him with a sense of patriotism that went well beyond home rule politics. When he arrived home to Inniskeen 'bonfires blazed from hill to hill all over Farney, and there was general rejoicing and jubilation'.[13] He was immediately elected chairman of the Carrickmacross board of poor law guardians.[14] This was not so much a mark of defiance as a belief among his fellow guardians that his arrest had been a mistake. However, after a brief honeymoon period, especially after he had begun to tour the southern constituency from June 1916 promoting SF, his new politics brought him into conflict with the old home rulers.[15] When, in April 1917, O'Rourke introduced a resolution in favour of SF to the Carrickmacross board of guardians, it led to a physical brawl when insults of 'mongrel' and 'liars' were exchanged. The resolution was defeated by twelve votes to four.[16] P.J. McCabe was 'astonished at Mr O'Rourke changing his attitude in such a short time. Heretofore he was a great Parliamentarian and a great supporter of the Irish Party.'[17] As these acrimonious exchanges continued, O'Rourke found his position as chairman untenable and in June 1917 he stepped down to be replaced by Alexander Fennell, the magistrate who had sat with him in the Donnelly, Quinn and Ross trial. Fennell believed that 'they couldn't have an Irish republic and the leaders of Mr O'Rourke's party [SF] know this very well.'[18] Throughout 1917, the views of old Ireland were coming into sharp contrast with those of a new cadre of political activists. The majority of long-standing middle-class guardians remained loyal to Redmond while some, like O'Rourke, threw themselves determinedly into SF politics.[19]

As Alvin Jackson has remarked, 'home rule was still viable in the early summer of 1916₃.[20] In May–June, Lloyd George convened talks to address the Irish question and, in particular, the issue of partition. In June, Monaghan

County Council called on all other local government bodies to pass resolutions that 'The division of a whole nation at the bidding of a small minority of zealots and political wirepullers is at once unnatural and we pledge ourselves and our constituents never to submit to it'.[21] Monaghan unionists were in more of a quandary; they had to consider the interests of the empire. Lloyd George allowed Carson believe that the cabinet favoured immediate implementation of the 1914 Home Rule Act and the exclusion of the six north-eastern counties. On 6 June 1916, Carson laid these proposals before the UUC and strongly urged their acceptance. On 12 June, the Monaghan, Cavan and Donegal delegates to the UUC issued a protest statement, complaining that this represented a desertion of Covenant principles. However, they agreed to allow negotiations to continue in the interests of the war effort.[22] For Carson this was 'the greatest piece of lasting evidence of their devoted, unselfish loyalty to the king, constitution and empire' that he had ever witnessed.[23]

Shortly afterwards, the leading Cavan unionist, Major Somerset Saunderson, discovered that Lloyd George had been duplicitous and, backed up with corroborations from Lords Lansdowne and Selborne, he wrote to Carson arguing that the agreement of 12 June could not possibly stand, based as it was on misconception.[24] Saunderson solicited the support of the North Monaghan Unionist Association (NMUA) but its secretary, William Martin, informed him that Monaghan unionists would stand firmly behind Carson and in July a resolution to that effect was forwarded to the UUC.[25] Carson described Saunderson's claims as 'a tissue of misapprehension from beginning to end' and welcomed the support of the NMUA: 'no one has suffered more than I have from the knowledge that it was impossible to include the three counties'.[26] Carson's sincerity was questionbable given that the UUC had progressed towards the geographical area of political stability to which it aspired. Revealingly, in June 1916, Hugh de Fellenberg Montgomery wrote to Carson: 'I believe that though this would look like a forsaking of our brother covenanters in Monaghan, Cavan and Donegal ... they would really be safer on the borders of a secure six county Ulster than inside the very insecure citadel of a nine county Ulster'.[27] While Lloyd George's initiative foundered, in hindsight Monaghan unionists were to regret their loyalty; Dr J.C. Hall later lamented that they had signed 'away their liberties' when they left responsibility for the exclusion negotiations in the hands of the unionists of the six counties.[28]

The Lloyd George conference took place against the backdrop of one of the most traumatic eras in Monaghan unionist memory. The devastating losses at the Somme alerted some to the sacrifice made by the unionists of the three counties but by July 1916 others understood that a state of partition, however unfavourable to the three counties, was inevitable. On 8 July 1916, Edith Wheeler wrote to Lady Londonderry suggesting that every woman and girl who desired to leave the three counties should be given the opportunity to do so but she had mentally accepted partition: 'Today we are all overwhelmed by the loss of our men … the only thing left to us is to support the principles for which they have died & to stand by those who are left especially those belonging to the men of *the deserted counties* [author's italics]'.[29]

The UUC's intransigence at the 1917–18 Convention, another initiative by Lloyd George to prepare and submit a scheme for the government of Ireland, was further proof of the position it was going to adopt. M.E. Knight was selected as the unionist representative of the three counties of Monaghan, Cavan and Donegal. Thomas Toal represented Monaghan nationalists. SF was not represented, which the Church of Ireland bishop of Clogher, Maurice Day, considered a most positive thing.[30] The UUC delegates clung to the exclusion principle. Carson's right-hand man, James Craig, summed up the situation: 'if they could not save the whole country for the Empire, they could at least save themselves'.[31] The die had been cast for Monaghan unionists. They paid dearly for their loyalty, while the IPP's ineffectiveness in the summer of 1916 and at the Convention had fatal consequences.[32] As Alvin Jackson has contended, the party's abject failure 'ruined both the credibility of the convention and the residual popularity of Home Rule' and, therefore, signalled its end 'as a popular cause'.[33] Sir Shane Leslie of Glaslough, who occupied the rather unique position of being the nationalist son of an entrenched unionist and Orangeman, later wrote that the IPP's impotence and 'the folly of the government' in 1916–17 made 'Sinn Féin the supreme and only party to which Irish Nationalists, who desire to be called Nationalists, can belong'.[34]

By the end of the summer of 1916, the geography of SF support had changed little from its pre-rebellion character in Monaghan. It remained predominantly localized with only Clones joining the traditional areas of Carrickmacross and Rockcorry. The identification of Clones as a SF area was, however, significant; it marked the beginning of the rise of Owen O'Duffy as the most important activist in the county.

O'Duffy had been born near Castleblayney on 28 January 1890, the youngest of seven children of a small farmer. His father also worked on the roads, thus he had a supplementary income which meant that the O'Duffys were much better off than many of their neighbours; the suggestions by O'Duffy's biographer that he came from an impoverished background should not be exaggerated.[35] His mother was a typically hard-working farmer's wife, rearing hens to sell eggs, and churning butter every day for the local market. Coming from a respectable background herself, she had strong ambitions for the social improvement of her children. One of her brothers was a national school teacher and another, Patrick Feely, ran a public house and grocery in Ballybay between 1912 and 1935.[36] Family friends included the owner of the Provincial Hotel in Clones, where O'Duffy stayed for a time when he began working in the town; indeed, he was socially confident enough to ask for a testimonial from Bishop McKenna of Clogher when applying for a position.[37] O'Duffy was an intelligent youth, and keen to meet his mother's aspirations of improving his status in life. When his mother died prematurely, his maternal uncle took him under his wing at Laragh national school. There, the education he received was far from 'basic', as Patrick Long has suggested.[38] O'Duffy had the opportunity of a scholarship to train as a school teacher but opted instead for a position as a clerk in the county surveyor's office in Monaghan. He showed an aptitude for hard work and had excellent organizational skills, rising quickly to assistant county surveyor and engineer.

O'Duffy was astute in progressing his career. In February 1916, he informed the county council that 'there was a more lucrative assistant surveyorship vacant in County Fermanagh, for which he considered he had a good chance'. Toal told the council that 'They would be very sorry to lose the services of one who had done his work remarkably well'.[39] It was agreed to raise his salary from £100 per annum to £110 and then £20 every three years to a maximum of £150.[40] O'Duffy was advancing professionally but there remained very traditional social class barriers that would inevitably inhibit further progression. Such issues concerned many young men of his generation, background and talent, including Dan Hogan, a young railway clerk with the Great Northern Railway (GNR) in Clones, recently arrived from Grangemockler in County Tipperary. Together, they would form a formidable alliance in the years ahead. Hogan's story is relayed in more detail in chapter 9.

In 1912, O'Duffy had moved to Newbliss, a village very much divided on politico-religious lines; it was a stronghold of Monaghan Orangeism but there were also strong republicans there such as the Tummons family with whom O'Duffy boarded for a time. The Tummons family were related to another Newbliss notable, Patrick Whelan, chairman of the Ulster Council of the GAA. He introduced O'Duffy to the local Gaelic League branch in Greenan's Cross – O'Duffy's first mention in the newspaper seems to date to May 1912 when he recited 'Hugh O'Donnell Roe' at a ceilidh there.[41] Whelan was also instrumental in having O'Duffy appointed as secretary of Monaghan GAA county board in September 1912. Just two months later, O'Duffy's success in Monaghan, based on his extraordinary energy and organizational ability, led to his appointment as secretary of the Ulster council.[42] Between 1912 and 1917, O'Duffy transformed the GAA in the county (and Ulster as a whole); he healed north–south GAA divides in Monaghan, largely a result of political constituency lines on a map, and put together a team under his management, drawn from clubs all over the county, that won the Ulster senior football championship in 1914, 1916 and 1917 (as well as the hurling championship in 1914). However, it is notable that Monaghan did not win another

'The Sinn Féin party is gaining strength in all parts' 63

championship between 1917 and 1921. This was undoubtedly related to O'Duffy's concentration on political activism and the GAA's contribution to the independence struggle in Monaghan (which will be described in chapter 6). In 1917, O'Duffy met with Luke O'Toole, general secretary of the GAA 1901–29, in Dublin who is said to have 'played a delicate juggling act of safeguarding the progress of the GAA while remaining committed to Ireland's march towards independence'.[43] O'Duffy later explained, with no little degree of hyperbole, that he 'went back to Monaghan a Volunteer and within a short time had recruited virtually every able-bodied member or supporter of the GAA into Volunteer activities'.[44] In November 1917, O'Duffy met Michael Collins for the first time and was initiated into the IRB, thereby making him a powerful figure in both GAA and republican circles.[45] O'Duffy's subsequent rise owed much to Collins' patronage and the respect they had for one other was to last until Collins' death.[46]

As Fearghal McGarry points out, one of the most telling remarks about O'Duffy's personality came from a fellow GAA officer in 1915 that 'O'Duffy was a Gael of unflinching courage, and with it he fired his followers to an enthusiasm that was invincible'.[47] It seems that from January 1917, before he met O'Toole or Collins, he had begun to use the newly acquired premises of the GAA club in Clones for SF meetings; by June the CI was reporting: 'the Sinn Féin party is gaining strength in all parts and particularly in Clones district where the influence of the GAA is successfully working in that direction'.[48] At the same time, O'Duffy was re-organizing the Irish Volunteers in Clones, Newbliss, Scotstown, Carrickmacross, Ballybay and Castleblayney. The young recruits were not merely content to be entertained by parades and marching bands and clapping crowds so typical before 1916; they were keen to learn the techniques of guerrilla warfare for 'the overthrow of British rule in Ireland', as O'Duffy put it in June 1918.[49] Some of these young men were goaded into activity by government blundering. On the night of 17–18 May, seventy-three prominent Sinn Féiners were arrested throughout the country as suspects in the so-called 'German plot', but ostensibly because of the prominent role of SF and the IV in the anti-conscription campaign.[50] These included Willie Loughran in Carrickmacross who had already been interned in Frongoch for his 1916 activities. Rather than these arrests being a crippling blow to the separatist movement, they gave it further momentum.[51] In the East Cavan by-election of 20 June 1918, Arthur Griffith won the seat for SF and the Monaghan CI reported an increase in SF membership and 'a good deal of excitement and rejoicing in Sinn Féin circles'; several Sinn Féiners were tried at Carrickmacross for marching in military formation when attending an election meeting in Cavan; and a few days later an estimated 5,000 gathered at meetings in Castleblayney and Tydavnet to protest against the internment of Sinn Féin leaders.[52]

When the authorities banned GAA matches in order to prevent seditious gatherings, O'Duffy simply refused to look for permits to stage them. The Ulster Council, of which he was secretary, backed him and on 4 August 1918, Gaelic Sunday, twenty-seven games were organized in Monaghan. An estimated 54,000 members participated throughout the country in a show of defiance that went a long way towards politicizing the GAA.[53] A few months before, the county inspector had reported that the GAA was 'causing disaffection to spread amongst the young men of Clones'.[54] For over a year, the police had strongly suspected that GAA football matches and meetings were covers for SF gatherings and that O'Duffy was the 'the only openly active Sinn Féiner in the co[unty]'.[55] Exactly two weeks after Gaelic Sunday, O'Duffy organized a cycle ride of thirty 'Sinn Féiners' from Clones to Cootehill and back; after which they marched in formation in pairs through the town of Clones and the village of Newbliss. Two nights later, the first meeting of Cumann na mBan reported by the police was held in Clones attended by about forty members.[56] According to O'Duffy, Cumann na mBan had been set up in Monaghan about a year previously in 1917.[57] At its height in 1921, there were five branches in south Monaghan with an estimated total of forty members (with Mary Nolan as president), and seven branches in north Monaghan with 117 members (under the presidency of Alice Mullan).[58]

In September 1918, O'Duffy and Hogan were both convicted of illegal drilling as a result of the cycle ride and sentenced to two months imprisonment in default of posting bail.[59] Michael Collins, then adjutant-general of the reorganized Volunteers, thought O'Duffy's imprisonment 'another hellish loss' for he regarded O'Duffy as the 'best man by far in Ulster'.[60] By the time of his arrest, there were seventeen SF clubs in Monaghan with around 760 members.[61] The growth was most pronounced in the south and mid-west of the county. In the southern barony of Farney, the remnants of factionalism from the bitter 1910 general election contributed to the supporters of John McKean switching allegiance to SF. Further north, such factionalism did not exist because nationalists in the past had retained a united front in face of unionist opposition that was absent in the southern constituency, and the old order, led by experienced men such as Thomas Toal, Denis Carolan Rushe and James Lardner MP, continued to hold sway. In September 1917, Éamon de Valera, Arthur Griffith and Seán MacEntee addressed a SF demonstration outside Carrickmacross attended by an estimated 4,000 people.[62] With the rise of SF, the UIL organization in that area found itself under great strain and there were reports of branch leaders resigning where SF clubs were organized.[63] In September, in an attempt to stem the exodus of members, the south Monaghan executive of the UIL decided to reduce the branch affiliation fee from £3 to £2 'as it was hard in those days when there was so many turning away from the constitutional movement to Sinn Féin to make up the larger sum'.[64]

That month, the death of Thomas Ashe, a founding member of the Irish Volunteers, while on hunger strike in Mountjoy Prison, Dublin, was another catalyst in altering the political landscape in north Monaghan. The county council indicted the British government for his death:

> The tragic circumstances which surround his early demise have burned themselves into the hearts of Irish people, and we condemn the government in trying to shift the blame from themselves to their employees and underlings. The conduct of the English government in Ireland is in accordance with their historic dealings with this country. The treatment of political prisoners savours only of the most degraded action of the most debased government in history.[65]

Before the war, a council protest such as this, condemning British policy as misrule, was rare. The council indictment revealed how the optimism felt before the war – that with the enactment of home rule, Ireland would be looked upon as Britain's equal – was now withering away to be replaced by old ancestral hostilities. More experienced politicians and observers could see this. In April 1918, Rushe wrote to Shane Leslie that 'men who were unknown a few years ago fill the public eye at present' and concluded that people were beginning to believe 'Ireland would be freed by a Spanish chief in the person of de Valera'.[66]

Meantime, in 1917–18 there were rumours that conscription was to be extended to Ireland. There were some unionists who were opposed to this but, in general, attitudes were summed up in the county's Grand Orange Lodge support for 'the extension of the Military Service Act to Ireland, as being the only means whereby the people of this county as a whole can have an opportunity of bearing their share in the great struggle'.[67] As was to be expected, the threat of conscription further inflamed nationalist public opinion. Back in December 1916, Eddie Kelly had asked his fellow nationalists to pledge themselves 'to resist the imposition of such a blood tax on our country and call on the Irish Party as the only legitimate weapon in our hands to stop it'.[68] In April 1918, Thomas Toal proposed an anti-conscription resolution to the county council, seconded by Bernard O'Rourke, denying the right of the British government to conscript Irishmen against their will; notably his motion incorporated SF's alternative slogan to home rule, 'the right of the principle of self-determination in this matter'. The resolution promised that the council would use 'every means at their disposal' to oppose 'such iniquitous attacks on the Irish people'.[69]

A few weeks later, Bishop McKenna of Clogher, Cardinal Logue and Bishop Edward Mulhern of Dromore issued a statement denying a claim by Lord Curzon in the Lords on 20 June 1918 that the Roman Catholic clergy had told 'their flocks to resist conscription under pain of eternal damnation' but McKenna still supported his diocesan clergy in their opposition to conscription.[70] It was important for the clergy to be seen to be leading the campaign, to ensure they retained control over the Catholic people. Some SF priests stressed the legacy of 1916; Fr Eugene Coyle, for example, told his parishioners that had it not been for the Easter rebels their sons' 'bones would be crumbling in the soil of Flanders, Mesopotamia and Gallipoli'; it was now time 'to die at home rather than fight for their oppressor'.[71] In April 1918, thirty anti-conscription meetings were organized by SF throughout the county, in towns, villages and at rural crossroads.[72] The police noted that 'the matter was referred to in practically all the chapels by the priests.'[73] In Carrickmacross, Revd Daniel O'Connor (who had so vociferously condemned the Easter 1916 rebels) formed an anti-conscription committee that comprised three Sinn Féiners and three nationalists.[74] At the end of the month 'a solemn covenant to resist conscription' was administered in all the Catholic churches of the county: 'Denying the right of the British government to enforce compulsory service in this county, we pledge ourselves solemnly to one another to resist conscription by the most effective means at our disposal.'[75] It was, indeed, the era of covenants to pledge resistance to the British government.

In April 1918, CI Tyacke was forced to admit that membership of SF had greatly increased because of the conscription crisis. The threat had provided SF with a national, political cause to mobilize the youth.[76] By the end of the year, there were thirty-nine clubs with 2,824 members.[77] This placed Monaghan in the top one-third of the counties in Ireland in terms of the ratio of inhabitants to SF clubs.[78] Only after the armistice in November 1918 did the sense of nationalist solidarity against conscription show signs of weakening, by which time SF had replaced the IPP as the party of nationalist Ireland.

Thus, a confluence of factors had propelled SF to the forefront of Irish nationalist politics: the government reneging on home rule; its conciliatory attitude towards Ulster unionists; its reaction to the Rising; the arrest of scores of young men in the county under the DORA; the conscription crisis; the prohibition of public meetings in July 1918, which prevented nationalists from holding *airidheacht* while the police did nothing to prevent the county's Orangemen reviving their 12 July celebrations; and, not least, the economic and social changes during the war years.

There was also the significant fact that SF retained the widespread support of the Catholic clergy. By 1919, of the eighteen members of the SF comhairle ceanntair of north Monaghan, twelve were priests and the president was Fr James McPhillips, PP of Tydavnet.[79] Fathers Hackett, McPhillips, Maguire and McKenna were all in their late forties or fifties by 1916, demonstrating that activism was not the preserve of the younger curates. Curiously, the bishop of Clogher had chosen to transfer to Monaghan individuals identified as troublemakers during the Easter Rising. In May 1916, Fr Eugene Coyle went to Clontibret and Fr James O'Daly to Ballybay. Both were allegedly members of the IRB who, according to Seosamh Ó Dúfaigh, were exempted from the oath by Thomas Clarke. They had been heavily involved in the IV in Tyrone.[80] In November 1917, Fr Coyle, on establishing a SF club in Clontibret, declared that he had been a supporter of the IPP 'until I saw that instead of being the servants of the Irish people they had become the tools of the garrison'.[81] Fr O'Daly was moved from Ballybay to Clones in 1916 where he became friendly with Owen O'Duffy. After the rebellion, Fr James McPhillips, described as 'a warm-hearted Irishman and deeply interested in the Sinn Féin movement', arrived in Donagh parish, while Felix McKenna brought stories of SF home to Glaslough from St Patrick's College Maynooth where he was a seminarian.[82] In Inniskeen, Fr Bernard Maguire ensured that SF was given full access to the parochial hall and school for its meetings.[83] He deliberately prevented the UIL from using either. It was forced to meet in Drumcatton, at the periphery of the parish; geographical marginalization could lead to political marginalization. However, his old friend and Monaghan's most radical priest, Fr Lorcan Ó Ciaráin, was moved in the opposite direction to Pettigo on the border of counties Fermanagh and Donegal, where he would spend the rest of his life.

The ever-astute Thomas McGahon made another valid observation about the rise of SF: for the first time since the Great Famine there was a generation of young men in Ireland kept there by the closure of emigration outlets, who he believed were 'of adventurous disposition ... predisposed to support adventurous, not to say desperate movements'.[84] Between May 1851 and December 1913, a total of almost 60,000 people had emigrated from the county, an average of around 1,000 per annum.[85] However, by 1914 emigration had almost halted; in that year the annual total dropped to 304 and in 1918 to twelve.[86] Monaghan's rural economy and lack of occupational outlets in industry and trade probably meant that emigration in the past was in the main a social necessity. The requirement to travel overseas in search of work and a livelihood doubtless engendered a bitterness among those forced to leave and, indeed, those left at home to grieve the loss of children or siblings. In 1912, Patrick Whelan, at a Gaelic League meeting in Greenan's Cross, suggested the need for cross-class and religious support for the development of Irish industry so that 'home life could be made brighter with an absence of any desire for emigration'.[87] Owen O'Duffy had seen several of his siblings emigrate when he was young and suffered the sadness of the death of his eldest brother, Peter, in America in 1903.[88]

Arguably, the war locked into the country the young, more energetic and radically minded youth, a generation with a new confidence to exert their independence and fight for proper working conditions. Town workers began to unionize. The first branch of the ITGWU was formed in Clones in January 1918.[89] It is not clear by whom but the CI reported that a delegate from Dublin was expected in the town in February.[90] In March, the attendants in Monaghan asylum went on strike to demand a war bonus of 10s. a week. They settled for 4s. and union recognition. Another branch of the ITGWU was formed in Monaghan town in September 1918 and about sixty workers joined. In March 1919, the CI remarked that 'labourers are asking for higher wages and this may eventually lead to trouble', and that there was 'a minor strike of bakers and labourers in Clones.'[91] On 1 May, hundreds of people turned out for a Labour march in the same town. Three red flags were noticed in the procession. A smaller meeting was held in Ballybay addressed by the socialist Peadar O'Donnell. In June, there was a strike by seventeen workers in the firm of J.J. McCaul in Carrickmacross. It was settled by increasing wages from 22s. 6d. per week to 36s. per week. In October 1919, there was a strike of carters and labourers in Monaghan town and employees demanded an increase of 7s. 6d. per week. There were increased tensions when Pattons, the two McCaldin firms and Crawfords – the four largest merchants in the town (all unionist-owned) – refused to grant any increases.[92]

In rural areas, increased demand for food and increased tillage generated more work for labourers. By February 1917 they were campaigning for better pay and working conditions. In Killanny, labourers led the way by forming a parish union, demanding a ten-hour day at 6d. an hour with a one-hour midday dinner break. Labourers in Inniskeen soon followed suit.[93]

The clamour for a more equitable share in wartime profits had refocused minds on the land question. In 1914, 20 per cent of agricultural holdings in Monaghan were unpurchased and would remain so throughout the war as the Treasury diverted its resources to the war effort, much to the frustration of their tenant farmers. Simultaneously, smallholders wanted access to more land to increase viability. Judging from RIC reports, Monaghan had been almost totally free from agrarian unrest in the years prior to the war. However, in 1915–16, the unpurchased tenants on the Shirley, Brownlow and Maguire estates in south Monaghan agitated to have their farms sold to them. Their rent levels were estimated to have been 40 per cent higher than the annuities being paid by neighbours to the Irish Land Commission.[94] Eight men involved in the Brownlow estate dispute were given prison sentences, which led to a mass demonstration in Carrickmacross.[95] Over the next year, isolated agrarian incidents were reported all over the county in areas such as Clones, Aughnamullen, Rockcorry and Carrickmacross.[96] By September 1917, there were reports that in the South Monaghan constituency former McKeanites, predominantly small farmers, had deserted to SF.[97] They had supported McKeane's candidature in the 1910 general election, enticed by his promises to improve their position beyond tenant proprietorship through the redistribution of untenanted lands. But he had failed to do so.[98] A comparable pattern of events in other parts of the country presaged the growth of the final phase of agrarian agitation in Ireland from the spring of 1917 until the end of the Civil War and the passing of the 1923 Land Act.[99]

SF soon realized that it could exploit the land question as parliamentarians had done in the past.[100] At a meeting of the county council in January 1917, SF's Bernard O'Rourke drew attention to the 'terrible hunger for land' in south Monaghan and that smallholders were paying the totally extortionate rates of £20–£22 an acre for conacre when the county council had proposed that £3 an acre was appropriate.[101] With the introduction of a Compulsory Tillage Order in January 1917 – a government measure designed to counteract the food shortage – O'Rourke called for the break-up of the 300 or so holdings of over fifty acres in the county.[102] With little consideration for economic pragmatism, SF pitted itself against the strong farmers who had remained loyal to the IPP. The livestock farmers may not have wanted to purchase ploughs, harrows and pulpers but they did so in the interest of self-preservation. By the end of February the *Democrat* reported: 'It is a considerable time since the plough was so much in evidence in County Monaghan as during the present week. All available ploughs were at work turning up land that in some cases had not been broken up for years.'[103]

While SF became the dominant party after 1918, the IPP did not disappear overnight. For a time, old Redmondites in Monaghan stood firm, unable to comprehend the revolutionary change that was in the air. At the end of May 1916, Eddie Kelly proclaimed: 'So far as his support of the Irish Party was concerned he would continue on until he went down with that ship (hear, hear), and when it was raked up out of the bottom of the sea, he would be found on deck'.[104] In November 1917, the CI reported that the 'men of stake in the localities', men like Kelly, were 'holding aloof from Sinn Féin'.

In particular, the AOH remained strong in the southern constituency as well as in religiously mixed areas further north such as Aghabog. In June 1917, there was an impressive turn out when around 2,000 people attended the unfurling of a new AOH banner in Ballytrain.[105] In February 1918, the Killanny AOH congratulated the nationalists of south Armagh 'on their splendid victory over Sinn Féin and factionalism': Patrick Donnelly polled just over 63 per cent of the vote in his victory over SF's Patrick McCartan. In May, they sympathized with nationalists in east Cavan on their by-election loss when Arthur Griffith defeated J.F. O'Hanlon.[106] The following month, the police reported that Clones Volunteers had marched to Newbliss to counter an AOH demonstration there.[107] And a few months later, Arthur Treanor organized an anti-SF demonstration on the eve of the general election; in the War of Independence he would pay with his life for his prominence.[108]

In September 1917, at a convention in Carrickatee it was announced that Bernard O'Rourke was selected to contest the nomination to be the SF candidate for South Monaghan in the post-war general election.[109] He seemed a natural choice given his high profile, his association through his arrest with the 1916 Rising, and his long experience in local politics. However, on 14 September 1918, the Carrickmacross notes in the *Democrat* suggested that

> his past record as a staunch advocate of the constitutional movement and the Irish Party may render his candidature a trifle distasteful to the republican advocates.[110]

It was prophetic: O'Rourke lost the nomination to Seán MacEntee, who had been sentenced to death for his role in the 1916 Rising in neighbouring County Louth. He was fifteen years younger than O'Rourke, and possibly it was felt that he would appeal more to the younger voters now enfranchised under the Representation of the People Act (1918) that tripled the electorate and gave women over thirty the right to vote for the first time. If O'Rourke was disappointed he did not show it publicly but instead canvassed indefatigably for MacEntee. Ernest Blythe, from a Presbyterian northern unionist background, was selected for the northern constituency. He had only been in Monaghan once before when arrested in Fr Ó Ciaráin's parochial house in Rockcorry in 1915 but his credentials were sound: he had an impressive record of arrest and imprisonment, and was a fellow prisoner of O'Duffy and Hogan in Belfast jail at the time of his selection.[111]

Polling day did not pass without factional outbreaks. Patrick Kavanagh later recalled that the Inniskeen AOH, armed with thick ash-plants and blackthorn sticks, gathered in the village, prepared to fight the younger Sinn Féiners armed with hurleys. There was a degree of symbolism here: the old Ireland with primitive weapons versus the new with the hurleys of the Gael. Kavanagh could remember only one old man on the SF side, 'old Mat Kearney, a man of close on eighty, with a white woolly beard on his face'. A major fracas broke out near Dan McNello's pub. St Patrick's banner was torn to shreds as the Hibernians allegedly fled in disarray.[112] Elsewhere, the *Democrat* reported that 'an army of Sinn Féin motor cars' had been 'let loose on the [southern] constituency'. Tom Carragher later admitted to being involved in the intimidation of voters, while P.V. Hoey recalled that 'the Volunteers' ... presence in military formation had a deadening effect on the anti-national activities of the followers of the Irish Party'.[113] In the 'Orange stronghold' of Drum, eight Sinn Féiners armed with hurleys took up position outside the polling booth to act as a 'Peace Patrol' but were run off by the

Orangemen. When they returned with reinforcements they were run off a second time. When another SF police patrol arrived at the AOH stronghold of Killybrone they were also scattered by the Hibernians.[114]

In a massive turnout of 87 per cent of the 16,175 electorate in the northern constituency, Blythe received 6,842 votes (49 per cent); Michael E. Knight, the unionist candidate, 4,497 votes (32 per cent) and John Turley, nationalist, 2,709 votes (19 per cent). More than half of the electorate in North Monaghan voted against SF. It is probably fair to conclude that the vast majority of unionists voted against Blythe; but they had turned out again in impressive numbers to emphasize the continued existence of a distinctive political culture in north Monaghan. In the predominantly Catholic southern constituency, where there was a 74 per cent turnout, MacEntee polled 7,524 of the 11,937 votes cast (63 per cent). The nationalist candidate, T.J. Campbell, polled almost 4,413 (37 per cent). In the country as a whole, SF won 73 out of 105 seats, Unionists 22 and the IPP a meagre 6. The SF percentage of the Monaghan vote was higher than the national total of 46.9 per cent, and much higher in the southern constituency. But Campbell also bucked the national trend: while the national vote for the IPP was 21.7 per cent, Campbell had captured 37 per cent of the vote in South Monaghan. The endurance of old nationalist politics there was due in large part to the continued strength of the AOH, which would remain active in Monaghan well beyond independence.[115]

In the aftermath of the election, T.J. Campbell claimed he had been beaten by 'a neglected register, by imported mobs, [and] by misrepresentation', warning that 'the new ascendancy with which the nationalists were threatened promised to be worse than the old ascendancy in its tolerance and persecution'.[116] Campbell would have known deep down that this was not why he was defeated. As early as October 1917, Thomas McGahon had recognized that the several thousand 'fine young men and women, well dressed and well behaved', who attended a SF meeting in Monaghan town had lost all sense of what had taken place in their parents' and grandparents' era; there was, he lamented, an 'ignorance of the average man under 30 of the revolution that has been affected in the condition of Ireland during the past half century by the constitutional methods which he is taught to despise'.[117] After the 1918 election, he recognized that the jaded IPP political machine had been ground down by the more energetic vigour of the younger, more enthusiastic Sinn Féiners.[118] For them the leaders of 1916 had already been enshrined as martyrs; as south Monaghan IRA leader, Tom Carragher, later recalled: 'After the Rising there was an awful silence, then a murmur which grew and grew into an awful roar and by 1918 the profile of Patrick Pearse was hung on every kitchen wall'.[119] Young Sinn Féiners had been in sympathy with the German plot prisoners (most of whom were of their generation); they had opposed conscription and the banning of their games; they had simply become fed up with a lack of opportunity; while young women, given the vote for the first time, were also looking for change and did not see the potential for it in the wearied IPP. The older men of property, including the South Monaghan home ruler who pronounced at a board of guardians meeting in Carrickmacross after the Rising that he was not going to be sidelined by 'social upstarts, and the discontent[ed]', were outmanoeuvred by democracy.[120]

Moreover, as the *Democrat* noted, the SF candidates in Monaghan had the unremitting support of the Catholic clergy who canvassed relentlessly on their behalf.[121] The most resolute Redmondite Thomas Toal recalled that SF activist, Fr James O'Daly, persuaded him to join in the celebrations to mark Blythe's election. Toal, it seems, had not intended to participate. It must have been a huge disappointment to him that not only was the establishment of a home rule parliament now in doubt but SF had taken in outsiders to fill the Monaghan seats. The election revealed to him where he now stood so when he took up Fr O'Daly's invitation he 'made a speech which pleased the crowds, explaining that after all efforts to effect a settlement by principle[d] means the English had again deceived us'.[122] He had come to recognize that if he did not jump on the SF bandwagon his political days were numbered.

The vast majority of SF's elected representatives were in prison at the time of their election in 1918, but the twenty-seven who were not convened the first Dáil Éireann on 21 January 1919. They rejected any form of British administration in their attempt to create a counter-state. A few weeks later, in his Lenten pastoral of 1919 Bishop McKenna, reflecting on the end of the First World War, spoke of the terrible conflict that had been fought 'for the destruction of the rule of might, for the liberties of small nations, for the right of people everywhere to choose their own form of government and shape their own destiny' and yet, he concluded, 'in our small nation, one of the oldest in Europe, might rules supreme'.[123] McKenna did not believe in violence and he regularly condemned atrocities on all sides during the later conflict, but the message in the pastoral of 1919 could have been interpreted as justification for a war of independence in Ireland. Tellingly, on the very same day that the Dáil met for the first time, Volunteers led by Dan Breen ambushed an RIC patrol guarding a consignment of gelignite at Soloheadbeg in Tipperary, killing two police constables. Traditionally, the incident is regarded as the beginning of the War of Independence.

Meanwhile, all that Monaghan unionists could now hope for was that if the British government implemented home rule, which it was obliged to do after the war, it would make provision for the partition of the entire province of Ulster and not just the six-county area that had been accepted in 1916.

6 'Private vengeance exacted its toll over cover of civil turmoil',[1] 1919–21

> Men were shot down on the country roads, in city streets, in their homes, in railway trains, on the threshold of the house of God. Every such shooting was the prelude to a bloody reprisal ... in such conditions, mere suspicion seals many a death warrant.[2]

Thus, Thomas McGahon finished his last editorial of 1921. It had been a bloody and violent year in Ireland, at least the first six months up to the calling of the Anglo-Irish truce on 11 July, and bloodier and more brutal in some counties than others. Monaghan's IRA brigade was the most violent in Ulster and the third-most lethal outside Munster.[3] Its victims were not all military. Nor were all IRA casualties inflicted by Crown forces. McGahon's contemporaneous summation captured aspects of the War of Independence that later became part of a collective amnesia when the 'four glorious years' came to be written about: reprisal, counter-reprisal, the shooting of civilians and 'private vengeance', all of which have more recently become the focus of attention in contentious historical debate.

In a work of this length it is impossible to address every dimension of the War of Independence in Monaghan in depth. Detailed narratives of major events such as the general raid for arms on unionist homes in the spring of 1920; the taking of Ballytrain Barracks; the daring rescue of IRA leader, Matt Fitzpatrick, from Monaghan hospital; the Ballybay ambush of 1 January 1921; the burning of Roslea (across the Fermanagh border but the work of the Monaghan IRA) and other episodes, belong to a separate study. While these events are, of course, alluded to in what follows, the main focus is on questions raised by other historians: who joined the IRA and why, who were its enemies, how did they deal with them, and how did those opposed to the IRA attempt to counter its activities?

In January 1919, when Owen O'Duffy and Dan Hogan were sentenced at Clones for their role in 'unlawful assembly' the previous September, 500 people saw them off at the train station.[4] This was very much part of the continuing cult of the hero that had emerged after the Rising – men being hailed as they were sent to jail or upon their release. The CI's reports over the course of 1919 clearly illustrate how busy SF became: north and south Monaghan SF executives were formed and in February began to plan for their candidates to take control of local government in the forthcoming elections; the same month seditious literature was seized suggesting the spread of SF propaganda material; and the Gaelic League was back to prominence, 'holding many classes'.[5]

On 22 December 1919, a meeting was held in Monaghan, presided over by Bishop McKenna, at which 'all shades of nationalists' were said to have been represented. A resolution was passed calling on President Woodrow Wilson to support self-determination for Ireland.[6] By the following autumn it was perfectly clear that the Irish delegation's efforts at the Paris Peace Conference were going to prove fruitless.[7] As part of an alternative strategy, the Dáil turned its attention to countering the British administration in Ireland; this had to be underpinned by the raising of a Dáil loan. Bernard O'Rourke became a key figure.[8] From late 1919 through 1920, bonds were sold to individuals across the country, a massive logistical operation, in denominations ranging from £1 to £100 and bearing interest at 5 per cent per annum, redeemable within twenty years of the international recognition of the Irish republic. From October 1919 to the end of January 1920, O'Rourke collected £766 for the Dáil loan from businessmen, farmers and labourers in Inniskeen, including subscriptions of £50 each from himself and Fr Bernard Maguire. By September 1920, he had successfully raised over £5,700 throughout south Monaghan, the most successful contribution from an Ulster constituency.[9] Neighbouring Tyrone, as a whole, had raised just over £5,300 and the national average by constituency was just over £3,600.[10] Following a raid on his home in 1920, O'Rourke was arrested when documentation relating to the loan was discovered and he was imprisoned in Belfast for several months.[11]

Around the same time, figures of national prominence – including Seán MacEntee, Ernest Blythe, Mrs Wyse-Power and Mrs Sheehy Skeffington – flooded into the county to promote SF ideology; meetings were held outside chapels with the support of the Roman Catholic clergy; audiences were roused by speeches condemning the treatment of prisoners in Belfast jail; and SF clubs began to involve themselves in local agrarian disputes.[12] However, some of the SF meetings were matched by AOH demonstrations, such as the one at Corduff on 11 May 1919, attended by an estimated crowd of 2,200. Demonstation and counter-demonstration reflected the tensions that continued to exist between old school nationalists and separatists.

Owen O'Duffy and the other Belfast jail internees were released just prior to the local government elections of 1920. These were contested in a politically charged climate where SF was again accused of intimidation by nationalists, particularly in the South Monaghan constituency.[13] The AOH and UIL held joint pre-election meetings in Carrickmacross, Inniskeen and Killanny to keep the nationalist vote intact but there was a noted reticence among potential candidates to put their names forward, despite James Shevlin of the south Monaghan UIL executive contending that 'the promises of Sinn Féin have not been fulfilled and there is nothing left to the people but a return to sanity and the constitutional movement'.[14] The assault on one prominent nationalist, Phil Magee of Inniskeen, by an armed gang in his own home forced him to withdraw from the elections and prompted nationalist outrage. The *Democrat* contended that such 'disgraceful political thuggery' was 'not freedom. It is tyranny.'[15] The incident, however, led to the withdrawal of all nationalist candidates in the southern constituency.[16] In their notice of withdrawal, the dozen or so candidates asked supporters to protest by abstaining from voting. However, as in the 1918 general election, it was a very changed electorate that cast their votes and when the results were counted, SF took control of the county and other local councils. McGahon accepted that they had to be regarded as 'representative of the popular will' and urged that 'Toleration towards those Irishmen who have disagreed with them [SF] should be the keynote of their home policy, just as unabated opposition to an alien government should be the keynote of their foreign policy.'[17]

Bernard O'Rourke and Toal (who now wholeheartedly supported SF) were the only two of the old nationalist block returned to the county council. Others such as as Eddie Kelly were gone (temporarily), to be replaced by young, politically uninitiated Sinn Féiners; one of them, James McKenna, later recalled: 'we were all inexperienced but the chairman, Thomas Toal ... was very helpful to us.'[18] Toal was proposed as chairman by John Coleman (SF) on the grounds that he had 'always been very fair and very impartial and had always served the interests of the council very well'. He was seconded by Owen O'Duffy who now found himself a member of the council, as well as its employee.[19] This must have come as something of a shock to the likes of J.C.W. Madden, born into the landed ascendancy and Big House tradition who found himself sitting on the council alongside a working man (and furthermore a leader of the IRA). Toal welcomed O'Duffy as 'one of the most intelligent and competent men that they had in the service of the council' and had no reservations about praising his activism 'while on the run and in prison'.[20] This was a very public pronouncement of support for the separatist agenda that O'Duffy now pursued.

The unionists retained their minority representation but soon found the tenor of political debate within the council chamber to be objectionable. At the first meeting, O'Duffy and Toal were instrumental in Monaghan becoming the first county council to forward a message of allegiance to the Dáil.[21] The four abstentionists were the unionists: Knight, Madden, J.C. Holdcroft and Samuel Nixon. When Madden called for the removal of the 'Sinn Féin flag' from the courthouse, where the council gathered, arguing that Ireland was still part of the United Kingdom, he was taunted with 'loud laughter' from the Sinn Féiners. Even Toal was much less diplomatic than in the past:

'if Col Madden and his party had been well disposed and allowed the foreign government to settle the Irish question at the proper time, there would be no trouble in Ireland today'.²² And O'Rourke reminded Madden and Knight that a few years previously they had drilled the UVF in Hilton Park 'preparing to fight the English government'.²³

The change in the political landscape meant that the 1921 general election passed almost without notice. The three SF candidates – Blythe, MacEntee and O'Duffy – were elected unopposed. By then O'Duffy and Dan Hogan (who deserved much of the credit) had built up an impressive IRA structure in Monaghan. It was later estimated by Dr Conn Ward, intelligence officer for the IRA in Monaghan, that by the time of the Anglo-Irish truce in July 1921 there were 1,827 IRA members in the 5th Northern Division divided into two brigades and six battalions. The 1st Brigade (parts of which were in Tyrone and Fermanagh) consisted of three battalions (Clones, Scotstown and Bragan) with thirteen companies in Monaghan, comprising 418 men of all ranks, as well as nine other companies of 279 men that were in Tyrone or Fermanagh. The 2nd Brigade also consisted of three battalions (Ballybay, Carrickmacross and Monaghan) with a total of twenty-seven companies (plus one in Tyrone) comprising 1,030 men of all ranks.²⁴ Organizations, companies and leadership changed over time according to changing circumstances, growing strength, depleting numbers due to arrests and so on. O'Duffy began as O/C Monaghan Brigade before it was divided into two and before he was promoted to IRA GHQ staff. In July 1921, Dan Hogan was O/C 5th Northern Division, having replaced O'Duffy, James McKenna was O/C 1st Brigade and Thomas McGee commanded the 2nd Brigade.

Historians are in general agreement that the GAA was important to the revolutionary movement but there were few counties where it was as vital as in Monaghan, or at least where it was used to such effect by IRA leaders. Dónal McAnallen has convincingly argued that 'there can be few examples in the world of someone interweaving sport and revolutionary activity so successfully as Owen O'Duffy and the GAA in Ulster'.²⁵ In later years O'Duffy claimed: 'So far as Monaghan is concerned, the Volunteers minus the GAA organization would have been negligible … The GAA had gathered and trained the manpower along the right lines, physical and mental; the Volunteer organization brought it into the front lines when the time came.' This meant that 'hardened and vitalized by Gaelic games, our men could wear the enemy out in speeding across country, in braving the weather's worst rigours of rain or cold through long nights and tiring days'.²⁶ This may be true but many of those the IRA fought against had survived more horrific conditions in Flanders or Gallipoli and, indeed, at least as many of O'Duffy's men died as a result of illnesses seemingly brought on by the 'worst rigours of rain or cold' as died fighting in the War of Independence. Andrew Sherry died of tubercular peritonitis in January 1923; James Marron reportedly died 'following hardship and rheumatic fever'; Henry Duffy whose terms in Ballykinlar 'had [a] major effect on his health ... suffered from enteric fever'; and John Brennan died of chronic colitis said to have been due to activities from October to December 1921.[27]

It is hardly surprising that O'Duffy contended that the GAA in Monaghan contributed to the bulk of IRA membership; after all he was leader of both. If there were other motivating factors they are less easy to determine. For example, the role of the Christian Brothers has been highlighted by some historians as important but there was only one such school in the county – in Monaghan town – and its influence is not obvious from witness statements. The role of the Christian Brothers has often overshadowed that of primary school teachers, some of whom were equally adept at kindling the spirit of Irish nationalism, especially those who embraced the Gaelic Revival and promoted the Irish language, Gaelic games and Irish history in their schools. O'Duffy had come under the influence of his own uncle who taught him in Laragh national school, as did other contemporary pupils including the MacMahons – Peadar, Brian and Sorcha.[28] Peadar fought in the War of Independence outside County Monaghan, becoming a member of Collins' wider 'squad' (not the so-called 'twelve apostles') and later chief of staff of the National army. On retirement from the army he became secretary of the Department of Defence, remaining a lifelong friend of O'Duffy, who was godfather to Peadar's second son. Brian MacMahon also became a member of the IRA and fought in both the War of Independence and Civil War, after which he became a civil servant. Sorcha, as noted previously, was a founding figure in Cumann na mBan, a courier for the Volunteers during the Rising, and, along with Kathleen Clarke and Áine Ceannt, co-founder of the Irish Volunteers Dependents' Fund, which raised funds for the families of dead or imprisoned Easter rebels.[29] Brian MacMahon made several references to the influence of national school teachers when interviewed by the BMH: the captain of the Broomfield Company was 'one of the many outstanding products of the nationals schools, intelligent, well read, especially in matters relating to Irish history and poetry'; Paddy Corrigan of the Lisdoonan Company was 'an exceptional character, very intelligent, very well read, patriotic and idealistic – another fine product of the rural national schools of the country'.[30]

There was a link between SF priests and the diocesan seminary, St Macartan's College in Monaghan town. Frank O'Duffy, one of the earliest IRA leaders in Monaghan, was a teacher there and he was passed information by priests such as Frs Coyle, O'Daly and McPhillips, stationed in neighbouring rural parishes, who were also known to meet in each other's parochial houses with prominent IRA leaders and to shelter men on the run.[31]

At the beginning of 1920, Thomas McGahon was somewhat cynical in his claim that the appeal of a republic 'was a prospect to fire the blood of any young Irish patriot'.[32] However, time and again history has shown that youth, enthusiasm for a cause, and patriotism often go hand in hand. The appeal of republican patriotism is difficult to measure but when O'Duffy arrived in Belfast jail, he found: 'About 160 of the cream of Ireland gathered together, all intelligent, robust & exemplary young men, whose only crime is intense love of country, & irresistible desire to secure the freedom of their mother land.'[33] Similarly, P.V. Hoey recalled: 'The IRA was not an army in the modern sense, it was a guerrilla force of patriotic men banded together in a life and death struggle for the nation's freedom, carrying on under most difficult circumstances, and pitted against the might of an empire.'[34] If combative leadership was a determinant, O'Duffy and Dan Hogan certainly had the necessary charisma to bond young men together in both the GAA and the Volunteers.[35]

Patriotism was not only allied to creating a better country, it was also linked to more personal ambitions for self-improvement among lower-middle-class employees such as O'Duffy and Hogan, stymied by the existing social class system. As Monaghan was a predominantly rural county, one cannot easily dismiss the recasting of the land question as an inducement to young men to join the IRA. In March 1920, James Shevlin of the south Monaghan UIL criticized the fact that 'The republican party said "help us to get a republic and then we'll settle the land question".'[36] Similar inducements were being held out to young men elsewhere; in Clare, for example, IRA leader Michael Brennan later noted that he 'hadn't the slightest interest in the land agitation, but I had every interest in using it as a means to an end ... to get these fellows into the Volunteers.'[37] The agrarian issues that had been simmering during the war years came to the fore after 1920, as happened in many parts of Ireland. In their witness statements Monaghan IRA veterans, no different to any others in this respect, remembered the turbulent years as a struggle with Britain for independence and not as a struggle for a revolutionary transformation of society conditioned by post-war economic dislocation. However, had their recollections been prompted by a set of questions that, for example, included land acquisition and redistribution, it is very possible they might have responded differently, admitting that a desire for social and economic improvement on the back of Irish independence was one of their main motivating factors.

As elsewhere in the country, there was a diversity of occupations represented in the Monaghan IRA and no clear social profile emerges, at least not one that has yet been mapped.[38] Patrick McPhillips was a carpenter in a local Big House, Bellamont Forest (near Cootehill in County Cavan).[39] Charles Emerson was a teacher in the technical school in Monaghan. Thomas

Gillanders was a postman. Conn Ward, the battalion's intelligence officer, was a medical doctor, as was Patrick McCarville. Joe Shevlin was a post office clerk. Pat McDonnell was a foreman on the roads with responsibility for collecting gelignite in the Curragh, a useful man to have on board when explosives were required.[40] P.J. O'Daly was assistant county surveyor to O'Duffy, his south Monaghan battalion was made up of captains who 'were foremen on the Direct Labour road scheme'.[41] Council workers and engineers were an asset to trenching roads or attacking barracks: at the raid on Ballytrain in February 1920, O'Duffy brought one of his road gangers and a team of quarry-blasters with him to dig under the gable walls and set the explosives. Indeed, O'Duffy and his council employees were being paid for repairing the same roads they were blowing up to hamper the movement of police and troops.[42]

Francis Tummons seems to have been more typical of Monaghan IRA membership; he was the son of a small farmer from Derrykerrib, north of Clones.[43] James Mulligan stated that the members of the Slieve Beagh Active Service Unit (ASU) were 'all small farmers'.[44] Paddy McCarvill's father farmed six acres of 'bad land' in Threemilehouse.[45] However, a major exception were the MacMahons of Coas who came from a wealthy farming background. Patrick Donnelly from Carrickmacross and James Marron from Corduff were labourers. Because so many were farmers or farmers' sons, involvement in the fighting had its attendant problems. When Thomas Brennan was imprisoned in Ballykinlar in 1921 he worried about the corn, the red heifer and his mother not being able to get all the farm work done; but he told his sister, Ellie: 'As long as mother and Kate [another sister] are not suffering I'll manage to survive all other troubles and the triumph of our cause will amply repay those who have suffered'.[46] The impact of the revolutionary period on agriculture has yet to be fully considered but at the end of the War of Independence, the County Monaghan executive of the Irish Farmers' Union complained that 'the abnormal times through which we have passed had a very bad effect on the general work, and resulted in a big reduction both in membership and finance … A large number of branch secretaries and chairmen were either interned or on the run.'[47]

From the outset, family connections were important. John, Peter, Patrick and Michael Woods from Annyalla were brothers who were IRA members and their three sisters – Mary, Cassie and Brigid – were in Cumann na mBan.[48] The two Mohan brothers from Killanny were officers in the local company while their two sisters were also prominent in Cumann na mBan. In poorer areas of the county – around the Bragan mountain and Knockatallan, for example – young men may have been drawn into the movement by a tradition of resistance. As Seamus McKenna remembered, 'An intelligent old man in our midst would then tell us of the efforts made for freedom down the years by such men as the Fenians, the United Irishmen, the Whiteboys, the Landleaguers etc. and tell us we were fighting in their footsteps under the best leader ever Ireland had, Michael Collins.'[49]

Whatever the reasons for joining the IRA, the vast majority of Volunteers, as elsewhere throughout the country, were young and unmarried, some still under parental control. Phil Marron wrote to his mother in April 1920: 'I'm sure you will be surprised to hear that I am a prisoner in the city of Derry'.[50] He had evidently kept his nocturnal adventures from her. When James Keenan was court-martialled for his role in an ambush, a local RIC officer gave evidence that his father, a substantial farmer, 'was a man of excellent character, and had always been associated with the Constitutional Nationalists'. His father told the court how the generations had divided: 'there was a wide gulf between Hibernians and Sinn Féiners in south Monaghan. One party supported constitutional government; the other was revolutionary.'[51] Nor did every mother want her son(s) involved. The mother of Frank O'Duffy 'was very much opposed to his politics, due to the fact that she was an English woman, two of her brothers were officers in the British army, and she was of the English mentality'.[52] Guerrilla warfare was best suited to young single men; Monaghan Volunteer, Thomas Donnelly, later made the pertinent point about Charles Emerson, who had been one of the leading early Volunteers in the county, that 'on account of his family responsibilities, [he was] displaced in favour of a young man who would be more suitable for the position'.[53]

Volunteers were exclusively Catholic (and, it seems, devout). One veteran recalled that in safe houses there 'was always plenty of Holy Water around & Rosaries said before going off but never any drink'.[54] The strict ban on alcohol was largely determined by traditional Catholic teaching. In his pastorals, Bishop Patrick McKenna perennially denounced the 'scourge of excessive drinking'.[55] O'Duffy stringently upheld similar regulations against drinking. Joe McCarville recalled that if O'Duffy heard of an IRA volunteer going into a public house 'he would sack you at once';[56] and James McKenna recalled O'Duffy's insistence 'on strict temperance in the ranks'.[57] Throughout the county, O'Duffy's IRA waged war against illicit distillation.[58] And IRA commanders knew there were more practical reasons to discourage alcohol: as Ernie O'Malley put it, 'drink meant an open mouth, talk and rumour', all of which could have dangerous consequences for IRA men and their plans.[59] Alcohol consumption may have been a common problem among Volunteers throughout the country, as Joost Augusteijn's work contends, and sometimes young men required Dutch courage before embarking in nocturnal ambushes or having to shoot someone, sometimes as part of an execution squad.[60] (On 1 February 1923, during the Civil War, the quartermaster in Collins Barracks received 'accounts for whiskey which was purchased on the order of General [Dan] Hogan, and supplied to the firing squads who carried out the executions'.)[61]

Not all of the IRA's work was done in fields, from behind ditches, and in the streets of towns and villages. There also had to be safe houses for men on the run. Joe McCarville could name nine such houses in the Newbliss–Clones area alone.[62] James Mulligan of Scotstown remarked: 'We could get no digs only barns and cattle sheds and depend on the generosity of the poor people of the mountain side for food and these poor people gave us all they had, often not having enough for themselves'.[63] What this suggests, as other historians have argued, is that certain economic thresholds determined whether people supported the IRA. In Monaghan, the less well-off mainly did so, while the strong farmers tended to remain aloof. They did not want to contemplate a revolution that might endanger their social position and economic security. There were also safe townhouses. In 1942, O'Duffy wrote to the secretary of the Military Services Pension Board on behalf of Alice Mullan of Park Street in Monaghan who had been county president of Cumann na mBan. Not only had she 'organized branches all over the entire brigade area; she spent a very considerable amount of her money on the movement, and allowed her business (spirit and boot merchant) to almost lapse.'[64] There were many others like her. James Mulligan claimed he could name almost thirty families whose daughters were involved, often sisters such as the Connollys of Feeha or McCruddens and Sherlocks of Carna.[65] Brigid Fitzgerald of Ture was 'one of the most prominent members of the Cumann na mBan organization'. Her father's house was a regular meeting place of O'Duffy, Hogan, Fitzpatrick and the other Monaghan IRA leaders. Brigid 'frequently kept watch from the hilltops to prevent a surprise raid by the British authorities'.[66] Some IRA men even fell in love in safe houses; in 1932, Brian MacMahon married Rose Finnegan of Killanny whose family had sheltered him on several occasions.[67]

During the course of 1919, the Monaghan IRA did not engage in acts of violence but they did engage in unlawful activity, including marching and drilling, and patrolling illegally held football matches or *aeridheachtaí*.[68] Most particularly, they actively pursued a campaign of social ostracization of the RIC according to the terms of a boycott drawn up by the Dáil the previous August that stated they had been 'judged guilty of treason to their country ... [and] unworthy to enjoy any of the privileges or comforts which arise from cordial relations with the public'.[69] The general aim was to neutralize the RIC as a law enforcement body and prevent them from gathering information that would disrupt IRA activity. The boycott was extended to those who associated with the police. By September 1919, the widespread posting of printed notices in south Monaghan threatening anyone found speaking to the RIC with the penalty of death was reported to have caused a good deal of apprehension and fear.[70] There were sporadic incidents including assaults on policemen and family members; the breaking of windows in RIC homes;

threatening letters; and the kidnapping of RIC employees. One young woman was threatened with death if she went through with her marriage to an RIC constable and another had her hair shaved after she was seen talking to a policeman.[71] Anti-police violence became common throughout Ireland, often hemming police into their barracks; during 1919 sixteen policemen were killed.[72] By August 1920, the crisis was so severe the RIC inspector general reported:

> Boycotted, ostracized, forced to commandeer their food, crowded in many instances into cramped quarters without proper light or air, every man's hand against them, in danger of their lives and subjected to the appeal of their parents and their families to induce them to leave the force and so put an end to the danger and annoyance to which continued service exposes them all.[73]

From the beginning of 1920, the RIC in Monaghan were targeted for arms badly needed by the IRA. In December 1919, Constable Fox of Ballytrain got cut off from two fellow constables on his way home from court in Castleblayney; the CI simply stated that 'Constable Fox's cycle went wrong and after some delay the other 2 constables started for Ballytrain leaving Fox in Castleblayney to follow later'.[74] Fox was attacked by five men and his carbine taken from him. Less than two months later, in February 1920, the IRA attacked and sacked Fox's barracks at Ballytrain (no connection is inferred), nine miles north-west of Carrickmacross and close to the Cavan border. The raid, led by O'Duffy and Hogan, marked the beginning of the War of Independence in earnest in Monaghan.[75] The attack was a huge propaganda success for the local Volunteers, making national newspaper headlines in the days after, and adding to the cult of hero status.[76] This was a raid for arms; the IRA had not come to kill RIC men and those who were injured in the siege were looked after by the IRA medical officer.[77] As Fearghal McGarry points out, at this stage O'Duffy was very much against killing policemen.[78] After Ballytrain, the IRA concentrated on destroying barracks in villages such as Scotstown, Tydavnet, Emyvale and Smithboro (a later attack on the major town barrack in Carrickmacross was unsuccessful); all of these buildings were subsequently vacated, leaving large swathes of the countryside unpoliced (see map 6). This cleared the way for O'Duffy's next offensive, this time against the unionist population who he believed were in possession of arms from the old UVF days. On 31 August 1920, O'Duffy ordered a county-wide raid for arms. John McGahey of the Rockcorry Company recalled that the first house raided, which belonged to the Millar family, 'resembled a military fortress in size and strength'. There were six fully armed men in the house, four family members and two employees. A

1 Michael E. Knight (*right*), his father George Knight (*seated*) and brother, George Walter Knight (*left*).

2 Thomas Toal (1862–1946), chairman of Monaghan County Council 1900–42, and his wife, Susan, who travelled to Bundoran to have their portrait taken by John J. Thompson, 'Patronised by their majesties, the king and queen'.

3 (*left*) Thomas McGahon (1868–1941), the Redmondite editor of the *Dundalk Democrat*.
4 Edward Kelly (1883–1972), Essexford, painted when he was chairman of Monaghan County Council.

5 (*left*) Bernard O'Rourke (1874–1956), Inniskeen, politician, miller and entrepreneur.
6 Charles Laverty (?–1951), Castleblayney solicitor and politician, president of Incorporated Law Society, 1923.

7 Household staff at Glaslough, taken at golden wedding anniversary celebration of Sir John and Lady Constance Leslie, 1905.

8 Sir John and Lady Constance Leslie and family at golden wedding anniversary celebration, Glaslough, 1905.

9 Banner of Ballybay LOL No. 211.

10 (*right*) Banner of Aghabog AOH.

11 Monaghan UVF officers at Knockballymore training camp, January 1914. Included from Monaghan are (*from left, front row*) Michael E. Knight, Revd E. Stack, Sir John Leslie, Capt. Richard Dawson & Lt.-Col. Gerald Madden.

12 Monaghan Ulster Volunteer Nursing Corps being inspected by its president Ms Murray Ker and Col. John Leslie at Newbliss, 28 July 1914.

13 Edward Carson (1854–1935) at Newbliss House, 28 July 1914.

14 'Raising the colours', UVF demonstration, Newbliss, 28 July 1914.

15 (*above*) 'Orange Proclamation': popular postcards issued in the aftermath of the Larne gun-running incident, 1914.

16 Monaghan UVF badge.

17 Monaghan senior football team, Ulster champions 1916. Owen O'Duffy is first on the left, second row.

18 General Owen O'Duffy (1892–1944).

19 James Vogan (*far left*), head gamekeeper on Leslie estate at Glaslough, with fellow gamekeepers. Men such as these made it difficult for the IRA to raid Big Houses.

20 Fr Lorcan Ó Ciaráin (1863–1945), one of Monaghan's most radical priests in the lead up to the 1916 Rising.

21 Smithboro Loyal Orange Lodge Brass Band, *c.* 1920.

22 Funeral of Lt.-Col. Gerald Madden (b. 1872) of Hilton Park who died from wounds on 12 November 1915.

23 Monaghan RIC after discovering a poitín still near Carrickmacross, c.1918.

24 Carrickmacross Comrades of the Great War, c.1920.

25 '1st man to enter RIC barric': unidentified IRA volunteer outside Carrickmacross RIC barracks, 1921.

26 Mary Nolan (*centre*), president of south Monaghan Cumann na mBan.

27 General Dan Hogan outside Lough Bawn House during the truce period.

28 Castleshane House, destroyed by fire in February 1920.

29 William Black of Gola House, Ballyleck; the house was burned in 1921.

30 Funeral of William and Robert Fleming, St Maeldoid's Church of Ireland cemetery in Castleblayney, March, 1921. The coffins are draped in Union Jacks and carried by men in paramilitary uniform.

31 Free State soldiers at the Ballybay crossroads, outside Carrickmacross, 1922.

32 Unidentified Monaghan IRA volunteers.

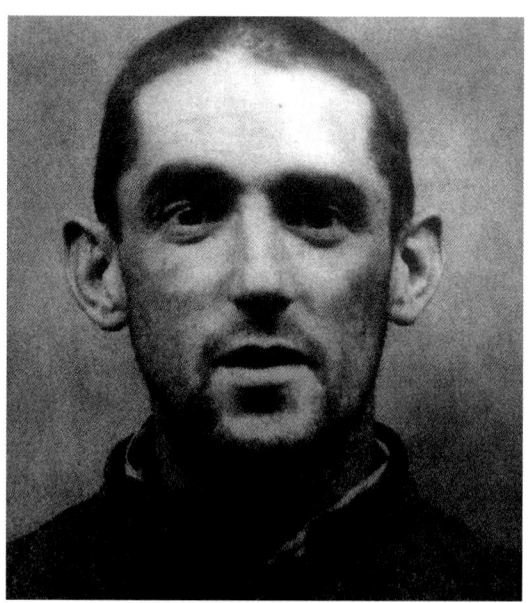

33 Patrick McCarville (1893–1955) in prisoner uniform. He was medical officer of 5th Northern Division and later TD for Monaghan, 1922–7.

'Private vengeance exacted its toll over cover of civil turmoil' 83

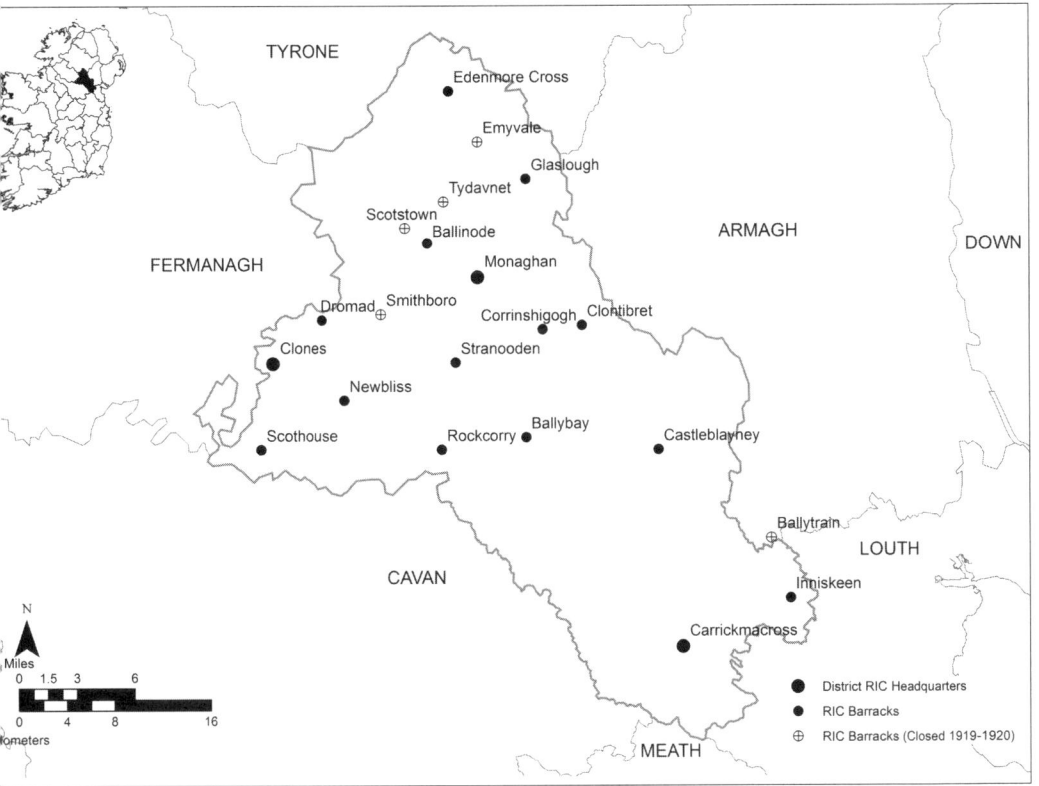

6 Distribution of the Crown forces

gunfight lasted around half an hour before the IRA was forced to break off their attack.[79] Towards daybreak the same company made its way to Crawford's outside the village of Drum. When McGahey and Volunteer Peter O'Reilly forced the front door with an axe they were met with a hail of fire from Crawford. The raid was abandoned with O'Reilly later dying of his wounds, having been shot in the chest. McGahey later reflected: 'this tragic affair which happened so quickly, cutting off a fine young life in the prime of its manhood and snatching from us a dear comrade and friend, shocked us all that even at the present day the survivors of this shooting have not been able to forget.'[80]

John Wright and his two sons successfully fought off a raid against their home in Killybressal. Patrick McCluskey was severely wounded in a raid on the Hazlett home.[81] During a raid on Raddocks, Eugene Sherry was wounded. He later recalled: 'Young Raddock's determination in defence of his house forced us to retreat and we failed to disarm the young man as we did not relish the endangering of the lives of his father and mother.'[82] Bernard Marron was killed in the raid on McCauls and Owen Keenan of Corcaghan was killed in another incident. In the raid on the Fleming home at Drumgara outside Castleblayney, Patrick McKenna was shot dead by William Fleming and quietly buried by his comrades. He was later reinterred in the family plot in St Mary's churchyard, Castleblayney.[83] In Monaghan, more IRA men were killed by well-armed unionists in this general raid for arms than by the Crown forces during the entire of the War of Independence.

In the second half of 1920, tensions understandably escalated. The fact that most outlying barracks had been destroyed prior to the general raid meant that in the weeks and months that followed there was no protection against IRA reprisals. McGahey claimed that 'all the Unionists in our area and the surrounding districts went into both Ballybay and Cootehill looking for police or military protection for their houses and persons', but patrols were not the answer.[84] Reprisals began two weeks after the raids. An estimated 100 men arrived back at the McCaul household, where Bernard Marron had been killed, shot the father and ordered the son out of the country.[85]

At the 12 July celebrations, a motion was passed by Monaghan Orangemen appealing to the government to deal resolutely with 'the cruel and treacherous warfare which is being carried on in this county involving the sacrifice of the lives of loyal men and the senseless destruction of life and property'.[86] In September, a large meeting representative of unionists throughout the county was held in Monaghan town. It criticized the attitudes of the local Roman Catholic clergy for not openly condemning the outrages perpetrated by 'the advocates of a republican government'.[87] The meeting decided to appoint committees with authority to form 'town guards', the first of which was established in the village of Drum: its aim was to defend property 'against the marauding bands of ruffians who under the guise of political organizations are robbing and terrorizing the peaceful inhabitants in other parts of the county'.[88] Shortly after, a meeting was held at Smithboro where steps were taken for the formation of a County Monaghan Protestant Defence Association, in order to bring the local organizations under a central authority.[89] The constitution and rules of the association specified 'closer co-operation and unity of action amongst the Protestants and Loyalists at this present crisis'. The use of the term 'Loyalists' indicated how (former) unionists had more or less given up hope of remaining within the United Kingdom but they still wished to retain their loyalty to the Crown.

Less than three weeks after this meeting, on 12 October 1920, Michael Kelly, a nationalist hackney driver, was killed as he drove Fr Murray of Tydavnet home. Kelly's parish priest, Fr James McPhillips, happened to be president of the SF comhairle ceanntair of north Monaghan. His death at the hands of loyalists was interpreted as a reprisal for local arms raids, although he is unlikely to have been a participant in these actions.⁹⁰ The incident signalled a change in the dynamic of violence in Monaghan. As one Volunteer later recalled, the widespread prevalence of loyalists 'scattered over the area created somewhat of a problem', as they maintained 'a most hostile attitude to everything republican', acted as informers, and opened fire on suspected Sinn Féiners.⁹¹ Peter Woods of the Annyalla company recalled that there were townlands 'with practically an entire Unionist population' who 'had the remnants of the Ulster Volunteer organization and held a lot of the Ulster Volunteer rifles'.⁹² An escalating cycle of violence was to be one of the clear impacts of the general raid for arms.

In the months that followed, the Monaghan IRA also faced the added threat of the Ulster Special Constabulary (USC), more commonly referred to by contemporaries in Monaghan as the B Specials, and the arrival of additional Crown forces to supplement the police: the Black and Tans and the Auxiliaries. The Specials arose out of the UVF, which had been revived in many areas.⁹³ It is not entirely clear when they were first organized in Monaghan but quite probably soon after the September 1920 unionist meeting; therefore, so-called 'town guards' were essentially B Special companies comprised of former UVF men and ex-soldiers. The Black and Tans arrived later in the winter and were stationed in the major towns, while a company of Auxiliaries took over Hope Castle in Castleblayney. The Black and Tans had arrived shortly after the events of 'Bloody Sunday', 21 November 1920, when Michael Collins' 'squad' shot dead fourteen suspected British secret service agents in Dublin, and a company of Black and Tans retaliated that afternoon by firing into the crowd gathered at Croke Park for a game between Dublin and Tipperary. They killed twelve civilians, including Tipperary footballer, Michael Hogan from Grangemockler, brother of Dan. The Monaghan IRA intelligence officer, Dr Conn Ward, later claimed that: 'Bloody Sunday affected him [Hogan] and [he] wanted to get using [the] gun at all opportunities'.⁹⁴ The statistics would seem to verify this: in the eight months after Bloody Sunday eighteen people were killed by the IRA in Monaghan in comparison to only three up to then.⁹⁵

Aggression was met by counter-aggression. On Christmas Eve 1920, the Black and Tans went on a rampage in Castleblayney; when a reporter of the *Democrat* visited the town, he found the people in a state of terror.⁹⁶ Carrickmacross publican, William Daly, recalled 'a good night' until a brawl broke out because of his refusal to serve Black and Tans any more drink. He experienced '20 minutes in the wild west' as pistols were pointed and the row spilled out onto the street.⁹⁷ Daly also reported the police being 'very aggressive' in the area as a whole, forcing people to provide food and money to them and even stealing clothes off hedges as they dried.⁹⁸ In February 1921, Patrick McCabe of Rockcorry was arrested and while in custody 'was maliciously beaten with the butt ends of rifles, his ribs broken and his body left a mass of bruises. His boots were stripped off and he was made walk through the village of Rockcorry with a Union Jack wrapped round his head.'⁹⁹ These aggressive actions lived long in local memory, even if the towns and villages of Monaghan got off lightly when compared with Balbriggan in Dublin, Trim in Meath, Tuam in Galway, Thurles in Tipperary and many more places that were burned and sacked by Black and Tans.

Reprisal and counter-reprisal bred a cycle of violence that particularly characterized the War of Independence from January to July 1921. On the night of 1 January 1921, a patrol of four policemen was ambushed on Main Street, Ballybay. Constable Michael Malone was killed, two others were wounded and a civilian, John Somerville, a Presbyterian loyalist butcher from Main Street, was found dead beside Malone. Shot as he ran from Coyle's pub, he might have been going to the aid of the wounded policemen or he may have been deliberately targeted since he was known to have been friendly with the police.¹⁰⁰

On 22 January, three policemen were ambushed and killed after they left Leonard's public house in Corcaghan.¹⁰¹ Philip Marron recalled that for the weeks previously the police had been acting in a 'blackguardly manner', searching local houses and generally causing mayhem, so the IRA decided to put an end to it.¹⁰² J.C.W. Madden raised the incident at the county council meeting, calling on its members to 'condemn murder which might bring about retaliation and loss to their county'. Toal deflected the issue, stating he did not know the full facts of the case but Patrick Duffy of SF called on England 'to withdraw her army of occupation'.¹⁰³ The Corcaghan incident led Bishop McKenna to denounce crime and violence on both sides, reminding young IRA men of their Catholic teaching, although he did blame the violence on the denial of rights and liberties to people who were 'oppressed'.¹⁰⁴ Around the same time, Monaghan Presbyterians were told that their General Assembly wished for its people 'to live in peace with their Roman Catholic fellow-countrymen'.¹⁰⁵ However, in October 1921, James Carson paid a visit to his ancestral home at Monanton, near Ballybay, and later recalled: 'there were no social relations between Protestant and Roman Catholic. Religious, social and political differences were deep. They were two peoples living in one community.'¹⁰⁶

On 30 May 1921, a police patrol was ambushed between Carrickmacross and Castleblayney. Constable Walter Perkins, a veteran of the First World War, was killed.¹⁰⁷ William Daly recorded in his journal that Perkins was the 'nicest fellow [that] could be got' and that he had been engaged to a local girl.¹⁰⁸ There were local repercussions: the following day the police ordered all schools and shops in the town to close and people from the rural areas coming into the town were turned back. The Thursday market was almost empty and Daly claimed that 'some of the Black and Tans ordered men and women off the footpath, clouted and kicked a good many of the boys', and intimidated Fr Cullinan.[109]

In total, five policemen were killed in Monaghan by the IRA during the War of Independence. The only IRA fatalities suffered in combat with Crown forces were the McEneaney brothers, Michael and Thomas, killed on 30 June 1921 when an ambush at Carnagh railway station, on the Castleblayney–Keady–Armagh line, was surprised by a party of Auxiliaries.[110] In total, therefore, only seven men were killed in what might loosely be termed military combat.

The IRA also waged war against perceived civilian enemies. Shortly after the attack on the barracks at Ballytrain, a number of leading IRA men were arrested, including O'Duffy, and imprisoned in Belfast. There, O'Duffy organized a hunger strike that won certain rights for the prisoners. When Phil Marron wrote to his mother of the success of the strike, he hinted at the presence of another IRA enemy in Monaghan: 'Our fight is won and we have proved ourselves to be Irishmen. Our success is wonderful propaganda in the city of Belfast and after a little while the Joe Devlinites will be Sinn Féiners.'[111]

'Joe Devlinites' were the members of the AOH. From the moment SF came to prominence in Monaghan, there were bitter tensions between the two organizations, as became evident during the 1918 general election. Patrick McMeel lived in the mountainous area of Bragan where there was a large AOH population 'bitterly opposed to the Volunteers and Sinn Féin'.[112] In August 1919, Sinn Féiners attacked AOH dances in Clones and Castleblayney.[113] A couple of weeks after the raid on Ballytrain, there was a huge AOH demonstration in Carrickmacross, its organizers wanting to emphasize 'that far from being a dwindling power in south Monaghan, Hibernianism is flourishing and calmly waiting the summer to assist in marshalling once again the wandering children of our land into the solid ranks of constitutionalism'.[114] There was an obvious and deliberate biblical allusion to the Jews in search of the Promised Land. The reasons for this internecine strife are not hard to find. The AOH was primarily supported by traditional middle-class supporters of the IPP. These were the men who had vociferously condemned the 1916 Rising, believing it the work of socialist revolutionaries.

On 13 November 1920, an AOH member, Michael O'Brien, was on his way home from a fair in Shercock in neighbouring County Cavan when he came across a number of IRA men lying in the ditch. O'Brien recognized them and called out their names.[115] He was shot and subsequently died from his wounds on 2 December. On 9 March 1921, two young Catholic men – Patrick Larmer, aged 23 and Francis McPhillips, aged 21 – were found dead in a laneway in Aghabog. A note was pinned to Larmer's body which read: 'Tried, Convicted, & Executed by IRA'; that on McPhillips' body read: 'Convicted informer. IRA'. According to the police reports, both 'were shot through the heart, over which a small piece of paper was pinned', suggesting execution by firing squad.[116]

McPhillips had been abducted earlier that night from the family farm at Corleck where he lived with his mother and six unmarried sisters, ranging in age from fourteen to twenty-five. His widowed mother farmed around thirty acres, a decent-sized farm for Monaghan at that time. McPhillips was a member of the AOH.[117] In 1918, Aghabog was a stronghold of Hibernianism. That June an Aghabog Ladies Auxiliary was founded with 500 people in attendance who were told that 'Aghabog was a very staunch and nationalist parish' and that 'the criminal lunacy of Sinn Féin was turning all Ireland's friends against her'.[118] In 1919, the division unfurled a new banner dedicated to the late John Redmond.[119] The local AOH despised the SF movement.[120] McPhillips had been suspected for some time of providing information to the police and it was also believed that he was too loose in his conversation with Presbyterian neighbours about local republicans. A few months before his abduction he had been warned by the IRA and in a very public punishment tied to the railings of the church at Aghabog for all his neighbours to see as they filed out from Mass. Not heeding the warning, a short time later he was duped by IRA officers disguised as police, subsequently tried by court martial in March 1921, over which O'Duffy is said to have presided, and executed.[121]

In her subsequent compensation claim, McPhillips' mother maintained that the loss of her only son meant hardship for her and her daughters who struggled to work the farm. County court judge Johnson described the case as 'the most tragic and appalling' brought before him, made all the more so because his murderers shared McPhillips' religion: 'They went out every day', he reflected, 'and they saw the spires of churches pointing to heaven, and they knew they were living in a Christian land'. He awarded £1,400 in damages 'to be a county-at-large charge'.[122] McPhillips' mother claimed that her son's only crime had been the fact that he was a member of the AOH.[123] Similarly, in March 1921, a Monaghan Hibernian wrote to Joseph Devlin that McPhillips was murdered 'for no other reason than that he was a staunch Hibernian. That's the treatment meted out to Nationalists at Sinn Féin hands.'[124] Years later, Hugh McArdle, county president of Monaghan AOH, claimed the killing was 'an attempt to scare the rest of the organization'.[125] Thirteen years after his execution Fr Tom Maguire, the SF-sympathetic parish priest of Aghabog, who had heard McPhillips' final confession, believed that the boy should not have been put before the squad ... To my judgement the deceased was deserving of every human consideration, because he was generally acknowledged as not up to the normal mental standard. Moreover, it was commonly stated then and since that local bitterness influenced the evidence and court-martial decision.[126]

His last sentence suggests that while McPhillips was executed as an informer, there were other circumstances related to local factionalism, such as his AOH membership and his antipathy towards the IRA.

On 25 June 1921, Arthur Treanor's body was found with the customary note alleging that he had given information to the police. Treanor, from Dunmadigan in Emyvale, was the most prominent local politician to be killed; he was a poor law guardian and rural district councillor as well as a member of the north Monaghan executive of the UIL, and president of Davagh AOH. The *Democrat* claimed that he was 'a steadfast and consistent supporter of the constitutional movement and gave much of his time in devotion to the best interests of his county'.[127] A substantial farmer, he was a vociferous opponent of SF and, as noted previously, organized an anti-SF demonstration before the 1918 general election. His opposition to a local council vote of sympathy for Terence MacSwiney and Kevin Barry brought him into further conflict with SF. In IRA eyes, anti-Sinn Féinism was tantamount to treason against the republic. Thus, Joseph McKenna accused Treanor of being 'a notorious British supporter from the time the Volunteers first started'; his guilt, McKenna claimed, was proved when a cheque payable to Treanor from Dublin Castle was intercepted in a raid on the mails.[128] Patrick McGrory, however, believed that Treanor 'was too intensely Irish to stoop to betray a fellow Irishman'.[129] Contradictory claims obscure the exact motivation for abductions and killings but equally they reflect the fact that there may have been local as well as national reasons; Thomas McGahon was canny enough to know that sometimes 'private vengeance exacted its toll over cover of civil turmoil'.[130]

Patrick Larmer's body was found beside McPhillips. Unusually, Larmer was a member of the IRA, or at least he was carrying dispatches for them when he was arrested outside Rockcorry Catholic church while playing a game of pitch and toss – a popular pastime. After he was released from Belfast prison he informed his IRA superiors that he had only told the authorities what they already knew. However, a round-up of suspects in the Rockcorry neighbourhood in the days after his release cast doubts on his claim.[131] John McGahey knew that Larmer 'was an intelligent country boy who unfortunately for everybody concerned was timid and easily scared', and he could have forgiven him for 'his weakness in yielding to threats under torture by the Tans'.[132] At the court martial, McGahey believed he had convinced O'Duffy not to execute Larmer until 'Dan Hogan arrived on the scene and intervened in a manner most aggressive towards myself'. McGahey regretted that but for Hogan's arrival the boy's life might have been spared, and for the rest of his life McGahey's conscience obviously played upon him, so much so that he used his witness statement as an opportunity to vindicate Larmer for whom execution 'was much too drastic [a] punishment'.[133]

Just over two weeks after Larmer's execution, on 25 March, Henry Kerr (sometimes cited as Carr), a 65-year-old Catholic bachelor farmer, was abducted from his house at Corvoy. A card bearing 'Convicted as a spy, executed by the IRA' was pinned to his chest. Police conducted exhaustive enquiries but no one was arrested.[134] John McGahey claimed he had been given several chances but his alleged treachery had been revealed in an intercepted letter.[135] The CI also admitted that a few weeks before Kerr had been 'visited & he chatted with the military officer'.[136] Furthermore, he was known to have been 'One of the old school of nationalism' who 'expressed his opinions freely and fearlessly'.[137] Kerr was shot six times in the head, chest, knee, leg and shoulder.[138] Anne Dolan has suggested that multiple wounds such as Kerr suffered may have been the result of 'panic or enthusiasm or inaccuracy' on the part of the execution squad or intended to make the victims 'foul in death to all who beheld them, to make mourners shiver at the sight of what might be done to them in turn, to cause a body to be waked in a closed coffin because it was too damaged for the grieving to look upon'.[139] Whatever the reason, Kerr was not the only victim to experience a particularly brutal death.

Early in 1920, a British soldier, Joseph Gibbs, who had allegedly tried to infiltrate the IRA, was found out by Patrick Corrigan, executed and secretly buried on a lonely hillside.[140] In April 1921, John McCabe, an ex-soldier and pedlar of drapery, hardware and religious memorabilia (the only way he could make a living following demobilization) was shot several times and left in a barn in Tullyvaragh to die.[141] That McCabe survived was described as 'almost a miracle'.[142] A sign around his neck stated: 'Convicted spy, IRA'.[143] CI Tyacke reported: 'No reason is known for the attempt on him. He was not in communication with the Monaghan police & in his occupation he does not seem to have made enemies.'[144] It may have been because he was a tramp or an ex-soldier, two classes often targeted by the IRA.[145] There had been a long antipathy towards the tramp class in south Monaghan. The 'Carrickmacross notes' in the *Democrat* in January 1912 referred to 'the tramp pest'.[146] In March 1916, 'the tramp, McCusker' was brought before a special court for an attack on a woman near Ballytrain.[147] These incidents occurred before the advent of the IRA. During the War of Independence, the IRA treated tramps as social outcasts. For instance, in July 1920, publicans were ordered by the IRA not to serve 'the tramp class' and warned that non-compliance would be 'severely dealt with'.[148] Peter Hart has argued that after the Protestant minority the main target groups of the IRA were 'ex-soldiers, tinkers and tramps, and others seen as social or political deviants'.[149] The Monaghan experience hardly corroborates this; McCabe seems to have been the only case of an ex-soldier or tramp targeted, while Gibbs was an alleged soldier-spy.

Hugh Duffy from Rockcorry was an army pensioner who delivered telegrams for Rockcorry post office. He was shot on 1 April 1921 in a lane at Moylemuck after having been sent with a bogus telegram to Greacons. The usual notice, 'Spies and informers beware', was pinned to his chest. He had three large wounds on the side of his head, one from a bullet and two caused by a blunt instrument; there were also numerous puncture wounds on the left side of his chin possibly caused by buckshot; and two other exit and entrance wounds on his left shoulder and left side of his chest.[150] Again, this was a particularly vicious killing where the multiple wounds suggest a vindictive sadism beyond the routine execution of a spy. His wife, Margaret, claimed that 'he had no personal enemies and was very popular as far as I am aware ... He was an army pensioner and was well known as a loyal subject'.[151] In her naivety she probably revealed the motivations that lay behind his murder. The CI came up with another motive rooted in neighbourly jealousies regarding patronage: 'He was acting in the absence of the regular postman who was sick & though he had so acted for years it is believed that those who opposed his appointment thought that this was a good time to use the terror of the IRA name to remove him.'[152] However, one IRA veteran later claimed that O'Duffy was a B Special.[153] This may be significant as this was around the time of the Roslea burnings, the motivations for which, as discussed below, were rooted in USC activity along the border.

On 17 April 1921, Kate Carroll, a middle-aged Catholic spinster, who lived with her elderly parents and mentally challenged brother near Duffy's Cross, Tydavnet, was taken from her home by a number of armed men and killed; once more the usual warning to spies and informers was pinned to her chest.[154] Her execution contravened an IRA general order issued in November 1920 that stated in the case of a female found guilty of being a spy, only 'consideration of her sex prevents the infliction of the statutory punishment of death'.[155] While the contemporary newspapers stated that Carroll was a Protestant, thereby suggesting a sectarian dimension to her murder, she was in fact a Roman Catholic who had come to the IRA's attention for illicit distilling, a practice, as noted earlier, against which the IRA waged war. In June 1920, about forty IRA men had been involved in extensive poteen seizures in Clones, Newbliss and Aghabog, and in Farney they displayed 'marked activity in hunting down poteen-makers'. Around Ballytrain, the distillers 'declared war on their assailants' and posted armed guards around the stills.[156] However, the IRA did not kill poteen-makers;

they simply smashed their stills and warned them not to reoffend. But Kate Carroll had compounded her offence by writing to the RIC informing on other illicit distillers, who were effectively her competitors. This letter was intercepted by the IRA.[157] Fearghal McGarry's contention that 'the charge of spying appears to have been a convenient rationale for the execution of an obvious anti-social security risk' is highly plausible.[158] At the end of the day, Carroll was nothing more than a harmless, impoverished, middle-aged spinster 'handicapped by the helplessness of the other members of her family'. When the police sought help for her family, 'none was forthcoming'; nor could they identify the perpetrators in an area where the population was divided between those who were 'hostile, and the remainder terror-stricken'.[159]

Of eight individuals executed as spies in Monaghan, five were Catholics, two were Protestants and one (Gibbs) was an outsider whose religion was unknown. As McGarry has concluded, the ruthlessness of these spy killings has to be seen in context: the IRA believed they were essential to their freedom of movement.[160] And the campaign must have been successful in this respect because it was reported in April 1921 that people were generally living 'in fear of their lives'.[161] Before the War of Independence began, Richard Mulcahy had been forthright as to how war would have to be waged for the struggle to be successful:

> Freedom will never come without a revolution, but I fear Irish people are too soft for that. To have a real revolution, you must have bloody fierce-minded men who do not care a scrap for death or bloodshed. A real revolution is not a job for children, or for saints or scholars. In the course of revolution, any man, woman or child who is not with you is against you. Shoot them and be damned to them.[162]

Did these brutal acts, as McGarry asks, 'cast the darkest shadow over O'Duffy's good war'?[163] Acts that are expedient in the eyes of some are atrocities in the eyes of others. All across post-war Europe, paramilitary actions were seen as justification for nationalist struggle.[164] What is noticeable is that there were no 'spy' casualties in Monaghan until after 'Bloody Sunday' in November 1920; it is speculative but that may very well have had something to do with the impact 'Bloody Sunday' had on Dan Hogan.

The low incidence of sectarian murders in Monaghan may have been largely due to the unionist community's ability to protect itself. By April 1921, O'Duffy estimated that there were 620 men from Monaghan serving in the USC, drawn predominantly from border areas with strong unionist populations. Clones (including the Protestant enclave of Drum) had the highest number with an estimated 200. McCluskey contends that in Tyrone 'The

USC essentially executed an indiscriminate terrorist campaign against the entire nationalist population'.[165] In Monaghan, the USC was not so violently active but Monaghan Volunteer, John McGahey, certainly resented their existence in his area of Rockcorry.[166] He and other local IRA men took umbrage at their participation in full uniform in police search parties; when Francis Tummons was arrested on 29 April 1921 he recalled that 'the raiding party included military, RIC and Special Constabulary, the latter well known Orangemen and neighbours of our own'.[167]

In February 1921, certain USC, operating along the border, were accused of intimidating and searching nationalist boys in the small Fermanagh village of Roslea for IRA dispatches. This type of activity hardened O'Duffy's antagonism towards the USC. He ordered the execution of one notorious Special who was subsequently shot and wounded on the morning of 23 February.[168] As a reprisal, ten nationalist homes in Roslea were burned, two nationalists wounded, and one Special accidentally shot dead. Fearing further reprisals, many nationalist families fled across the Monaghan border to Scotstown and Knockatallon.[169] An incensed O'Duffy wrote to headquarters: 'we cannot let this wanton conduct to go unpunished' and asked: 'Am I right in assuming I have a free hand in this matter?'[170]

Permission was granted. On the night of 21 March the IRA burned fourteen houses belonging to B Specials, shot two dead and wounded two other members of the force.[171] According to the *Standard*, the sectarian nature of Roslea left unionist families along the county border watching and waiting every night in fear of attack; tired and sleepless, they would turn out to the fields for work the following day.[172] The same must have been true for nationalist families. Thomas McGahon feared the worst, writing in the *Democrat*: 'If this thing spreads, which God forbid, nothing can save Ireland from a hideous war of extermination in which Catholic and Protestant will suffer as have those of Roslea'.[173] A few nights later the most brutal sectarian killings in Monaghan took place in reprisal for the shooting of Patrick McKenna in the general raid for arms seven months previously. Between forty and fifty IRA men returned to the Fleming homestead, set it on fire and smoked the inhabitants out.[174] The *Democrat* contained a graphic description of what followed:

> Fleming and his son opened up the door and handed up the gun. Neither man was fully dressed ... they were escorted from the house, through a bye-road some perches from the house ... They were placed against the ditch by the armed men and a volley of shots directed at them. Robert fell mortally wounded. A big discharge from a shotgun – probably the weapon which had been handed up – caught him in the lower jawbone. The side of his neck was almost blown away ... The father was seriously wounded. He was shot in the back and stomach.

Though very seriously wounded, he crawled back to the outhouse and there, in the presence of his mother and children, lay on the floor and covered himself with hay.[175]

The report claimed that the elder Fleming had been on good terms with all of his neighbours until McKenna's death. He was described as a 'quiet, inoffensive man, a unionist in politics, but not mixing much in political matters'.[176] However, a surviving photograph of the Fleming funeral at St Maeldoid's Church of Ireland cemetery in Castleblayney (see plate 30) clearly illustrates that it was a paramilitary-style affair. The hats on the coffins and the uniformed escort suggest both men may have been Specials. Moreover, McKenna's father in his application for a posthumous pension for his son had no doubt but that the Flemings were members of the USC.[177] The Flemings were not killed because of their religion – they were killed because the IRA believed they had chosen to throw their lot in with the enemy.

O'Duffy was smug in his report to GHQ for March: 'this lesson [Roslea] had apparently the right effect as leading Unionists have since approached some of the Catholic clergy with a view to having a truce'.[178] An all-party conference was duly held at Clones, at which representatives of all denominations from Roslea, Tydavnet, Clones, Killevan, Corcaghan and Smithboro gathered.[179] It was indicative of how the majority of people in north Monaghan wanted to carry on with their lives, free from inconvenience and fear. However, O'Duffy was becoming more belligerent and informed those present that 'there would be no truce until the B Special constables surrendered their arms and ceased all hostility towards us'.[180] It was around this time that he was promoted to divisional commandant of the 2nd Northern Division that covered Tyrone and Derry. While he was reluctant to leave his base in Monaghan, Dan Hogan's promotion in his place meant he still effectively held sway and his authority was further strengthened by his position in the Dáil.[181]

McGarry is probably right that but for O'Duffy's restraining influence, the number of sectarian casualties would have been much higher in Monaghan, citing how he 'prevented one company from killing local Protestants to avenge Michael Kelly's death'.[182] By extension this suggests that the rank and file *were* intent on sectarian violence, motivated by revenge possibly embedded in historical ancestral grievances or jealousies as much as contemporary events. However, the wider public, nationalist and unionist, condemned the escalation in civilian murders, and after the brutalities of March and April 1921 even the SF-dominated county council called for an end to the killings.[183] Thus, O'Duffy and the IRA were arguably constrained by the continued influence of middle-class men such as Thomas Toal and Denis Carolan Rushe with whom O'Duffy continued to meet during the War of Indepedence; in fact, both often provided him with safe shelter. Neither Toal nor Rushe would have condoned murder. Nor did Bishop McKenna who yearly railed against violence perpetrated by all sides in his Lenten pastorals, or the leaders of the Anglican and Presbyterian churches. The IRA had to be careful not to alienate support for 'the cause' by attracting odium from the majority because of their actions.

Finally, there was another dimension to the War of Independence in Monaghan, not unique to the county, but more effectively policed there than anywhere else due largely to Monaghan's geographical location: the Belfast boycott. Until 1920, Monaghan was more commercially linked to Belfast and other Ulster markets than Dublin. A prolonged dislocation of trade was not in the best interests of businesses in County Monaghan, nationalist or unionist. But this became inevitable after the creation of Northern Ireland. Moreover, as the troubles escalated in the south, so also did the sectarian tensions in Belfast. In the course of 1920, an estimated 11,000 Catholic nationalists were expelled from their jobs in Northern Ireland, and of 455 people killed, 58 per cent were Catholic even though they made up only 24 per cent of the population.[184] These events had repercussions in Monaghan, giving rise to low-level sectarian crimes of a nature that traditionally accompanied increased tensions in the county's historical past. In June 1920, there were seventeen outrages reported by the CI including the burning of Braddox Orange Hall, raids on Protestant houses in Clones and south Monaghan, and malicious damage to a Protestant shop in Carrickmacross. In July, seventeen crimes against unionists were reported including cases of intimidation, robbery, malicious damage and the burning of Lough Fea Orange Hall.[185] That October, the secretary of the First Monaghan Presbyterian Church wrote to Fr James McNamee in Monaghan town to 'point out to him that some more panes of glass in the church window were broken since our last interview'.[186] Windows had, in fact, been broken repeatedly between 1918 and 1920.[187] In July 1920, there were reports from Carrickmacross that very few Belfast commercial travellers received orders for goods and in one of the hotels, where they frequently stayed, a notice was posted warning Belfast travellers 'not to return to the town until such time as the present religious warfare was at an end'.[188]

The following month, on 6 August, Seán MacEntee, TD for South Monaghan, a native of Belfast, read a petition in the Dáil drawn up by four SF members of Belfast Corporation and other prominent nationalists in the city, appealing for help in 'the war of extermination being waged against us'.[189] The petition called for a boycott of goods from Belfast and a withdrawal of funds from Belfast-based banks by people in the rest of Ireland.[190] The Dáil was at first divided on the issue; the other Monaghan TD, Ernest Blythe, was opposed and forecast that it would destroy forever the possibility of any union.[191] His advice went unheeded and the Belfast boycott was initiated in September 1920. Within four months the Dáil had appointed a director and voted £2,500 for the campaign.[192] Given both Monaghan's border location and its long tradition of sectarianism, it was inevitable that the boycott would have significant consequences.

By the end of August 1920, the *Standard* claimed that a movement 'with powerful and co-ordinated support' was in train throughout the county.[193] Shopkeepers were cautioned by the IRA not to deal with Belfast firms, and members of the public were warned not to enter the shops of those who were supplied from Belfast.[194] On 19 August 1920, a deputation of four, said to be representative of a newly formed committee of nationalist traders, visited all the shops in Monaghan town with a declaration 'not to deal directly or indirectly with Belfast unionist firms or traders until such time as adequate reparation has been made to the Catholic victims of the recent Belfast pogrom'. All nationalist shopkeepers were reported to have signed but unionist traders did not commit themselves, arguing: '[It would] limit our capacity to buy in the best markets' and 'punish those as innocent of persecution as we are ourselves'.[195] Unionist merchants were consequently subjected to more stringent tactics such as pickets outside their premises, which inhibited trade and led to loss of custom, earnings and, inevitably, redundancies.[196]

At the unionist meeting of September 1920, the Belfast boycott was condemned as sectarian discrimination; it contended that now a commercial war as well as a physical war was being waged against Protestants.[197] McCaldin's bakery in Monaghan town repeatedly refused to observe the boycott, with the result that by April 1921 five of its bread vans were burned.[198] In April 1921, O'Duffy reported to GHQ that 'Several merchants, including Unionists, have fallen in with our wishes and paid stiff fines to have their names removed from the Black List'.[199] The Scotstown SF club prevented the circulation of the unionist *Belfast Telegraph* and the *Standard* in the district and on 27 November passed a motion protesting against the acceptance by Monaghan Asylum Committee of a 'unionist tender' that was 2s. 6d. more expensive than the one from Jim Treanor, a local nationalist; a copy of the resolution was sent to the clerk of the asylum and the Monaghan boycott committee.[200]

The IRA also prevented Belfast goods entering the county by rail and road. On 4 March 1921, at Inniskeen, a train containing sugar, bacon, bread and hardware was emptied and burned. The following month at Glaslough, another goods train was burned. O'Duffy was delighted that the captured railway invoices and mails gave a list of the firms still dealing with Belfast.[201] Soon it was reported that 'orders to Belfast were reduced to a minimum'.[202] Goods traced back to boycotted premises were seized from purchasers and destroyed. 'In this way', McGahey contended, 'the boycott campaign became more effective as the country people feared to visit shops on which the boycott ban was placed'.²⁰³ The *Standard* could not help concluding in April 1921, and probably with some justification, that there had to be 'greedy and unscrupulous traders' who were using the boycott 'to bring custom to their shop'.²⁰⁴ However, there were those who continued to defy the IRA. In August 1920, angry Newbliss shopkeepers, who were picketed for refusing to honour the boycott, organized themselves to travel to Belfast to get bread. On their return, their bread carts were escorted into the village by fifty UVF men.²⁰⁵

The inconvenience caused to the consumer should not be overlooked. As deliveries became more uncertain, prices continued to rise and it was estimated that the working man in Monaghan town who observed the boycott had to pay 5*s*. per week extra for the cost of living.²⁰⁶ A report on the town of Ballybay claimed that 'where only a limited number of traders are engaged in the different branches of business it is only natural in the case of a boycott to find the consumers exploited when half the sources of supply are cut off or blacklisted'.²⁰⁷ Thus, the boycott added to the woes of the ordinary man and woman on the street, fuelled sectarian tensions, and ultimately had a detrimental effect on unionist trade.

P.S. O'Hegarty argued at the time that the boycott 'turned apathetic Protestant unionists into bitter partisans', and regarded it as 'an utterly shameful episode in the history of Sinn Féin'.²⁰⁸ One can understand why unionists would become embittered: livelihoods were threatened and that threat coincided with the struggle for an Irish republic to which they were opposed. There is little doubt, as was the case in neighbouring Tyrone, that unionist businesses in Monaghan suffered, and probably more so than its neighbour for, as Fergal McCluskey concludes: 'Monaghan, located outside the proposed six-county area and with a seventy-five per cent Catholic population, had advantages in maintaining the monopoly of legitimate force that Tyrone did not enjoy'.²⁰⁹

And all this time, Monaghan unionists were facing yet another major crisis. In December 1920, the Government of Ireland Act had been passed making provision for the establishment of the state of Northern Ireland. After the May 1921 election, unionists in Northern Ireland gained their expected majority winning forty seats to six each for SF and the nationalists, and James Craig was appointed prime minister. As Winston Churchill, now chairman of the cabinet committee on Irish affairs, put it: 'from that moment the position of Ulster became unassailable'.²¹⁰ In a bid to have the whole of the province excluded, the Monaghan, Cavan and Donegal delegates made a plea to the UUC in the form of a pamphlet entitled *Ulster and Home Rule: no partition of Ulster* (1920). It presented a comprehensive and in many respects sound economic argument as to why the province should not be divided. However, the 1912 Covenant remained the central issue for Monaghan unionists – it would be sacrilege to break it, a peace with dishonour as J.C.W. Madden had earlier put it.[211] At a meeting of the UUC on 10 March 1920, with Edward Carson presiding, Lord Farnham of Cavan moved, and Michael E. Knight of Monaghan seconded, a resolution that the UUC would not accept anything other than the exclusion of the 'whole geographical province of Ulster'.[212] The resolution was rejected. Monaghan unionists condemned the 'selfish policy' of the UUC; worse still, in their eyes the Covenant had been shown to have been nothing more than 'a mere scrap of paper', brushed aside by the UUC so as 'not to endanger their precious six-county safety'.[213] In April, the Monaghan delegates resigned from the UUC and at the Orange celebrations on 12 July J.C.W. Madden denounced Carson and encouraged his fellow Orangemen to give their allegiance to a southern parliament should it be established.[214]

The attitude of grassroots unionists can perhaps be gauged from the pronouncements of their religious leaders. Revd Robert Burns of Drum, for example, was vociferous in his denouncement of the UUC: 'in this country it does not pay to be loyal'.[215] In May 1920, the editor of the *Standard* complained that 'no array of figures could form an excuse for breaking such an undertaking as the Ulster Covenant', and concluded that Monaghan unionists had to realize that since Belfast had thrown them over, they needed to 'look at matters political from a new viewpoint ... like it or not'.[216]

It was no wonder that most people welcomed the Anglo-Irish truce called on 11 July 1921 in the hope that it would signal a return to peace and that all could resume their lives in an atmosphere free from fear and threat. The public was war weary after almost a decade of dislocation to their lives. Peace brought respite to the non-combatants who, at the most basic level, had been incommoded by travel restrictions; to take but one example, restrictions had prevented the old age pensioners collecting their weekly payments in Shantonagh post office.[217] In the run up to Christmas 1921, businessmen of all classes and creeds were said to be looking forward to a return to prosperity.[218] People looked forward to a halt in the rising cost of living, and to an end to the continuous threat of violence arriving to their doorstep. In August, the *Democrat* rejoiced at the renewal of social events: 'It is a long time now since we had occasion to refer in happy terms to a successful entertainment'. Several areas saw a revival of GAA activities, Gaelic League classes and Protestant soirées. Towns, villages and rural crossroads were the scenes of jubilation and celebration as IRA prisoners arrived home after several months in jail.[219] And republican courts, under Dr Conn Ward, were freely operating in most areas, establishing order but also attempting to deal with the ratepayers who were almost £14,000 in arrears; these sums were badly needed to get the county 'back on its feet'. Of course, ignoring the British judicial system was not to everyone's liking and J.C.W. Madden warned Ward that any attempt to bring unionists to republican courts would be a breach of the truce and would be resisted.²²⁰

Meanwhile, Owen O'Duffy was promoted to deputy chief of staff to Michael Collins and Richard Mulcahy, while Dan Hogan became commandant of the new 5th Northern Division. It had been a meteoric rise for both men and entirely based on their record during the War of Independence. The day after the truce was called Hogan sent out orders calling on his units to be vigilant and prepared: 'Now is the time to push on our training with the utmost vigour. All arms must be carefully kept and where possible damaged weapons fixed. The Old Drill halls are to be used again and care is to be taken that our haunts during the war are not known to anyone outside our own men.'²²¹ In September and October, the IRA formed training camps at Coolfore, near Carrickmacross, at Lough Bawn House commandeered from Colonel Tennison, and near Tyholland chapel. These activities were clearly breaches of the truce, and, according to the CI, local unionists perceived them as preparations for a threatened religious war in the North.²²² Hogan's bullishness was conditioned by the calling of the truce, but, in actual fact, the truce came at a time when the Monaghan IRA was coming under increased pressure. In the middle of June, scores of Volunteers had been arrested when a large-scale police and military operation had swept through the countryside, north and south, taking in men aged between sixteen and sixty-five for questioning in camps at Lough Egish, Carrickatee and Latton. The *Standard* delighted in the fact that 'the military were gaining the upper hand forcing the IRA on the run into the mountainy areas of the north.'²²³ With depleted numbers and arms, it is difficult to see how much longer they could have continued to operate.

The announcement of the truce had coincided with renewed sectarian strife in Northern Ireland. On 10 July 1921 – another 'Bloody Sunday' – 161 nationalist homes were burned and fourteen people killed, ten of whom were Catholic. By the end of the week the death toll stood at twenty-three, of which sixteen were Catholic, and 216 Catholic homes had been destroyed.²²⁴ Bishop McKenna railed against the Belfast pogroms and sarcastically castigated the administration: 'But, of course, Belfast is a loyal city and no voice thunders against its savage persecutions'.²²⁵ O'Duffy had now also been appointed IRA liaison officer by the Provisional government to work with Northern Ireland counterparts in an attempt to secure protection of northern nationalists. He took a belligerent approach. In October, at a public meeting at Ballyhaise in Cavan, he stated that while he was willing to extend the hand of friendship to unionists in the North, he was not prepared to stand aside 'and see Irishmen and women murdered because they were Catholics'.²²⁶ When he spoke in the Dáil in August 1921, he boasted about Monaghan IRA's response to unionist opposition: 'He had dealt with them by force in

Monaghan, Fermanagh and Tyrone, and these people were now silent.'[227] The threat was clear enough. In October, O'Duffy informed Collins that 'Orange aggressiveness' and attacks on defenceless people in the area of his command were becoming so serious that it was necessary to take active steps for their protection. He requested arms for local Volunteers in Monaghan.[228] Strife along the new border was far from being at an end.

7 'The best interests of the county demand ratification of the Treaty':[1] Civil War, 1922–3

The witness statements of Monaghan IRA veterans who fought in the War of Independence have little to say about the Civil War that ensued. Typical, for example, is Peter Woods' parting remark: 'This brings me up to the eve of the Civil War with which I do not want to deal'.[2] Over forty years later, the residue of bitterness remained. In 1967, Tom Armstrong wrote to Fr Laurence Marron: 'when I came back from prison the senseless, destructive Civil War killed my sense of pride in those "four glorious years", when the achievement and sacrifices of those who had died or suffered in the struggle seemed a dead loss'.[3] Even had Fr Marron and others pressed their interviewees to continue their conversations into the Civil War, they would most likely have been reticent. As Alvin Jackson has concluded, 'many Irish people dealt with this [the Civil War], as they had dealt with earlier psychological assaults, with the weapon of silence'.[4]

The ratification of the Anglo-Irish Treaty, signed on 6 December 1921, was supported by leading Monaghan Sinn Féiners including TDs Ernest Blythe and Owen O'Duffy, Bernard O'Rourke, and Dan Hogan.[5] Thomas Toal's comment echoed the famous remark of Michael Collins that the Treaty was 'the first step towards freedom', and he duly instructed his fellow councillors to support it.[6] In response, Monaghan County Council and all of the local government bodies passed strong resolutions of support.[7] When the South Monaghan comhairle ceanntair of SF met in Ballybay in December 1921, it resolved:

> That while adhering to our republican principles and maintaining Ireland's indefensible right to absolute independence, we believe that under the existing circumstances the best interests of the county demand ratification of the Treaty.[8]

The Treaty was popular with those who believed it delivered what the War of Independence had set out to achieve – the evacuation of British troops from Ireland and the end of British administration. When, on 2–3 February 1922, the police evacuated Carrickmacross Barracks, William Daly recorded the departure of the 'scum of England brought into Ireland to kill the Irish and destroy their property with fire and sword'. The following day he noted how the 'IRA entered the barracks for the first time in a quiet orderly manner … and hoisted the Republican flag. Victory for Ireland.'[9] The new elite wasted no time in jostling for position. The clerk of the Carrickmacross republican court immediately commandeered the home of Constable Walsh of the RIC, presumably leaving him homeless.[10] The Treaty was also decisively supported by the Catholic clergy.[11]

However, the county's Dáil representatives were divided. During the Treaty debates, Ernest Blythe, TD for North Monaghan, made several lengthy interventions in support; he believed 'the Republic was a means to an end and not an end in itself'; the republican form of government 'was a machine for securing the freedom of the country'.[12] Arguing that he was 'the only member of the Dáil who comes of the people who are going to exclude themselves or may exclude themselves from the Free State', he proposed that they could be encouraged to come over 'to the side of the Irish nation' but, if not, 'they might be coerced, and I would stand for it that we have the right to coerce them'.[13] Owen O'Duffy was also in favour of ratification. He too regarded the Treaty as a means to an end, and gloried in the fact that it would lead to the end of a British military presence in southern Ireland, but he made reference to the threat in border counties created by the USC and had a strong message for Monaghan Protestants: 'We made it very clear to them [during the War of Independence] that if they were prepared to join up with the enemy they would get the same treatment as the enemy. Nine or ten of them have got the treatment of the Black and Tans, and they admitted they did not get that because of their religious belief.'[14]

When Seán MacEntee, TD for South Monaghan, was approached by pro-Treaty Bernard O'Rourke and Fr Eugene Coyle, he said that he would sooner resign than support the Treaty.[15] MacEntee was vociferous in his condemnation, especially of the clauses he felt would make partition a permanent reality. His opposition signalled the difficulties that lay ahead. The *Standard* was of the opinion that if the future government depended on 'academic quibblers' such as MacEntee, 'who deliberately flaunt the unanimously expressed will of the people who elected him', then the outlook for the Irish Free State was hopeless.[16] MacEntee's pronouncements on local social policy had already made him unpopular in the southern constituency. For instance, in December 1921, he said he was not in favour of retaining Carrickmacross hospital but 'not more than one per cent of the people of the town' agreed.[17] In the June 1922 pact election, McEntee was not re-selected to contest the seat by the anti-Treaty side but instead was replaced by Patrick McCarville (whose wife, Eileen McGrane, was Michael Collins' secretary). O'Duffy and Blythe 'openly campaigned on the merits of the Treaty, criticized the anti-Treatyite candidate and urged their supporters to give their third preference votes to the independent'.[18] In the final results, the pro-Treaty side secured 11,792 votes, McCarville, 5,046 and the Independent, 3,681.[19] Blythe, O'Duffy and McCarville were thus returned to a Dáil comprising 58 pro-Treaty TDs, 36 anti-Treaty, 17 Labour, and 10 others. McCarville's success and the strength of his support showed there was still a hankering for a republic among a significant section of the Monaghan electorate.

Dónal McAnallen argues that O'Duffy as chief of staff of the National army continued to use the GAA in his plans and that 'far from keeping the IRA and Ulster GAA business separate, he blurred them quite deliberately'.[20] On 14 January 1922, the Monaghan football team left for Derry by motor car to partake in a game between both counties. The team included Hogan and six of O'Duffy's senior officers. Outside the village of Dromore, in County Tyrone, they were held up by a party of USC and arrested. They had been dressed partly or wholly in IRA uniforms and a number of them were armed.[21] The football match was merely a diversion. The real objective was to rescue three IRA men under sentence of death in Derry gaol. That they made their intentions so obvious may have been a combination of ineptitude and arrogance and was certainly rather curious. O'Duffy disingenuously looked on the action of the USC as being 'provocative in the extreme', while Collins, in a telegram to Churchill remarking on the 'gravity of the situation', supported O'Duffy's claim that the only reason the men were armed was for their own protection.[22] Craig advised that they apply for bail but Collins could not agree to this as it would recognize the northern courts.[23] The situation or crisis expedited meetings between Collins and James Craig in London to try to address the northern question. Collins wanted, for example, to improve the position of northern nationalists and to have Catholic workers reinstated to their employment in the Belfast shipyards.[24] Craig wanted an end to the Belfast boycott, more for political reasons, as it was probably impacting on no more than 10 per cent of northern businesses.[25] The terms of the agreement were published in the press on 21 January 1922: Collins would call off the Belfast boycott; Craig would aid the return to work of Belfast nationalists; and the terms of the Boundary Commission, as set out in the Treaty, would be revised by mutual agreement. Unfortunately, it proved a false dawn, and the agreement broke down largely due to mutual distrust.[26]

Paul Bew has argued that at this time 'Collins outlined tactics he intended to pursue with a view to destabilizing the northern parliament'.[27] Thus, the northern divisions of the IRA were reorganized and supplied with arms by Collins.[28] Great care had to be taken to ensure that any weapons supplied by the British government were not used in the northern campaign, as they would be recognized by their serial numbers. To avert this, weapons were exchanged between the military leaders of the IFS and the anti-Treaty IRA of the south led by Liam Lynch.[29] In early February a 'shadowy IRA Ulster council' under O'Duffy's command, and with the influential Frank Aiken on board, was set up in Clones.[30] On 8 February, IRA ASUs from Monaghan crossed the border with Northern Ireland into Aughnacloy, Clogher, Roslea, Newtownbutler, Wattlebridge, Belleek, Lisnaskea and Enniskillen. They kidnapped sixty unionists to be held as hostages for the release of Hogan and his fellow prisoners. Among those captured was Anketell Moutray, a member of the UUC, and Captain Coote, son of William Coote, MP. During these raids the IRA encountered the USC at Wattlebridge, Newtownbutler and Roslea, killing three officers and abducting twenty others.[31]

Craig immediately pressed the British government for the release of the hostages.[32] If the British failed to convince the Provisional government to do so, he was determined to carry out his own plans. Austen Chamberlain, the British Conservative Party leader, revealed that Craig intended to: 'arrest a similar number of known poisonous Sinn Féiners resident in the North', take them to a place along the border and use them to negotiate the release of the unionist prisoners.[33] The excitement was far from over on the Monaghan border and an incident at Clones railway station on 11 February hardened attitudes further and had grave repercussions throughout Ulster. A train carrying eighteen armed USC from a training camp at Newtownards to Enniskillen stopped at Clones for a connecting service. The Specials had not applied for a special permit to allow them enter the IFS. Matt Fitzpatrick, whose brother, John James, was a prisoner in Belfast jail, was then commandant of the 5th Northern Division based in Clones. When the presence of the USC was reported to him he immediately made his way to the station. The sequence of events is unclear but Fitzpatrick was shot dead when he boarded the train. The IRA on the platform, armed with machine guns, returned fire killing Sergeant Dougherty and three Specials; some of their colleagues made a run for it but a number of others were arrested and subsequently taken to Carrickmacross.[34] Collins placed the blame firmly on 'the people who did not inform our liaison officer of the journey'.[35] The Clones affray led to an eruption of sectarian violence in Belfast: between 13 and 15 February thirty-one people were killed, including six children in a bomb attack on a Catholic school off the York Road.[36]

There were further consequences in Monaghan. In March 1922, five unionist families were forced from their homes in Glaslough. As a reprisal, five nationalist families were evicted by USC in Caledon, just across the border in County Tyrone. On the southern side of the border, anyone suspected of being a Special attracted attention. Louis de Montfort, who lived in Fermanagh but had a solicitor's practice in Clones, was ordered to stay out of the town. Basil Brooke, the future prime minister of Northern Ireland, appealed on his behalf to the Home Office: 'This gentleman has been doing magnificent work for the B Constabulary. But owing to his connections to the force he has lost his means of livelihood.'[37] Brooke's statement revealed much about the hidden role of the B Specials in Monaghan.

Although the British government declined to send troops to Monaghan as suggested by Craig, Churchill continued to impress upon the Provisional government how inflamed public opinion was over the Clones affray, and that the release of the unionist hostages was a matter of urgency.[38] On 17 February, he telegrammed Collins that 'the North have ample forces to defend their territory but if not more troops will be sent them to any extent that may be necessary'.[39] At that stage, there were reports of movements of USC north of the Monaghan border.[40]

The impasse was broken on 21 February when the British government ordered the release of the Monaghan footballers and other republican prisoners.[41] The Monaghan GAA convention welcomed Hogan and his fellow prisoners as heroes.[42] In turn, the IRA released most of the unionists, although the USC captured in Clones were still detained.[43] The release of prisoners on both sides failed to ease the tension in Monaghan. All the roads along the Fermanagh border were trenched by the USC to prevent a recurrence of the kidnapping. Shortly afterwards, the main roads along the Tyrone–Monaghan border were also rendered impassable. With the trenching of the roads, people were unable to travel to their local markets and fairs. Those on the Fermanagh side of the border, who had traditionally used Clones markets in the past, now turned to Newtownbutler with detrimental economic consequences for the Monaghan town.[44]

By the end of March 1922, it was reported that there were considerable IRA forces on the Caledon–Aughnacloy frontier.[45] To accommodate these men, Mullen's Mills, Glaslough Orange Hall and a number of unionist farmhouses on the Monaghan side were commandeered.[46] A unionist farmer was shot dead just across the Tyrone border while tending his cattle.[47] At the end of March the *Standard* reported that 'many farmers in the district are far behind with their spring work as they are afraid to venture into the fields with their horses, owing to being exposed to snipers'.[48]

These incidents mirrored others further north where one of the most vicious occurred on 22 March 1922 when, in response to the murder of six policemen and USC in Northern Ireland, armed gunmen burst into the home of Owen McMahon, a Catholic businessman (but also director of Glentoran FC, a Protestant East Belfast soccer club), and murdered him, three of his sons (two others were injured) and one of his employees. The connivance of the police in this murder was suspected from the outset, further fuelling tensions.[49] In response to the continued atrocities, the British government supported a renewal of the Collins–Craig pact. On the eve of the meeting, Craig took a conciliatory approach stating that his government did not blame the IRA for the spiralling outrages in the North but 'he noted language explicitly supporting northern IRA violence had been used by senior figures closely associated with the regime', most particularly Owen O'Duffy.[50] The pact, which began 'Peace is today declared', included terms that were to allow for nationalists to join the USC with nationalist Specials patrolling nationalist areas (something which O'Duffy strongly favoured but northern republicans did not because they were not going to take a declaration of allegiance to the northern state).[51] All IRA activity north of the border was to cease and people expelled from their homes were to be allowed to return. The Northern Ireland government was to use every effort to secure the restoration of the expelled Catholic workers and both Irish governments were to agree to the release of political prisoners.[52] Accordingly, on 9 April 1922 Collins secured the release of the five Specials who had been held in Carrickmacross since the shooting of Matt Fitzpatrick.[53]

In the wider scheme of things, there was little support among republicans for the pact. Over the following few weeks the country slipped into civil war. Monaghan was largely spared the fratricidal struggle that characterized areas further south, particularly in areas of Munster. O'Duffy and Hogan played a significant role in ensuring that the majority of the Monaghan IRA favoured the Treaty. They had instilled loyalty in their men and O'Duffy was experienced in offering incentives where necessary. For example, he offered Dr Conn Ward the post of medical director general of the National army if he supported the Treaty.[54] A few prominent local leaders such as Paddy Corrigan and P.J. O'Daly opposed the Treaty but they withdrew altogether from the IRA 'rather than take up arms against their former comrades'.[55] When Todd Andrews came to Monaghan in 1922, he found the anti-Treaty side in disarray. Shortly before, Ernie O'Malley, assistant chief of staff of the anti-Treaty IRA, had received complaints about the inactivity of senior officers in Monaghan and sent Frank Aiken to Donaghmoyne to meet Tom Carragher. But as Andrews observed, the proposed changes to the local command structure made little difference 'because the large part of the Division had gone over to the Free State side. What was left was badly armed and poorly organized.'[56] The IFS forces also had the advantage of knowing the local terrain just as well as their enemies, and so safe houses such as Carraghers were frequently raided.[57]

Although no crime statistics exist, newspaper and military reports suggest that there existed a degree of banditry during the civil chaos of 1922–3, much of which was connected to the anti-Treaty IRA. Tom Carragher of Donaghmoyne and Jimmy Fitzsimons of Inniskeen held up trains on the Clones–Dundalk line, and raided banks in Kingscourt in neighbouring County Cavan, allegedly to pay their men.[58] In June, property belonging to Bernard O'Rourke was burned at Inniskeen railway station; cars and motorcycles were commandeered by the anti-Treatyites and bread vans hijacked and destroyed.[59] A civil war is no different to other conflicts in being a war of words as well as an armed struggle. This was vividly illustrated in the portrayal of an incident that occured in Monaghan town on 18 August 1922. Peadar Livingstone in *The Monaghan story* described how, in a series of raids, the anti-Treatyites stole £1,200 from the Ulster, Hibernian and Provincial banks, and Lieutenant Thomas Gillanders of the National army was killed.⁶⁰ However, according to the contemporaneous account of Patrick McCarville, elected anti-Treatyite TD, the anti-Treaty forces had no official sanction to carry out the bank raids and had been sent to Monaghan to capture National army positions. Following an investigation ordered by Frank Aiken, then O/C 4th Northern Division, £130 was retrieved and returned to the manager of the Ulster Bank with an apology. The remainder of the money was reportedly squandered and the ringleaders were said to have left Ireland.⁶¹ Thus, the raids could be variously interpreted as part of military operations to fund the anti-Treatyite cause or as an outrageous example of banditry. The condemnation of both by the Catholic clergy probably discouraged more similar activity. In September 1922, for example, Canon Patrick McKeown condemned the anti-Treatyites and 'appealed to the young men of the district to abandon this fratricidal strife and obey the teaching of the bishops who had already spoken out'.⁶² In February 1922, Bishop McKenna added his concerns about 'the great increase in serious robberies and crimes of violence to the person'. He urged people not to replicate the actions of the Crown forces which had 'showed little respect for life or property' and counselled Irish leaders to consider the 'depth of pain and suffering which the very idea of a split is causing amongst the people'.⁶³

The most serious military incident thereafter in Monaghan was an attack on Carrickmacross Barracks by the anti-Treaty IRA in early September 1922 that resulted in the death of Patrick McCabe from Bawn, a private in the National army. McCabe's death exemplified both the complexities of Irish society at the time and the hardship endured by some families; two of his brothers had been killed in the First World War and another had been wounded.⁶⁴ In the same attack, a shop assistant, John O'Leary, was hit by a stray bullet in the shoulder and died later that evening in Dundalk hospital.⁶⁵

A week before the Carrickmacross raid, another Monaghan native, Captain Francis Byrne from Killanny, had been killed in an attack on Dundalk jail. On 15 July 1922, Dan Hogan had led the 5th Northern Division on a raid on Dundalk that resulted in the capture of Frank Aiken and 300 men of the 4th Northern Division. At that stage, Aiken had not committed to the anti-Treaty side and had tried to prevent civil war. Matthew Lewis has pointed out that 'contemporaries and historians alike have agreed that Hogan acted on his own initiative in capturing Dundalk'.⁶⁶ However, Hogan's close relationship with O'Duffy raised suspicions that the latter was involved. O'Duffy had made it clear that he would not accept Aiken's neutrality and there were rumours that Aiken held northern unionist hostages who O'Duffy wanted released.⁶⁷ Aiken and his men were held in Dundalk prison before being rescued in a daring raid on 27 July by other members of the 4th Northern Division. On 14

August, Aiken, 'smarting over the fact that Hogan's capture of the town was being lauded as a great victory for the Provisional government', returned to Dundalk and retook the jail; the attack resulted in the deaths of four members of the National army, including Captain Francis Byrne, and the serious wounding of another Monaghan native, Brian MacMahon.[68]

Within days of recapturing Dundalk, Aiken and his men left the town and crossed the border into south Armagh and south Down. Around the same time O'Duffy moved south to counter the anti-Treaty IRA and as the Civil War intensified in Munster, cross-border attacks came to an end. After the death of Collins on 22 August 1922, one northern IRA leader complained: 'the attitude of the present government towards its followers in the six counties is not that of the late General Collins'.[69] Moreover, McAnallen has concluded that 'Collins' death represented a personal tragedy for O'Duffy and an end to his hopes of smashing partition'.[70] By August 1922, this had already been accepted by Ernest Blythe, TD for North Monaghan and minister for local government, who wrote that there was no likelihood of the unification of Ireland within any reasonable period of time and as there was nothing to be gained 'by attacking the North East, its forces or government ... all military operations on the part of our supporters in or against the North East should be brought to an end'. He repudiated Collins' policy of sending arms northwards, contending that all future pressure on Northern Ireland should be 'absolutely normal and constitutional'.[71] The result was that the USC now dominated the nationalist countryside on the Fermanagh border, north of Clones and were preventing people from coming into the town's markets and fairs. The *Democrat* reported that the 'vast area from Smithboro to Newtownbutler and along the foot of the Carnmore mountains, wholly nationalist in feeling, isolated from Clones by the destruction of the highways, and the inhabitants generally [are] subjected to every inconvenience and insolence that the Specials can devise.'[72] There is no doubt but that this period witnessed the beginning of the end of Clones as a commercial hub.[73]

Like the Anglo-Irish truce, the end of the Civil War in May 1923 brought some relief to the vast majority of Monaghan people. In October 1922, the *Standard* had been gracious enough to praise the work of the Provisional government in restoring law and order, the editor contending that it had gained a prestige both at home and abroad that Monaghan loyalists could not have contemplated a few months before.[74] In the June 1922 general election, O'Duffy's reputation and public profile helped him to top the poll in Monaghan with 7,290 votes, well ahead of his running mate, Ernest Blythe with 4,494 votes. The third seat went to the anti-Treaty SF candidate, Patrick McCarville, who polled 5,046 votes. If the Independent vote of Thomas McHugh (3,681) is taken as pro-Treaty, the Monaghan electorate voted 3:1 in favour of the Treaty, which largely reflected the national vote, but again McCarville's poll suggested considerable local opposition to the emerging new order.

The Civil War changed nothing and the election of August 1923 exhibited the same pattern. The Monaghan electorate returned two pro-Treaty Cumann na nGaedheal candidates in Blythe (11,290) and Patrick Duffy (1,316) who together accounted for just over 49 per cent of the vote. McCarville was again returned as a republican with 5,745 votes or just over 22 per cent of the vote. He was comfortably second in the poll, 4,400 votes ahead of Duffy. The Farmers Party won 11.5 per cent and Independents 16.9 per cent of the poll. O'Duffy did not contest this seat as he had just previously been appointed commissioner of An Garda Síochána, an unarmed police force, which the *Standard* deemed a positive step that 'should tend to hasten a new and brighter day for Ireland'.[75]

No unionist candidate contested the 1921–3 general elections in Monaghan. Growing awareness of the irrelevance of unionism in the south was reflected in the pages of the *Standard*: 'Even if we could return a candidate under PR the minority in the southern parliament would be so small that it would be unable to accomplish anything.'[76] On 8 October 1920, a meeting of the County Grand Orange Lodge moved that there should be two separate grand lodges in Ireland.[77] Although little came of the proposal that day, William Martin, formerly of the North Monaghan Unionist Alliance, raised the issue again in 1922. This time the Orangemen agreed to send a resolution to the Grand Lodge of Ireland meeting in Belfast in December, declaring that they could no longer pledge loyalty to a union abolished by law: 'If Orangeism is to exist at all it must have its own organization which will not clash with the laws of the Irish Free State'.[78] The separate IFS lodge never materialized due to a lack of support at a meeting at Clones in April 1923. That July, the only Orange demonstration in the IFS was held at Analore, near Clones. *The Weekly Bulletin* estimated that it was attended by up to 4,000 people and that 'they marched behind their old banners to the meeting place, in the full confidence that their rights as a minority would be fully respected', and it reported that 'not a single untoward incident marked the progress of the processionists to or from the rendezvous'.[79] Michael E. Knight urged his fellow Orangemen that 'by a strict adherence to their principles, by acting as a lawful, law abiding people, they could create and build up for themselves and for those who would come after them a strong position in that county'.[80]

This did not mean that all Orangemen were in agreement. In December 1921, the editor of the *Standard* admitted that many readers were no longer satisfied with some of the opinions on Irish political matters expressed in its columns.[81] At the July celebrations of 1923, William Martin commented on the number of Orangemen absent that day and wondered why this was so, knowing full well that this was down to their sense of deracination.[82] In time, 'matters settled down and relationships of trust and co-operation began to grow', as L.T. Brown contends in his history of Monaghan Presbyterians.[83] At first, this manifested itself in a gradual moving away from party and sectarian politics at local government level. When the *Standard* published the names of candidates for the local elections of 1925, 'force of habit' led it to use the term 'unionist' after the names of those Protestants who had formerly contested elections under that political label. The candidates duly informed the newspaper that they were contesting the elections as Independents, resolutely excluding party politics from their conception of their duties as members of a local public body.[84] Five Protestant members were elected to the council. Michael E. Knight, on seconding Toal as chairman, said that he hoped all members would attend to their duties in a spirit free from party politics, and that the desire of the council members should be to serve the best interests of the people whom they represented. Something then followed that would have caused surprise a few years earlier: a nationalist proposed Knight as vice-chairman. This motion might have succeeded but for a new controversy that was brewing. Instead of the old unionist versus nationalist divide, there was now a growing friction between members from the south of the county and those from the north. The southern members claimed that the vice-chairman should come from their region, and in order to avoid any further division, Knight withdrew his nomination.[85] Knight consistently (from the time he joined the council) acted in what he considered to be the best interest of the county. In May 1922, Toal had paid him an appropriate compliment: 'They held widely different views in political matters, but Mr Knight was always a gentleman and always approached things in a friendly spirit ... He sincerely hoped that they would soon have a settled government in which all could unite together for the general good of the country.'[86] While they did forsake their unionist principles (though not necessarily their loyalism), Monaghan unionists maintained a keen interest in politics.

In the decades after independence, it is fair to say that Protestants in Monaghan living under Dublin rule had less to grieve about than Catholics living in neighbouring south Fermanagh, south Tyrone and south Armagh who were living under Belfast rule.

8 'Is everything we love gone forever':[1] the Big House, 1912–23

A little more than a generation before 1912 the dominant elite in Monaghan, as was the case in the country as a whole, was the landed class – the gentry and the aristocracy – whose positions of economic dominance and socio-political power were symbolized in their Big Houses. Those who have featured most prominently in this study so far, such as Sir John Leslie, J.C.W. and Gerald Madden, Edward Lucas Scudamore, the earl of Dartrey and Lord Rossmore, were all born at a time when their families were lords of the soil, their fathers (and some of themselves) high sheriffs, lieutenants of the county, members of the grand jury, chief officers on the boards of poor law guardians and MPs. Wealth may have been slipping away from them for generations but they still remained the social elite and therefore expected, and usually received, the deference of their estate employees and tenants; this was not as grudgingly given as orthodox nationalist history has traditionally claimed. If revolution can be defined as turning the world upside down, then undoubtedly this was the class that lost the most; yet it has received relatively little attention from historians dealing with the period from 1916 to 1923.[2] This chapter attempts to redress this imbalance drawing mainly on a case study of the Lucas Scudamore family of Castleshane, and is based on the recently discovered archive in the family's possession in Kentchurch Court in Wales.

The 'county snobocracy', as Rushe disparagingly called them, had been seriously affected by the dramatic political changes and social reforms from the end of the Famine to the outbreak of the First World War, a period that also witnessed the emergence of a very publicly articulated resentment towards the Big House and its inhabitants, especially during the Land War era of the 1880s. In April 1912, the *Democrat* reported on the sale of Rokeby Hall in neighbouring Louth, purchased by the 'Irish' Clinton family, and seen as evidence that 'the pendulum of fortune seems to be swinging the other way'.[3] Monaghan readers would also have read McGahon's tirade against the visit of Lord Roden to Dundalk in July of that year where he spoke against home rule, and his advice that Roden should not 'speak of intolerance to Irishmen who know the history that was written in the blood and tears of a persecuted people by those who went before you'.[4]

Despite revolutionary change, most of the old Monaghan gentry families clung on; the proceeds from the 1903 Land Act subsidized their continued residence in their country mansions surrounded by modest to extensive demesnes. As indicated in chapter 2, the third home rule crisis had provided them with another opportunity to lead. They used their military experience to train the UVF, financing its arming, and allowing their demesnes to be used for drill purposes, and their homes and Orange lodges on their properties as stores for arms and ammunition. It was this type of flagrant opposition to home rule that brought old ancestral resentments to the fore and projected the Big House to the forefront as a symbol of imperial rule in Ireland.

The First World War exacted a heavy toll on the gentry. The death of Norman Leslie in October 1914 came as a great blow to the family. Neither Sir John nor his wife, Leonie, ever recovered; when their granddaughter, Anita, arrived at Glaslough for the first time in 1919, she found that 'one room frightened us. It had been that of our Uncle Norman, who had been killed five years previously and it was kept just as he had left it ... a bunch of withered flowers lay on the pillow'.[5] After the war, Anita claimed: 'Many of the old aristocrats never reappeared; they remained in their country estates grieving our lost sons or they disliked the new mixed society'.[6] They grieved and resented in equal measure.

For them, the 1916 Rising was the ultimate act of treason against the empire in what they believed to be its darkest hour of need. Sir John Leslie ordered the Monaghan brigade of the UVF, or at least those he could muster, on stand-by during the Rising.[7] He derided 'my friend the Countess Markovitch [sic]' who 'massacred the Dublin police with her own fair hands [and] is doing nothing for her sins beyond a little fancy sewing in detention'.[8] Captain Anketell Moutray (kidnapped by the Monaghan IRA in 1922) recorded in his diary that 'we are inclined to treat the whole stunt with utter contempt', adding a few days later: 'I was, I admit, much distressed that we were not able to pull off a scrap with the rebels – I would love to have been able to swot them – dirty dogs.'[9] The Madden papers contain J.C.W. Madden's copies of the constitution of the Irish Citizen Army, and a pamphlet entitled *Independent Labour Party of Ireland: appeal to the Irish working class* which told of the empire being founded on 'the misery of the toiling masses' and called upon the 'slaves' to rise up. He kept them not because he was a socialist but rather, like the nationalist middle class, he and his peers feared the rise of labour and socialism that the Rising could portend. While it may just have been coincidence, it seems that Sir Nicholas Gosselin was taking no chances, and he sold Aughnamullen House and all its contents to move permanently to England shortly after the Rising.[10]

Seymour Leslie saw a poignant irony in the fact that when the 'gay twenties' started and 'the London season resumed ... many faces were missing; many were dead and ruined, or still mourning'.[11] At home in Ireland, the Leslies prided themselves on their claim that while 'mansions with memories and heirlooms were burned and families which counted as Anglo-Irish removed their capital future out of the country', they stayed put. However, the hard facts may tell another story, the Leslies were no different to the majority of their peers: their 'capital future' had been tied up in a fanciful international share portfolio designed by Ernest Cassels, with little investment in Ireland, and they lost their fortune in the post-war global economic collapse. Signs of encroaching penury were everywhere in the increasing neglect of their country house. In 1919, Anita Leslie discovered signs of dilapidation: 'We found bedrooms that had not been used for years, and a cobwebby boxroom lined with enormous hanging cupboards designed to hold dresses of the last century'.[12] The fact that the IRA did not burn Glaslough was not down to any particular fondness for the family among local IRA supporters; indeed, few Catholic nationalist families had benefited from employment in the house or demesne, which was mainly reserved for unionists, and Sir John had not endeared himself with his ardent unionism and Orangeism so entrenched that he disinherited his eldest son for converting to Catholicism and nationalism. Glaslough survived because it was located in a largely unionist village, with a number of former UVF men on the estate payroll, including gamekeepers like James Vogan who were good marksmen. Thus, the local IRA had the good sense not to raid it. The same was true of Hilton Park where Major J.C.W. Madden 'drew on his militia training to put Hilton into a posture of defence in 1920–2, with the result that (in common, as he always maintained, with the other houses in the county which were manned and not abandoned) Hilton escaped unburnt'.[13]

Other houses were not so fortunate. In March 1921, Gola House, the unoccupied residence of William Black, and said to be one of the oldest and finest in County Monaghan, was burned by the IRA, allegedly because of a rumour that the military intended to occupy it. Caution is, however, required when examining the motivation behind attacks on houses. While military considerations undoubtedly played a role these actions sometimes had ulterior motives. Gola and its lands had been purchased in 1903 by William Black. Born into a very small farm of around seventeen acres in 1857, he emigrated with his brother to South Africa in 1879 where he accumulated a vast fortune 'through a string of trading posts'. He returned to Monaghan to educate his five children and purchased two large estates: Ballyleck where he and his wife Sarah resided, and Gola where he set up his sister in residence and where he stabled his race horses and raised Shorthorn cattle. The circumstances of purchase are not known but they may have caused tensions at a time when small farmers were looking to the UIL to have large estates redistributed to supplement their own small uneconomic holdings. He became heavily involved in the unionist movement, becoming vice-president of the NMUA. His grandnephew believed that he 'was a typical target of oppositional violence'.[14] A great-grandson was more forthright: 'it's hard not to think that this [the burning of Gola] was political retribution for their unionism rather than for their economic advantage over their neighbours'.[15] The stones from the house are said to have been used to build the local Catholic church while the carved coat of arms was thrown down a nearby well.[16]

After the burning, Black sold his lands. On 11 September 1921, John Murray, the chairman of the Scotstown SF club, brought the proposed sale of the estate to the attention of its members and proposed that 'it should be divided into small farms and sold at a [reasonable?] price so that men in the neighbourhood or men who had sons in jail could have a chance, and that no strangers should be allowed to come in and give an unreasonable price'.[17] For the next twelve months or so there was a good deal of local tension and anyone defying this SF ruling was intimidated. One man, who took part of the demesne for grazing, had his cattle driven away and was assaulted when 'cow dung was forced into his mouth'. Another had his cattle driven from the demesne on four separate occasions, while another was expelled from the SF club 'for offering part of Gola lands to an ex-policeman' (although his authority to do so was not specified).[18] In the summer of 1922, Protestant demesne workers were ordered to leave the district 'or the coffins will be your lot'.[19] In 1924, Fr Philip Mulligan, the local parish priest, purchased the demesne for redistribution among local farmers.[20] William Black left Ireland and returned to the Umtata region of South Africa; according to a descendant he 'had no intentions of living with the politics of the Free State'.[21] The difference between Black and some of the more established landed families was that he could afford to leave; his fortune lay elsewhere.[22] In April 1921, application had been made for £10,000 in compensation for the loss of the house and just over £4,000 was awarded.[23] This was about the national average in terms of awards. Even if Black had wanted to stay in Ireland, the sum would not have been sufficient for him to rebuild.

In June 1921, Ballybay House, the residence of J.H.E. Leslie, was allegedly burned for the same reason as Gola, that it was to be used as a billet by the Crown forces.[24] Again, there may have been other factors involved. At the beginning of 1912, Leslie's relationship with the local community, estate and townspeople, had been excellent. The demesne was described as 'always in spick and span order for the visitor to traverse its well kept walks and avenues and benefit by an inspection of its profitably managed home farm and well conducted estate'.[25] Leslie had just donated part of the demesne for the construction of a golf course 'for the free use of the townspeople of Ballybay and surrounding district'.[26] The 'air of contentment and happiness' disappeared in the years that followed. It may have been related to the fact that Leslie did not sell his estate under the 1903 or 1909 land acts. By 1921, it was one of the few unsold estates in Monaghan and just before the burning there had been a rent strike by frustrated tenants who wanted to purchase their holdings; they also resented their high rents – driven up by market forces during the boom years – especially when they could see their neighbours who had purchased their holdings were paying more modest annuities to the Land Commission. As with Gola, it was reported that the house had been vacant and unfurnished for quite some time, probably because H.C.E. Leslie was posted to Rome as British ambassador (and therefore seen as a government official).[27] Nor can one discount the escalation of the third home rule crisis in the years after 1912 that may have diminished Leslie's 'generous dealings and kindly relationships' with the wider local community. A year after its destruction, the ruins of Ballybay were sold for £100 to a local tradesman for building materials. In March 1922, local businessmen, professionals, artisans, farmers and labourers gathered at a packed meeting organized by SF to discuss the sale of the demesne lands.[28] The composition of the meeting reflected the desire of all classes to gain access to land.

In early July 1921, Shantonagh House, home of the Fitzherbert family, was burned 'by armed men, some of whom were disguised'. The newspaper account again cited the fact that the house was to be used as a billet; however, a short time before the absentee Fitzherbert had visited the area to collect his rents and he was 'conveyed out of the house [on to] the roadway by armed men' and ordered to return to Queenstown in Cork where he resided.[29] Thus, agrarian grievances are just as likely to have been a factor behind the arson attack.

It is, therefore, not an easy task to determine whether alleged political or military reasons for the destruction of a Big House were entwined with additional social and agrarian motives. In Monaghan, as elsewhere, unresolved land questions were never far beneath the surface during the revolutionary period. For example, in February 1919, Matt Brown of Kiltybegs died and his widow put the estate of 500 acres up for auction. The local SF branch met 'for the purpose of securing the [demesne] farm for division amongst neighbouring farmers'.[30] Fr Bernard Maguire bid £9,000 on their behalf and said he would not make another advance. The message was clear: no outsider would be welcome. The police reported: 'The sum is below the value of the farm, other people wished to buy the farm but were apparently afraid to bid and the farm was not sold.'[31] Ten days later Mrs Brown decided to till some of the farm but one of her ploughmen was intimidated and so refused to do the work. When her brother-in-law took up the task he too was intimidated. The police were called in for protection, but the agitators remained at a distance and continued horn blowing from the neighbouring hills. In May, three horn blowers were arrested and one who refused bail was sent to prison for two months.[32] There were other cases like this. One IRA veteran, recalling the general raid for arms in August 1920, noted that of the four houses he raided two belonged to Protestants who had taken occupation of evicted farms during the Land League era; there obviously remained a good deal of residual bitterness.[33] Owen O'Duffy described the ostracization of land-grabbing neighbours: 'Hornblowing was only part of what they suffered. They never came of course to wakes or kaileys or dances. None of their neighbours spoke to them, none would buy or sell with them, lend them a box barrow or a pitch fork ... We would not show so much friendliness as even to glance at his gate.'[34]

When the First World War ended in 1918, the collapse in food prices should have meant a corresponding drop in the price of conacre and a return to pre-war rent levels (for those whose rents had not been judicially fixed in the past) but neither landlords nor those who rented conacre were prepared to acquiesce. Predictably, this resulted in protests. In March 1922, there were tenant meetings on three mid-Monaghan estates that had not been sold where the tenants demanded up to 50 per cent reductions 'owing to the failure in the prices of farm stock and produce this season'.[35] In January 1923, the unpurchased tenants on the Dartrey estate refused a reduction of 25 per cent on the grounds that it was inadequate. When William Martin, solicitor for its then owner, Lady Edith Wyndham, proceeded against some of the tenants, he received a threatening letter: 'Sir, be prepared yourself is going for a long visit to Magillycuddy Reeks. The Kerry air will do you good and when you come back you can go see Lady Edith Wyndham.'[36] The following month Glenburne House, the home of Henry Leslie, agent to the same estate, was burned, and large posters were distributed throughout the county calling on tenants on all unpurchased estates to pay no rent and 'to drive the last nail in the coffin of landlordism' in Monaghan.[37] These were in effect calls for compulsory purchase. In March 1922, after the Treaty had been ratified, Charles Laverty wrote confidently to the editor of the *Democrat* that landlords 'can rest assured that never again will a barrier between England's landlords and Ireland's farmers be made in London. We are masters now of our own affairs, and the English landlord who expects a continuance of ransom prices is living in a fool's paradise, the English landlord who has not sold will find he has over held his stock.'[38] He was largely correct as the case study of Castleshane illustrates.

Castleshane was a neo-Elizabethan extravaganza, built for the Lucas Scudamore family in 1836, to replace an original late sixteenth-century castle dating from the family's arrival in Ireland as part of the Elizabethan settlement. Edward Lucas Scudamore had been a prominent member of the Monaghan unionist movement until his death in 1917. His wife, Sybil, took over the management of the estate as her son, Jack, was still a minor.[39] The house was burned on 15 February 1920. At the time there was a good deal of IRA activity in the area; just a few days before a notice had been posted locally that 'anyone helping to fill in the trenches would be shot by order of the IRA'.[40] The house commanded a strategic position between Castleblayney and Monaghan town, and would have been an ideal billet for the military that would shortly occupy it. However, unlike the other houses burned, Castleshane was still very much occupied by the family, and the fire was not malicious but instead caused by a cinder falling onto the unprotected carpet in the dining room. It seems to have smouldered most of the night until discovered by a young maid the next morning who made the fatal mistake of opening the windows to allow out the smoke. The smouldering carpet suddenly burst into flames and fire engulfed the room and quickly spread. Lady Sybil Lucas Scudamore and her eight female servants escaped safely. The steward, George Morgan, attempted to quench the dining room blaze with a hose but 'was finally driven from the door of the room by the intense heat and smoke fumes'. When it was realized that attempts to extinguish the fire were futile, Morgan and some of the estate workers began salvaging as many valuable as they could.[41] The family silver, some furniture and valuable china, as well as part of the library, were saved but a James I bible was lost, as well as copies of the Nuremberg Chronicles, and most tragically (at least from the historian's perspective) the correspondence between Robert Peel, chief secretary of Ireland, and Edward Lucas, his under-secretary, covering the period 1841-6, including Lucas' brief sojourn as chairman of the Famine Relief Commission of Ireland.[42] Sybil's jewellery (locked in a safe upstairs), the family portraits and other valuable paintings and prints were all destroyed.[43] On Sunday crowds of townspeople from Monaghan walked out to witness the destruction. The local newspaper reported that the 'beautiful lawns around the house were sadly tramped and mutilated by the feet of men and wheels of carts brought to bring the salvaged furniture to a place of safety.'[44]

The burning may not have been malicious but the consequences were the same as those suffered by hundreds of other Big House families whose homes were burned at this time. The county gentry wrote in sympathy to Sybil. Miss Murray-Ker of Newbliss House said that she was 'just heart sorry' to hear the news.[45] Mrs Crayshaw regarded it as 'the greatest loss to all the countryside'.[46] Lady Dartrey felt 'absolutely ill to hear of the terrible calamity'.[47] The wider Protestant community also sympathized: the Monaghan War Pensions Committee lamented that such a tragedy should befall 'a lady who has always manifested a remarkable interest in the welfare of the people in general, and of the soldiers in particular'.[48] In 1919, Sybil had been awarded the Red Cross medal. At Christmas 1920, Mrs Cassidy, 'your very humble and obedient servant', sent a Christmas gift to Sybil of a chicken and a duck 'as a very small token of esteem and remembrance of what we all thought of you and your family'.[49] No evidence was found of any declarations of sympathy coming from nationalist Monaghan.

The burning of a country house meant the destruction of a family home and all that was precious to a family; and in this case, it also meant the destruction of a family's history and, indeed, a whole community's history. When Lady Dartrey sympathized with Sybil, her first query was about 'the picture', a reference to a portrait of Sybil and her late husband painted by the Welsh artist, Inglis. Sybil's son, Jack, was greatly saddened by its loss as it seems to have been the only surviving image of his parents together. He was also 'sick about the library going' and wondered had the gramophone 'pipped it' and had the records been melted?[50] Her daughter, Gill, was equally distraught at the loss of their home: 'This is the third letter I have tried to write to you, the other 2 I have torn up ... I can't believe it ... it seems everything we love goes ... is everything we love gone forever. I did so love Castleshane, I don't seem to think we have any real "home" any more.'[51] This came from a young woman who was capturing the mood of a post-war generation: 'What a perfectly beastly world this is. Whenever we try to be happy something seems to spoil it all ... I don't feel as though I ever want to do anything ever anymore.'[52]

Lady Sybil left for her family ancestral home at Kentchurch Court in Wales, never to return to Castleshane. Her departure had several consequences. The house staff (of at least eight maids) and most of the demesne labourers were made redundant, with obvious financial repercussions for a number of families, the post office, small village shops and the wider local economy.[53] One employee, Poppy Geddes, lamented that 'this neighbourhood cannot be the same again without Castleshane'.[54]

This economic blow was followed by a loss of patronage and influence traditionally exercised by the family. In January 1923, while Civil War was ongoing, Jack came of age. In time honoured tradition, the members of Clontibret select vestry presented a gift with an accompanying address that praised 'the good will and generosity' of the family for many generations towards Clontibret parish. It went on to 'deplore the fact that regrettable circumstances have rendered it impossible now for Mrs Lucas Scudamore and family to reside amongst us', and concluded with the hope that 'more propitious days ... may soon dawn for our country [which] will enable them to rebuild and reoccupy the old historic seat at Castleshane'.[55] There were former tenants and estate employees who regretted the loss of the traditional influence the Lucas Scudamores had used to help them in the past. Mrs Phil Cassidy, for example, wrote to Sybil that her son had been made redundant in the post office because of the continuous disruptions caused by the IRA's cutting of wires and the robbery of the mails.[56] It was 'a great loss' to the family as he had been earning a pound a week. Mrs Cassidy asked Sybil if she might write to Monaghan County Council 'as we were always used to you doing us so many favours'.[57] Sybil had no influence with the SF-dominated county council, but as a gesture of traditional estate paternalism, she sent parcels of gifts to the Cassidy family.[58]

The destruction of the Big House represented the end of an historical epoch and a way of life that had been consistent for generations. Sybil had no intention of returning to Castleshane. Some newspaper clippings kept by her are perhaps revealing of her attitude to the times and the new Ireland. Headlines blazoned with sensational accounts of 'Rampant Bolshevism in the south', the violation of the truce, and a 'typical' threatening letter that was 'received daily by Loyalists in Southern Ireland' must have resonated with her:

> If you don't give back the money to the grabbers of the farms you sold and also give up the other farms ... we are a few men who fought for Ireland and who burned your house, who are looking on and are determined to see justice done .... no protection, official or unofficial, will save you from our vengeance. We might also say we hate Protestants as they would grind us, and did when they had power. Our day has come.[59]

In Sybil's absence, management of the estate was taken over by George Morgan, the steward. He was soon reporting how difficult matters were. In August 1920, farming was disrupted by 'the most awful weather nothing but rain and very cold, nothing seems to grow ... potatoes are blighted very bad all round'. Until then pigs were doing well, selling at £12 a hundredweight, but by the beginning of August, just as the second lot of pigs that year were ready for market, Morgan reported the negative impact of the Belfast boycott on the pork market.[60] With the landlord presence removed, farmers who had taken untenanted Lucas Scudamore lands and parts of the demesne on conacre became reluctant to pay their rents. The family solicitor advised the issuing of writs but Morgan was of the opinion that this would only lead to a boycott of the Castleshane demesne.[61] By March 1921, the demesne was being pillaged. One old friend informed Sybil that people were 'making a total hand of the woods' with 'large farmers taking their firing out of it. Three out of the one house in it at a time carrying them out the road and wheeling them home in a barrow, and others even pulling up evergreen shrubs by the root to set.'[62] The fear among ordinary men and women is palpable in these letters and was compounded by the killing of the Flemings not far from Clontibret. Mrs Cassidy urged Sybil: 'please Madam do not say I wrote you anything about it or mention my name as the times are curious'.[63] And another: 'Please if you should mention this to Mr Morgan don't mention my name as you know the kind of times that are here and if he spoke my name it would do me no good'.[64]

Two wings of the house survived in a reasonable state. In May 1922, they were taken over by an anti-Treaty ASU and Morgan reported: 'it was impossible to get work done as you could not call your life your own'.[65] The yard offices were occupied by officers who left them in 'a disgraceful condition'.[66] The house was eventually attacked by the National army in August 1922 and the ASU arrested and sent to Dundalk jail.[67] The *Standard* reported: 'The cleaning up of this nest of rebels has caused a deep feeling of relief among the inhabitants of the district'.[68] But it did not ease local tensions in relation to the demesne. In August 1923, Gibson Whinnery, the elderly estate herd, turned grazing cattle out on the road because they had strayed among the dairy cows but Morgan pointed out to Sybil: 'He may have been able to do that in days gone by, but I can assure you and Whinnery it will not pay the Castleshane estate today to do these things'.[69] Morgan knew that the Whinnerys, both staunch loyalists, had been upset at his allowing a Gaelic football match to be held in one of the demesne fields but Morgan pleaded: 'The Revd Father McGarvey and Dr Kierans were interested in the match and if they brought the band from St Mary's I am no longer in a position to say you must stay outside'.[70] In January 1924, it was reported that a miniature distillery had been operating out of the house ruins. The following month the newly established Garda Síochána raided the yards again and this time found a dance in progress.[71] In the emerging Ireland, the ruins of a Big House and its demesne were now providing a playground for a class that in the past would not have been allowed inside the demesne gates.

After the destruction of Castleshane, the estate solicitor, T.F. Crozier, had strongly advised that the entire demesne should be sold 'as land is fetching such a high price at the present time', and further pointed out that 'the possibility of rebuilding any class of house that would be in keeping with the demesne is entirely out of the question'.[72] Crozier knew that in the future the upkeep of a Big House was simply unsustainable; in his letter he mentioned an unnamed house that the family had abandoned because 'it would take the majority of their income to keep it up in firing, lighting, servants, etc'.[73] While Crozier also knew that the attachment to the family's ancestral home was still in Jack's blood, he hinted to Sybil: 'I wonder will Jack ever be inclined to harden his heart and sell what remains of Castleshane. My own opinion is that he will have to do so eventually.'[74]

In Spring 1921, when Monaghan was in an 'unsettled state', Crozier advised against grazing Castleshane with the family's own stock in the absence of adequate protection and supervision.[75] Grazier rents from the demesne were £400 in arrears and Crozier concluded: 'I daresay it would be quite impossible to get anyone to serve civil bills'.[76] Less than a month after the Treaty was signed, Crozier told Sybil a land bill was being mooted: 'I should not be a bit surprised that there might be compulsory powers to acquire land situated such as Castleshane is now, namely the owners living in England, and the mansion house burned.'[77] Crozier again strongly argued for sale of the demesne: 'it will be very hard to find nowadays anyone who will be conscientious enough to protect yours and Jack's interests, particularly with the present state of the country.'[78] During the truce period, Morgan reported an attempt to destroy the remaining portion of the castle; he wrote to Sybil: 'all doors were forced and hay from the yard soaked in petrol laid up the stone steps'. There was a second attempt to destroy the entrance gates, and in early July 1921, forty yards of demesne wall were demolished.[79] These incidents showed there were those who wanted to destroy all evidence that the house ever existed and ensure that the Lucas Scudamores never returned. Sybil was now aware that there were 'Sin [sic] Féiners or otherwise' who were making the most of the difficult times.[80]

Sybil took Crozier's advice and sold off the untenanted lands in 1922 but she retained the demesne. Just under a decade later, in 1931, M.T. Henchy, an Irish Land Commission inspector, was sent to Castleshane to carry out a survey of the Scudamore lands that were to be compulsorily acquired under the powers that the Commission had been given in the 1923 Land Act for the relief of local congestion. As Charles Laverty had predicted, some families had held on too long. It was on the eve of a general election and Cumann na nGaedheal was under pressure to expedite land redistribution because Fianna Fáil was committed to this in its election manifesto. What Henchey found was in stark contrast to a previous time when the estate was efficiently run by the Lucas Scudamore family and maintained by an army of labourers: the lands were 'in very poor condition being for the most part overgrown with rushes and thistles'.[81] The following year, the demesne was compulsorily acquired for £3,715 payable in 4.5 per cent land bonds.[82] The Land Commission planted the demesne with pine trees. In 1961, Sir Shane Leslie wrote to Jack Lucas Scudamore: 'Castleshane is like a Norwegian pine forest but I think you were fortunate to clear out while the going was good'.[83] The following year he sent Jack a photo of his mother, Leonie, 'carousing with the duke of Connaught', and summed up the decline of the Big House in Monaghan in his own idiosyncratic way: 'The County Monaghan gentry were grand in those days entertaining royalty! Today they couldn't even get Lord Snowdon to take tea with them.'[84]

Attacks on residences and the eviction of gentry families were commonplace during the 1919–23 period, and into the future few republicans showed any cultural appreciation for the architectural grandeur and status of Big Houses and their designed landscapes. Tom Carragher, a leading IRA leader in the south of Monaghan during the War of Independence and later a prominent anti-Treatyite, commandeered Donaghmoyne House after it had been vacated by the Bolton family. A former comrade, Brian MacMahon, looked unfavourably at the subsequent actions of Carragher: 'The way in which he turned Bolton's wonderful grounds and priceless collection of shrubs and flower beds over to the pigs proved that he had no feeling with nature or no sense of beauty'.[85] It was more a case that Carragher had an antipathy towards the Big House, its demesne and all they stood for; indeed, he may even have felt that swapping herbaceous plants for livestock was a sign of progress in the new Ireland. However, the contrasting attitudes of these former comrades also illustrated the mixed feelings that the Big House could provoke; for some, like McMahon, the Big House still retained an aesthetic appeal, at least after it was divorced from its historical and political associations.

Families such as the Lucas Scudamores could have left Ireland after the 1903 Land Act but they chose to remain; however, two decades later the transformation in Irish politics and society convinced them and many others that resettling in England (or in the case of the Blacks elsewhere in the colonies) was a more preferable option. From the 1920s, the Big House went into decline. This, of course, was not unique to Monaghan nor was it merely due to tramsformations in local politics and society; it was also related to a dramatic economic dislocation due to dwindling investment portfolios (nothing had been so important to the sustainability of the Big House as its vast acres); the compulsory acquisition of demesne and untenanted lands as in the case of Castleshane and Dartrey; the unaffordability of servants and outdoor staff that led to the dereliction and decay of houses; and the rise of rates and taxes.[86]

The experience of the Monaghan gentry and aristocracy during and after the revolutionary period reflected the experiences of their counterparts further south.[87] By contrast, as Olwen Purdue has shown, their counterparts in the newly established state of Northern Ireland did not experience the same levels of violence, destruction of property, or dilution of their social and political power in the same period.[88] The Big Houses of Northern Ireland survived longer at least in part because of the more sympathetic political regime, whereas in the IFS and later the Republic successive governments and the wider public questioned the role of the Big House in the national patrimony, and for decades both were more inclined to view Big Houses as symbols of a colonial era best forgotten.[89] Of the great houses in Monaghan, only three now survive in the ownership of the original families: Glaslough, since re-imagined as Castle Leslie; Hilton Park owned by the Madden family; and Lough Fea, owned by the Shirley family but occupied only occasionally.

9 Revolution?

Revolutionaries dream of change, they fight for change. The photograph on the front cover of this book encapsulates the story of how events from around 1916 changed the life path of one young man. Dan Hogan, the eldest son of a relatively comfortable farmer from Grangemockler in County Tipperary, was born in 1895. His parents were of the Land War generation who had worked hard to effect social and political change. Their successful dairy farm had moved them beyond subsistence level to where they aspired to educate their sons and daughters; they did not want to see their sons slip down the social ladder into the labouring class. Dan was not kept at home to work the family farm; his parents believed he had the intelligence to make a life away from farming. His younger brother, Michael, was given that task; another brother, Thomas, entered the Christian Brothers in 1915 and was prominent in the GAA: in time the Hogan Cup presented to the winners of the All-Ireland senior colleges A football championship was named after him. Two daughters became nuns, further emphasizing the family's strong Catholic ethos. Thus, the Hogan family was firmly immersed in Catholicism and the GAA.

Hogan's life in Monaghan has been revealed in part up to now. In 1917, he came to Clones as a railway clerk with the GNR. The railway brought prosperity to Clones and Hogan arrived in a bustling, lively town where passengers congregated on their way to Enniskillen, Dundalk, Armagh, Cavan or for connections to Dublin and Belfast. It was also a town that had a very long tradition of sectarianism. Shortly after his arrival, Hogan came into contact with Owen O'Duffy through the local GAA club. Like his brother, Michael, Dan was an accomplished footballer and hurler. Before he left Grangemockler he had most likely been initiated into separatist politics. Michael was a member of the local Grangemockler Volunteers and when a SF club was formed there his home became a regular meeting place, as it did later for the IRA. This was the home territory of such later IRA leaders as Dan Breen, Dinny Lacey and Sean Treacy.[1] Edward Glendon, a member of the Grangemockler Volunteers, recalled Hogan coming home on holidays and bringing Owen O'Duffy and Seán MacEntee with him. MacEntee married Margaret Browne, a neighbour of Hogan's. Glendon recalled: 'When we all got together during holiday time in Browne's house, little else except the Rising, the executed leaders and the Volunteer movement was discussed'.[2] Glendon's memory was shaped by the popular nationalist memory of the Rising; by the time he set down his recollections, 1916 had become enshrined as an iconic site of memory: it was the defining event in the overthrow of the British administration in Ireland.

Hogan became O'Duffy's right-hand man; and Matt Smith went as far as to claim that Hogan was the real mastermind of the physical force movement in Monaghan.[3] As this study has highlighted, Hogan worked with O'Duffy to reinvigorate the GAA and later (or simultaneously) to establish an effective IRA structure in the county. O'Duffy remembered Hogan imbuing his men 'with the fine spirit of the Gaelic games he knew and loved so well'.[4] He became commandant of the 5th Northern Division after O'Duffy's elevation to GHQ. Before and after this promotion, Hogan commanded huge respect from his men. Tom Armstrong was profuse in his praise: 'I would like to record my regard for him as a wonderful character – of solid build and great physical strength, strong sense of humour with a hearty laugh, determined forceful drive, and utterly fearless of physical risk. He was a personal friend of every one of the boys, yet when a job was on he was very strict. He planned everything in great detail.'[5] Probably the best example of his attention to detail was his meticulous planning of the daring rescue of Matt Fitzpatrick from Monaghan infirmary, after he had been injured and captured during the Roslea incident in February 1921. This became one of the most talked about and best-documented incidents of the War of Independence in Monaghan.[6]

There also survives an illuminated address given to Hogan on 'behalf of the Catholic employees of the Great Northern Railway (Clones District)' that was presented in recognition of his 'untiring efforts in every cause that had for its object the well-being of your country and your fellow Irishmen', and praised his 'patriotism, high ideals and sacrifices cheerfully undertaken for "Holy Ireland's Cause"'.[7] It was a testament to the high regard in which Hogan was held, but also a reminder of the sectarianism in Monaghan during the War of Independence and the perception that Irish patriotism went hand in hand with Catholicism. In popular memory, both in Monaghan and in Tipperary, Hogan became 'a romantic figure whose exploits and youthful daring were the stuff of legends'.[8] In the 1930s, admittedly in an attempt to cast aspersions on his political enemies in Monaghan, O'Duffy publicly recalled that 'when there was fighting to be done those cowards would go into a rat hole rather than look Dan Hogan straight in the face either before or after the fight'.[9] Hogan was undoubtedly a charismatic, bellicose and, when necessary, ruthless figure of the type required in any revolution.

Hogan's ascent from lowly railway clerk to a national figure within five years was extraordinary, one that was only possible because of the dramatic developments of the time. As with many revolutionary figures, conflict and turmoil provided opportunities that might not have come his way had he remained with the GNR. Around 1920, he and O'Duffy established an auctioneering firm. Launching their enterprise, O'Duffy stated: 'It is not our desire to interfere in any way with the business of any Catholic auctioneer now practising, but every day we see Catholics placing their sales in the hands of non-Catholic auctioneers who are the avowed supporters of the British garrison.'[10] Given that this was in Clones, O'Duffy probably had Michael E. Knight's firm in mind. McGarry suggests that O'Duffy prospered during these years and if that was the case, then Hogan probably did likewise.[11]

The photograph of Hogan on the front cover of this book captures in a way that words cannot his personal progress. He sits resplendent in full military regalia of the post-truce period – much more resplendent than the average guerrilla fighter from the War of Independence. The trappings of bourgeois success – his impeccable uniform, silver watch and chain, and the car in the background – are clearly evident. The ultimate symbol of his military prowess sits on his lap, a Thompson sub-machine gun, a reminder that his military prowess brought not only political success but delivered a world in which he could prosper socially and economically. The photographic portrait is an image of self-aggrandisement. In this respect, the location is equally important: the photograph was taken at the front of Lough Bawn house, former residence of Colonel William Tennison, high sheriff of Monaghan, leading county unionist and local commander of the UVF. The IRA used the house as a training camp during the truce. There could be no better symbol of the end of the *ancien régime* than an IRA commander on the front steps of the Big House.

There is also a certain arrogance in Hogan's stare. A few months before, the last thing Hogan would have wanted was a photograph taken that would bring him to the attention of the authorities. But the War of Independence had made him a celebrity and now he basked in that. As P.S. O'Hegarty put it, 'The Volunteers became popular heroes, and their leaders began to get swelled heads'.[12] Victory always inspires confidence and the reception that fighters were given could clearly prompt such arrogance. When Thomas Carragher of Lislanley, injured in the ambush that resulted in the death of the McEnaney brothers, was released from Mountjoy in January 1921, he was met in Castleblayney by two SF bands, paraded through the town, and escorted by uniformed IRA men and 'an immense concourse of people', while all the houses in the town were brilliantly illuminated and bonfires blazed. Fr Ward, the curate at Annyalla, congratulated him and his comrades 'on the splendid victory they had won and counselled them to remain united in the future'.[13] The celebration typified the glorification of the IRA's War of Independence but remaining united was the great challenge presented by the Civil War.

The witness statements (both in the BMH and Marron collection in Monaghan County Museum) cover only a fraction of the number who fought; they may also reflect disproportionately the experiences of those who were satisfied with their lot post-independence. Fearghal McGarry makes the point that 'the numerous, well-educated, and socially frustrated middle classes from which they derived formed the main participants and beneficiaries of the Irish revolution: the most capable and ambitious among them would rise from humble origins to national leadership during this rapid period of "exciting meritocratic flux"."[14] However, this thesis remains to be tested in relation to Monaghan because there has, to date, been no systematic analysis of the social backgrounds of the rank and file there or of their post-independence status.

There were certainly some who fitted McGarry's stereotypes: medical doctors such as Conn Ward, Patrick McCarville and Charles Emerson; teachers such as Frank O'Duffy; surveyors including Owen O'Duffy and P.J. O'Daly; and even GNR employees like Hogan. These men already had a future before 1916, lucky enough to have made it to a respectable level of education or even university. However, for the majority the removal of the British administration alone could not guarantee social and political advancement. For that to be the case, military revolution had to be accompanied by a social revolution and this was less easy to define and deliver. There were those who attempted to promote social revolution, in large part through the land question, but not enough nationalists were committed to radical change. The witness statements reveal there were certainly a few Monaghan IRA veterans who subsequently made good for themselves in the National army or the Garda Síochána, largely due to the influence of O'Duffy and Hogan. But the fate of the many – the second and third sons of small farmers, the farm labourers and the shop assistants – remains to be elucidated. It is hard to tell what proportion of the rank and file from the working classes who fought in the 1916–23 period were satisfied – socially, politically, economically, culturally, emotionally – in the years and decades that followed or felt that their efforts had been vindicated. As the flush of victory faded and the hero worship from young women, and the boasting of daring deeds died away how did these former combatants feel about the fruits of their struggle? In February 1920 Thomas McGahon concluded:

> We can well believe that young men may be induced by fiery orators no wiser than themselves, by poets of the romantic order, by brooding over certain episodes of Irish history of a hundred years ago or more, to believe it a grand and noble thing to risk and even lose their lives in the pursuit of certain ideals – which in the opinion of others are unattainable and must remain so.[15]

In Monaghan it was not long before those 'others' who had been opposed to the social equality ideals of the 1916 Proclamation came back to prominence. As Kevin O'Higgins put it in relation to the wider national arena, he was part of a generation of the 'most conservative-minded revolutionaries that ever put through a successful revolution'.[16] John Regan has shown how, by the 1920s, Cumann na nGaedheal accommodated the 'ascendant Catholic nationalist middle-class' with Redmondite roots.[17] Similarly, Mel Farrell has found that 'many former Home Rulers, cut adrift and denied their birth right as a result of Sinn Féin's victory in 1918 ... subsequently found a new political home in the pro-Treaty movement'.[18] Significantly, despite its antipathy to SF, the Redmondite AOH remained strong in Monaghan until at least the 1930s and provided the springboard for the re-emergence of the former elites; in 1934 even O'Duffy referred to it as 'a great organization'.[19]

Within a short time, the Mr O'Rourkes, Mr Kellys and Mr Toals were back in control of local politics and society. O'Rourke was a patriot in the sense that he believed in the struggle for independence but he was never a revolutionary; he did not anticipate the expropriation of his business empire after independence: revealingly, his admiration for Pearse was not matched by a similar admiration for Connolly. In 1918, he bought Belleek Pottery. Under Lemass' industrial drive he was chosen to set up Arklow Pottery in 1934–5, of which he remained chairman and managing director until his death in 1956. He remained director of the family firms, O'Rourke & Co., Dundalk, and O'Rourke, Cuniffe & Co. in Dublin, and owner of O'Rourke Bros, Millers, in Inniskeen.[20] O'Rourke never contested a Dáil seat but in recognition of his services, President W.T. Cosgrave nominated him to the IFS Senate in 1922 where he served until its dissolution in 1936. After independence, he became a member of Cumann na nGaedheal, for many years serving as chairman of the local Inniskeen branch. He continued on Monaghan County Council until 1945.

Thomas Toal successfully reinvented himself in the years of the War of Independence as an ardent SF chairman of the county council who supported the severance of connections with the Local Government Board, who refused to submit the council's books for audit to the central administration, who, during the Belfast boycott, transferred the council's accounts from the Ulster Bank, and who had the resolution condemning the 1916 rebels, which he had ironically proposed, expunged from the record.[21] McGarry contends that O'Duffy had retained 'continued authority over Monaghan County Council' during the revolutionary period but this is debatable because a veteran like Toal was too astute to be outmanoeuvred.[22] It was not only his political cunning that kept him in the chair until the 1940s but also his wealth and influence as a major employer. Toal also became a member of Cumann na nGaedheal and in 1925 he was invited by Ernest Blythe to put his name forward for the Senate. In the election of that year there was a massive turnout of 80 per cent in Monaghan and Toal polled 80 per cent of that vote. He sat in the Senate for almost twelve years.

After a few years in the political wilderness, Eddie Kelly made a notable but unsurprising comeback; his social standing in south Monaghan made it inevitable in the post-independence conservative climate. Over time, he acquired the nickname 'the Twister' as he swung from one party to another.

Ever the consummate politician, and one with a sense of humour, he had a poster designed of himself, with his coat turned inside out, and twisting the starting handle of a tractor with the slogan: 'Vote for Eddie, the twister'. He became chairman of Monaghan County Council for a seventeen-year period and in 1954 achieved his ultimate political ambition when he was elected Fianna Fáil TD for Monaghan.[23] When he failed to get the Fianna Fáil nomination in 1957, he went to the Fine Gael convention and ended up as James Dillon's running mate. Little wonder that Ted Nealon in his *Tales from the Dáil bar* should remember Kelly as 'a man unmatched in any of the County Halls'.[24]

Kelly was the only one of the 'big three' to live to see the 1966 golden jubilee of the Rising. When he was interviewed by the authors of *Cuimhneacháin Mhuineacháin*, his selective memory of events served to reinforce the changes of the previous fifty years. His version of events placed him at the GPO on Easter Monday, willing to die for Ireland,[25] rather than in Carrickmacross where he had introduced a motion calling for the execution of the leaders.[26] No one contradicted him. The area of history and memory is increasingly becoming a popular field of research; Kelly's life and his version of that life are fertile ground for political historians as well as historians of memory. And in the process it is worth looking at how IRA contemporaries remembered men like Kelly. IRA veteran Brian MacMahon wrote:

> ... there were many fine people who believed in John Redmond and his constitutional movement and considered our policy to be sheer madness, as we could have no hope of success. They did not approve of the IRA but were willing to render us assistance in certain circumstances. Tom Daly of Bocks and Eddie Kelly of Essexford were typical examples. Almost all of this category held genuinely nationalistic opinions.[27]

MacMahon came from the middle class and was no different to Kevin O'Higgins, Patrick Hogan and others in the IFS government of the 1920s, conservative revolutionaries who believed in the protection of property. Kelly was a nationalist all his pre-independence political career; he just never became a Sinn Féiner. Ultimately, his wealth and his local social standing guaranteed his political survival.

What happened in Monaghan after the Civil War places doubt over the applicability of the term 'revolution' for the events of 1912–23. There was certainly no dictatorship of the proletariat. Lough Bawn, the house outside which Hogan had his photograph taken, was bought by local solicitor and land agent, Charles Laverty, the last home ruler to have contested a seat for south Monaghan in the 1910 general election, for the princely sum of £4,000. If there was a revolution, it did little to upset his way of life. He may never have achieved his ultimate political ambition but he was fortunate that the new Ireland had not been taken over by socialist revolutionaries of the type he and the middle-class local politicians had feared in 1916. One veteran, Thomas Carragher of Annyalla (not to be confused with Tom Carragher of Donaghmoyne), later wrote eloquently:

> During the period of the Truce, the politicians and respectables took over. It was they who interpreted our dream, the dream we fought for. It was they would decide the terms to which we must agree. In the mind of every soldier was a little republic of his own in which he was the hero. But his dream was shattered. The process-server that he once made easy to talk to was back in business, the same gripper, the same sheriff with the same old laws while the little hero was back at his plough.[28]

For the sons of small farmers and the agricultural labourers, drudgery became their lot once more. The Land Commission never had enough available land in Monaghan for redistribution that might meaningfully change family social circumstances; this was obviously as true for the small Presbyterian farmers as their Catholic neighbours. It is questionable if Patrick Kavanagh ever fought for Ireland, except briefly in his imagination, but no one captured more vividly the hardship of post-independence small farm life in Monaghan.[29] His wonderfully evocative *Tarry Flynn* (1948) encapsulates the frustrations of post-indepedence rural youth, in large part caused by the stifling effect of the Catholic Church, where, for example, in Clogher in 1924 Bishop McKenna condemned 'certain imported dances, which are so obviously direct incentives to sin', corrupting the 'innocent country boys and girls in ever-increasing numbers'.[30]

Thus, it is difficult to elucidate who in Monaghan could claim to be contented after 1923. Those who had anticipated a home rule parliament after the war were disappointed; unionists found themselves 'thrown to the wolves' by their northern counterparts; those Sinn Féiners and members of the IRA who wanted only an independent Irish republic had not achieved the objective of their struggle; those who supported the Treaty had to deal with aspects of the agreement they did not like, including the partition of Ireland and the sundering of Monaghan from a large area of its economic hinterland; ordinary men and women, from both sides of the politico-religious divide, especially those living along the border of the new Northern Ireland state, were unsure of their future and fearful of the impact that the proposed Boundary Commission might have; the aristocracy and the gentry were in irreversible decline, placed outside the United Kingdom, their spiritual and ancestral home; and those at the further end of the social spectrum who thought revolution would bring more equal opportunities soon found that nothing really had changed. Brian MacMahon remembered feeling that when the truce was called, 'the possible end had come before we had achieved anything worthwhile'.[31]

The Civil War left a bitter legacy as it continued to be fought out in Irish politics long after the guns had been put down. By the 1930s, former comrades such as O'Duffy and Dr Conn Ward had become bitter political enemies who aired their grievances time and again in public, casting aspersions on each other's character and their roles in the 1916–23 period. O'Duffy's anger with the distortion of historical fact (at which he was fairly adept himself) led him to record: 'Many who are forgotten today were to the fore then, as my diary records. Men who now claim to have been in the Irish vanguard during those days are curiously unmentioned.'[32]

One of those was Dan Hogan. On 7 January 1924, when still at the height of his powers, Hogan married Elizabeth O'Flynn from Ballinasloe from a wealthy farming background. O'Duffy, Hogan's 'one good & true friend', was best man.[33] *An tÓglach* pointed out that 'Major-General Hogan's name is a household word in County Monaghan, where his record in the Anglo-Irish war is so well known, and he is universally popular with the officers and men of the Army'.[34] In 1927, Hogan was made chief of staff of the Irish army, replacing General Peadar MacMahon, also from Monaghan.[35] In February 1929, he resigned from his post as the result of a dispute with Desmond FitzGerald, minister for defence, over pay and conditions for members of the army.[36] C.S. 'Todd' Andrews contended that Hogan struck the minister 'in the course of some disagreement'.[37] On 11 February 1929, full of cynicism, Hogan wrote to O'Duffy: 'As I suspected the competition is very keen here amongst the probables since they heard the "good" news' of his resignation.[38] He received a gratuity of £3,300 and a pension for life.

In August 1929, Hogan and his wife emigrated to the US; O'Duffy drove them to the ship at Cobh and provided Hogan with a written introduction to his friends in America, crediting him with being 'the author of the scheme of organization on which our army is established'.[39] Unfortunately, nothing is known of Hogan's new life in America, except that one night in 1939 he walked out of his family home in New York, never to return. He subsequently corresponded with the Department of Defence between July 1939 and February 1940 from two addresses in Dublin and finally one in Chicago. His last correspondence was in 1940 and he cashed his last pension cheque in 1941. There is no evidence in the file whether Dan Hogan's whereabouts or fate were ever established.[40] In 1968, Hogan's only child, Betty, a former nun who left the Order to look after her elderly mother, made enquiries about her father to Fr Laurence Marron in Monaghan.[41] Neither she nor her mother had heard anything from him since the night he left home but she remembered him as 'a wonderful person'.[42] Marron made exhaustive enquiries but to no avail. Dan Hogan had simply disappeared.

After O'Duffy's meteoric rise, his fall was just as spectacular. After his Monaghan years, O'Duffy became IRA director of organization, deputy chief of staff, IRA liaison officer, a member of the war council along with Collins and Richard Mulcahy from July 1922, GOC of the south western command (a major challenge given the brutal nature of the fighting in that region and the fact that he was a northern outsider) and commissioner of the Garda Siochána in 1922. However, like Hogan and many others, the bitter legacy of the Civil War, the continuous political bickering and struggles for power took from his achievements. Ironically, while the independence struggle gave him a status that he would probably have been denied under home rule, IFS politics denied him ultimate political and personal satisfaction and his earlier legacy of accomplishment was greatly diminished in the end by his own bitterness. This emanated from a series of career and political setbacks in the 1930s, including his sacking as garda commissioner by de Valera in February 1933, the suppression of the Army Comrades Association (the Blueshirts) later that September, his enforced resignation as president of Fine Gael of which he was a founding member, his fall out of favour with the GAA, his flirtation with fascism and an unsuccessful campaign on behalf of General Franco during the Spanish Civil War, all of which was eventually compounded by personal problems including his descent into alcoholism. O'Duffy died on 30 November 1944 in a Dublin nursing home at the relatively young age of fifty-four. He is the only Monaghan person to date to have received a state funeral.

***

The complexities of Monaghan society in 1912–23 make it difficult for historians to provide definitive answers to all the questions that might be asked. Every source has its bias and its weakness. For many of the important issues, for example, working- and middle-class Protestant responses to the 1912–23 period (other than newspapers) no sources exist that are the equivalent to the BMH statements or MSP files, although compensation files, those for example of the Irish Grants Committee, do provide valuable detail on violence and sometimes attitudes towards the same. Even with all the new sources that have recently become available, it is still difficult for the historian to understand what, for example, drove some IRA men to the depths of depravity that they would take the young life of a neighbour's child and execute him as a spy, or take the life of a Protestant neighbour in a brutal fashion because of their politico-religious beliefs. How did Protestant families feel in the immediate aftermath of shooting IRA raiders? How did the families of victims put acts of brutality behind them and continue to co-exist in small intimate communities knowing who was responsible for the murder of their loved ones (as some undoubtedly did)? For families whose sons were killed as informers it not only sentenced them to a lifetime of sorrow but also shame and bitterness. There were those who, in the future, spread malicious rumours and others who were burdened with secrets. Some of those associated with the executions, such as John McGahey, endured decades of regret.

The class that undoubtedly experienced most revolutionary change was the Protestant aristocracy and gentry, and that came over the extended period from 1879 when they lost their political and socio-economic standing, and it was primarily the result of British legislation, not IRA violence. Their experience of decline was, of course, mirrored among the aristocracy in the United Kingdom and wider Europe in the post-war decades.

Alvin Jackson has made the point that the unionist generation of 1912–20 'have assumed a mythic stature for contemporary unionists, as the selfless patriots who created Northern Ireland'.[43] From the southern side of the border the perception is very different. At a meeting between this author and Monaghan Orangemen in March 2013, what emerged most strongly was the sense of betrayal, obviously passed down through the generations, regarding the breaking of the Covenant. Many of those present stated that mention of the Covenant had never been allowed in their homes. It had been an oath 'humbly relying on the God whom our fathers in days of stress and trial confidently trusted'; moreover, it was in 'sure confidence that God will defend the right' to fight that men subscribed their names, while unionist women in their Declaration believed that 'from this calamity God will save Ireland'. In the end, Monaghan unionists did not feel it was God who had let them down. Thrown over by Ulster unionists, the Anglo-Irish Treaty did little to address their grievances, and the proposed Boundary Commission never had much chance of success.

Like the young men who fought in the IRA, the experiences of Monaghan middle- and working-class Protestants in the decades after independence deserves scholarly attention in the future. For many middle-class unionists who did not wish to live under a Dublin parliament, and who could afford to migrate, the new state of Northern Ireland provided an obvious focus. In the inter-censal period 1911–26, the total population of Monaghan declined by 9 per cent, the Protestant population by almost 23 per cent. There were various reasons for this disproportionate Protestant decline (other than natural rates), including the withdrawal of Crown forces, war casualties, the closure of country houses and the sale of estates, but migration was also significant. A private census of Free State Protestants who had migrated north to County Fermanagh between 1920 and 1925 listed almost 150 Monaghan families, comprising over 450 persons,[44] some driven out by the dislocation of unionist trade, and others who left voluntarily, determined to live under British rule.

Without intention to sound condescending, but rather based on the experience of one born and reared in rural Monaghan, those Monaghan Protestants who stayed remained resilient and continued to play an important role in the everday life of local communities as small farmers, shopkeepers, publicans, merchants and professionals. Ironically, in 2016, when the centenary of the 1916 Easter Rising was celebrated, 'that sense of duality and difference that marks out border Protestants as a unique species on the island of Ireland' was similarly celebrated.[45] In an interview in August 2016, Jim Mills, originally from the Protestant enclave of Drum, remembered that in his youth Protestants tended to 'stick to themselves … There was a sort of segregation and a kind of directive from your parents not to be going anywhere else other than your own [hall].' But he also recalled the inter-dependency in mixed communities epitomized in the story of a local farmer, Victor Turner, who once 'came home from the Twelfth and his Catholic neighbours had his hay baled for him'.[46] It is a charming anecdote but Mills and and the others who work with him in trying to understand 'how border Protestants came to terms with living in the new Irish state' know full well the challenges of the project. For example, this author found it regrettable that Protestant families are still reluctant to come forward with family papers or oral evidence that might have elucidated more their history during the years 1912–23 and beyond.

It may be fitting to conclude this book with the fact that the Fine Gael Minister for Arts, Heritage, Regional, Rural and Gaeltacht Affairs, Heather Humphreys TD, who was responsible for overseeing the 1916 centenary celebrations in the Republic of Ireland, descends from a strong Monaghan Protestant and Orange tradition, whose grandfather was a signatory to the Ulster Solemn League and Covenant.[47] In March 2015, announcing her plans for commemoration, she commented: 'Given my background as a Protestant and an Ulsterwoman, who is a proud Irish republican, I appreciate the need to respect the differing traditions on this island'.[48] It was a very well crafted political statement, but also one that could be read as a personal reflection by the minister on her life experiences growing up in Monaghan. In her own words, the place at which she arrived was somewhere her grandfather would never have imagined 'in his wildest dreams'.[49]

Notes

ACKNOWLEDGMENTS

1 Patrick Kavanagh, 'The Great Hunger' in Antoinette Quinn (ed.), *Patrick Kavanagh: selected poems* (London, 1996), p. 41.
2 G.M. Trevelyan, *Clio: a muse and other essays* (London, 1913), pp 151–2.

CHAPTER ONE *Frontier county: Monaghan in 1912*

1 P.J. Duffy, 'The territorial organization of Gaelic landownership and its transformation in Co. Monaghan, 1591–1640', *Irish Geography*, 14 (1981), 72.
2 P.J. Duffy, 'Population and landholding in County Monaghan: a study in change and continuity' (PhD, UCD, 1976), p. 68; C.D. McGimpsey, '"To raise the banner in the remote north": politics in County Monaghan, 1868–1883' (PhD, University of Edinburgh, 1982), pp 6–8; see also P.J. Duffy, *Landscapes of south Ulster: a parish atlas of the diocese of Clogher* (Belfast, 1993).
3 See Pádraigín Ní Uallacháin, *A hidden Ulster: people songs and traditions of Oriel* (Dublin, 2003).
4 McGimpsey, 'Politics', p. 85; see also L.T. Brown, *Shepherding the Monaghan flock: the story of First Monaghan Presbyterian Church* (Monaghan, n.d.), p. 4.
5 Countess of Dartrey to Lord Dufferin, 14 Dec. 1883 (PRONI, Dartrey papers, D1071/H/B/D/78/126).
6 *Northern Standard* (*NS*), 23 June 1883.
7 Quoted in J.W. Taylor (ed.), *The Rossmore incident* (Dublin, 1884), p. 13.
8 *NS*, 27 Nov. 1885. 9 Quoted in *DD*, 24 Jan. 1914.
10 *DD*, 16 Aug. 1913. 11 *NS*, 12 Jan. 1839.
12 Fearghal McGarry, *Eoin O'Duffy: self-made hero* (Oxford, 2005), p. 55; see also Patrick Kavanagh, *The green fool* (London, 1938), p. 58.
13 *NS*, 20 July 1912.
14 Denis Carolan Rushe, *Historical sketches of Monaghan, from the earliest records to the Fenian movement* (Dublin, 1895), p. 112.
15 McGimpsey, 'Politics', pp 46–9.
16 'A short sketch of the life of Thomas Toal' (MCM, Toal papers).
17 *DD*, 27 Mar. 1920.
18 On another of these Monaghan men, see Terence Dooley, *Inniskeen, 1912–1918: the political conversion of Bernard O'Rourke* (Dublin, 2004).
19 Unless otherwise stated, quotations in the remainder of this section on Toal are taken from his, 'Life of Thomas Toal'.
20 *Hansard* (*Commons*), 4 Apr. 1910, vol. 16, cols. 186–8, 13 Jan. 1913, vol. 46, cols. 173–5.
21 Malachy Roe, 'J.C.R. Lardner, MP, forgotten middle-Irelander', *Clogher Record*, 21:3 (2014), 225–32.
22 Taken from report in *DD*, 14 Sept. 1918.
23 *DD*, 6 Apr. 1912. 24 *DD*, 3 June 1916.
25 *NS*, 10 Feb. 1912.
26 Author in conversation with George Knight (grandson of M.E. Knight), 29 Nov. 2013.

27 *DD*, 24 May 1913.
28 Peadar Livingstone, *The Monaghan story* (Enniskillen, 1980), p. 364.
29 Ernie O'Malley, *On another man's wound* (Dublin, 1979 [1936]), p. 24.
30 Senia Pašeta, *Before the revolution: nationalism, social change and Ireland's Catholic elite, 1879–1922* (Cork, 1999), pp 148, 153.
31 R.V. Comerford, *Ireland* (London, 2003), p. 42.
32 *DD*, 9 Oct. 1915.   33 McGarry, *O'Duffy*, p. 2.
34 O'Connor to Dillon, 18 Sept. 1908 (TCD, John Dillon papers, MS 8,771).
35 *DD*, 24 May 1913.
36 *Table showing by poor law union, the number of holdings, their size in statute acres, the number of holdings owned and tenanted, and the division of land in the year, 1913*, Cd. 7429, 1914, xcviii, p. 24.
37 See David Seth Jones, *Graziers, land reform and political conflict in Ireland* (Washington, 1995); Fergus Campbell, *Land and revolution: nationalist politics in the west of Ireland, 1891–1921* (Oxford, 2008).
38 Minutes of Monaghan County Council, 8 Jan. 1917 (MCM).
39 *DD*, 15 June 1912.   40 *DD*, 1 Feb. 1913.
41 Cumann Seanchais Mhuineacháin, *Cuimhneachain Mhuineacháin* (Monaghan, 1967), p. 8.
42 See for example, *DD*, 3, 10 Jan., 14 Feb. 1914.
43 Alvin Jackson, *Ireland, 1798–1998* (Oxford, 1999), p. 159.
44 See Seamus Mc Phillips, 'The Ancient Order of Hibernians in County Monaghan with particular reference to the parish of Aghabog from 1900 to 1933' (MA, Maynooth University, 1999).
45 *DD*, 25 Mar. 1916.   46 *DD*, 6 May 1916.
47 *DD*, 27 Jan. 1912, 8 Mar. 1913. The RIC also reported the health of the AOH and UIL.
48 Minute book of Killanny AOH (NAI, LOU 5/1).
49 Quoted in Seosamh Ó Dufaigh, 'Social and political comment in the Lenten pastorals of Bishop Patrick McKenna (1916–22)' in H.A. Jefferies (ed.), *History of the diocese of Clogher* (Dublin, 2005), p. 180.
50 John Privilege, *Michael Logue and the Catholic Church in Ireland, 1879–1925* (Manchester, 2009), p. 88.
51 CI Monaghan, Jan. 1916 (TNA, CO 904/99).
52 The average number of members was slightly higher at 2,555 but this was for only four of the counties as there were no individual membership returns for Longford; Michael Wheatley, *Nationalism and the Irish party: provincial Ireland, 1910–1916* (Oxford, 2005), p. 49.
53 Minute book of Killanny AOH (NAI, LOU 5/1).
54 *DD*, 30 Sept. 1916.   55 *DD*, 11 Apr. 1914.
56 *DD*, 20 Jan. 1912.   57 CI Monaghan, Jan. 1913 (TNA, CO 904/89).
58 http://www.hoganstand.com/monaghan/ArticleForm.aspx?ID=143664 (accessed 31 Mar. 2016).
59 Owen is the preferred version of his name used in this book, as it is the version used by him to sign his name.
60 CI Monaghan, Jan. 1916 (TNA, CO 904/99).
61 *DD*, 3 June 1916.
62 Dónal McAnallen, 'The radicalization of the Gaelic Athletic Association in Ulster, 1912–1923: the role of Owen O'Duffy', *International Journal of the History of Sport*, 31:7 (2014), 706.
63 Quoted in Paul Murray, *The Irish Boundary Commission and its origins, 1886–1925* (Dublin, 2011), p. 189.
64 Ó Dúfaigh, 'The Lenten pastorals of Bishop Patrick McKenna (1916–22)', p. 197.

65 Quoted in Proinsias Ó Muirgheasa & Peadar Ó Casaide, *A man of Farney: a short story of the life of Henry Morris* (Carrickmacross, 1974), p. 10.
66 Livingstone, *Monaghan story*, p. 359. 67 Quoted in McGarry, *O'Duffy*, p. 9.
68 *DD*, 25 Jan. 1915 69 CI Monaghan, Jan. 1916 (TNA, CO 904/99).
70 *DD*, 15 Apr. 1916.
71 Owen O'Duffy, 'Reminiscences', chapter 6, pp 1, 5 (NLI, Eoin O'Duffy papers, MS 48,300/2).
72 Ibid., p. 7.
73 *NS*, 20 July 1912; Inspector General's confidential monthly report, July 1913 (TNA, CO 904/90).
74 *FJ*, 31 July 1908.
75 This is discernible from his correspondence with the Madden family; see PRONI, Madden papers, D3465/3/37/62.
76 *Minutes of evidence of the Royal Commission on the Land Law (Ireland) Act, 1881, and the purchase of Land (Ireland) Act, 1885* [C4969-I], HC 1887, xxvi. 25, p. 170.
77 Shane Leslie memoirs (NLI, Leslie papers, MS 22,885).
78 See Seymour Leslie, *Of Glaslough in the kingdom of Oriel and of the noted men who have dwelt there* (Glaslough, 1913).
79 This case study was carried out by cross referencing the 1911 household schedule returns of fifty-one townlands with the valuation books in the Valuation Office and used originally in Terence Dooley, 'Protestant politics and society in County Monaghan, 1911–26' (MA, St Patrick's College, Maynooth, 1986), pp 6–7; for similar conclusions regarding the post-Famine period see Duffy, 'Population and landholding in County Monaghan', pp 97–9.
80 *NS*, 8 Jan. 1910. 81 *NS*, 16 July 1910. 82 *NS*, 30 Sept. 1911.

CHAPTER TWO *Home rulers and rebels: 1912–14*

1 See exhibition booklet by Natasha Martin & Stuart McConkey, *The Ulster Covenant and the people of Monaghan* (2013), p. 11.
2 For a stimulating piece on the Covenant and 1916 Proclamation, see Liam Kennedy, *Unhappy the land: the most oppressed people ever, the Irish?* (Sallins, 2016), pp 168–86.
3 Martin & McConkey, *Ulster Covenant*, p. 8.
4 Lord Rossmore, *Things I can tell* (London, 1912), p. 244.
5 According to David Fitzpatrick, the signing rates of non-Catholic males for the Covenant was just over 83 per cent and over 80 per cent for the Women's Declaration; David Fitzpatrick, *Descendancy: Irish Protestant histories since 1795* (Cambridge, 2014), p. 243.
6 *NS*, 9 Aug. 1913. 7 *NS*, 20 July 1912. 8 *DD*, 20 July 1912.
9 CI Monaghan, Aug. 1912 (TNA, CO 904/87).
10 CI Monaghan, July 1912 (ibid.).
11 Michael Laffan, *The partition of Ireland, 1911–1925* (Dublin, 1983), p. 33.
12 Gerald Madden to *Dundalk Democrat*, [?] Oct. 1913; *DD*, 1 Nov. 1913.
13 *NS*, 9 May 1914.
14 CI Monaghan, July 1913 (TNA, CO 904/90); CI Monaghan, Oct. 1912 (TNA, CO 904/88).
15 CI Monaghan, Jan. 1916 (TNA, CO 904/99); Tim Wilson, 'The strange death of Loyalist Monaghan, 1912–1921' in Senia Pašeta (ed.), *Uncertain futures: essays about the Irish past for Roy Foster* (Oxford, 2016), p. 176; Brendan Mac Giolla Choille (ed.), *Intelligence notes, 1913–16* (Dublin, 1966), pp 35, 40.
16 Fergal McCluskey, *Tyrone: the Irish revolution, 1912–23* (Dublin, 2014), pp 18, 29.

17 Gerald Madden to Jack [J.C.W.], 23 Dec. 1913 (PRONI, Madden papers, D3465/J/37/54).
18 Gerald Madden to Jack, 25 June 1913 (ibid., D3465/J/37/48).
19 CI Monaghan, Jan. 1913 (TNA, CO 904/89).
20 *Belfast Newsletter*, 16 Apr. 1914.
21 Madden to Tyacke, 24 Feb. 1914 (PRONI, Madden papers, D3465/J/37/62).
22 http://www.photoalbumofireland.com/george-knight-county-monaghan/ (accessed 13 Apr. 2016).
23 Ibid. 24 Ibid.
25 Stack to J.C.W. Madden, 12 May [1914?] (PRONI, Madden papers, D3465/J/37/78).
26 McCluskey, *Tyrone*, p. 29.
27 Talk given by Quincy Doogan, Monaghan County Museum, 12 May 2013.
28 For comparisons, see Timothy Bowman, *Carson's army, the Ulster Volunteer Force, 1910–22* (Manchester, 2007), pp 54–7.
29 G. Hacket Pain to the commander, Monaghan Regiment, 7 Feb. 1914 (PRONI, Madden papers, D3465/J/37/58).
30 Ibid.
31 Col. F.H. Crawford to Craig, 10 Dec. 1936 (PRONI, Crawford papers, D640/30/2).
32 CI Monaghan, May 1914 (TNA, CO 904/93).
33 *DD*, 2 May 1914; the wider cynicism of nationalist Ulster can be seen in the postcard in the plate section of this book.
34 Ibid.
35 UVF return of arms for month ended 28 Feb. 1917 (TNA, CO 904, part vi).
36 *DD*, 18 July 1914. 37 Ibid. 38 *NS*, 26 July 1913.
39 *NS*, 13 May 1911. 40 *NS*, 22 Nov. 1913. 41 *NS*, 1 Aug. 1914.
42 Ibid.
43 CI Monaghan, Apr. 1914 (TNA, CO 904/93).
44 Quoted in Agnes O'Farrelly (ed.), *Leabhar an tAthar Eoghan: the O'Growney memorial volume* (Dublin, 1904), pp 60, 80–2, 102.
45 Quoted in ibid., p. 137.
46 http://ansionnachfionn.com/2015/06/08/the-battle-of-pettigo-and-belleek-may-to-june-1922/ (accessed 29 Mar. 2016).
47 Earnán de Blaghd, *Slán le hUltaibh* (Dublin, 1971 ed.), pp 167–74.
48 J.J. O'Connell, typescript 'History of Irish Volunteers' (NLI, Bulmer Hobson papers, MS 13,168).
49 De Blaghd, *Slán le hUltaibh*, p. 167.
50 'To the people of Ematris', n.d. (in author's possession).
51 John McGahey (BMH, WS 740), pp 1–2.
52 Livingstone, *Monaghan story*, p. 368. 53 *DD*, 24 Jan. 1914.
54 Ibid. 55 Ibid., 14 Mar. 1914. 56 Ibid.
57 Eddie Kelly (MCM, Marron papers).
58 CI Monaghan, May 1914 (TNA, CO 904/93).
59 *DD*, 9 May 1914. 60 *DD*. 61 Ibid.
62 Ibid. 63 CI Monaghan, May 1914 (TNA, CO 904/93).
64 Ibid. 65 CI Monaghan, May, June 1914 (TNA, CO 904/93).
66 CI Monaghan, July 1914 (TNA, CO 904/93).
67 Quoted in Éamon Phoenix, 'Partition, the Catholic Church and the diocese of Clogher, c.1912–1928' in Jefferies (ed.), *Clogher*, p. 207.
68 *NS*, 4 Mar. 1914. 69 *IT*, 18 Feb. 1914.
70 Phoenix, 'Partition', p. 208. 71 *NS*, 28 Mar. 1914.

72 Alvin Jackson, *Home rule: an Irish history, 1800–2000* (Oxford, 2003), pp 129–31.
73 *Anglo-Celt (AC)*, 28 Mar. 1914.
74 CI Monaghan, May 1914 (TNA, CO 904/93).
75 *DD*, 23 May 1914.
76 Quoted in A.T.Q. Stewart, *The Ulster crisis* (London, 1967), p. 218.
77 Quoted in Patrick Buckland, *Irish unionism ii: Ulster unionism and the origins of Northern Ireland, 1885–1922* (Dublin, 1973), p. 100.
78 Ibid., p. 99.   79 *DD*, 25 July 1914.   80 *DD*, 1 Aug. 1914.
81 *DD*; CI Monaghan, July 1914 (TNA, CO 904/94).
82 CI Monaghan, Aug. 1914 (ibid.).   83 Ibid.

CHAPTER THREE *'It's a great war for the farmer'*

1 Kavanagh, *Green fool*, p. 57.   2 *DD*, 4 July 1914.
3 Ibid., 8 Aug. 1914.   4 Quoted in Jackson, *Home rule*, p. 144.
5 *DD*, 8 Aug. 1914.   6 Ibid.
7 Quoted in *DD*, 3 Oct. 1914.   8 CI Monaghan, Sept. 1914 (TNA, CO 904/94).
9 Ibid.
10 CI Monaghan, Apr. 1915 (TNA, CO 904/96); *DD*, 5 June 1916.
11 *DD*, 3 Oct. 1914.   12 Quoted in Jackson, *Home rule*, p. 145.
13 CI Monaghan, Sept. 1914 (TNA, CO 904/94); on similar 'excuses' being preferred elsewhere see Daithí Ó Corráin, '"A most public spirited and unselfish man": the career and contribution of Colonel Maurice Moore, 1854–1939', *Studia Hibernica*, 40 (2014), 98.
14 Joseph McKenna (MCM, Marron papers).
15 CI Monaghan, Nov. 1914 (TNA, CO 904/95).   16 Ibid.
17 *DD*, 3 Oct. 1914.
18 List of clergymen who came under notice owing to their disloyal language and conduct (NAI, Crime special branch reports, 1913–20).
19 CI Monaghan, Aug. 1914 (TNA, CO 904/94).   20 Ibid.
21 *NS*, 3 Oct. 1914.   22 *NS*, 17 June 1916.   23 *NS*, 22, 29 July 1916.
24 Timothy Bowman, 'The Ulster Volunteer Force and the formation of the 36th (Ulster) Division', *IHS*, 32:128 (Nov. 2001), 503.
25 'Return of Recruits who have joined the Army between 15th December 1914 and 15th December 1915', Intelligence Notes 1915, p. 55 (TNA, CO 903/19); I am grateful to Dr Daithí Ó Corráin for these statistics.
26 McCluskey, *Tyrone*, p. 53.   27 *DD*, 30 Jan. 1915.
28 *NS*, 30 Jan. 1915.   29 *NS*, 29 May 1915.
30 CI Monaghan, Feb. 1915 (TNA, CO 904/96).
31 CI Monaghan, Oct. 1917 (TNA, CO 904/104).
32 Donal Hall, *The unreturned army: County Louth dead in the Great War, 1914–1918* (Dundalk, 2005), p. 15.
33 Cullen, *Book of honour for Co. Monaghan*.
34 Shane Leslie memoirs (NLI, Leslie papers, MS 22,885).
35 See Ian d'Alton, ' "Lay spring flowers on our boy's grave": Norman Leslie's short war' in Terence Dooley and Christopher Ridgway (eds), *The country house and the Great War: Irish and British experiences* (Dublin, 2016), pp 76–86.
36 *NS*, 24 Aug. 1918.   37 *NS*, 3 June 1916.   38 *NS*, 19 Aug. 1916.
39 *DD*, 29 Aug. 1916.   40 Minutes of MCC, 1 Oct. 1915 (MCM, MCC minute books).
41 *NS*, 5 June 1915.   42 *NS*, 11 Dec. 1915.

43 CI Monaghan, Aug. 1915 (TNA, CO 904/97); Nov. 1915 (TNA, CO 904/98); Oct. 1916 (TNA, CO 904/101).
44 David Fitzpatrick, *Politics and Irish life, 1913–1921: provincial experiences of war and revolution* (Cork, 1998, 2nd ed.), pp 68–9.
45 See Chapter 5.
46 J.M. Wilson to *Irish Times*, Oct. 1916 (PRONI, Wilson papers, D989/A/8/7/1).
47 *NS*, 30 Jan. 1915; see also chapter 6.
48 CI Monaghan, Sept. 1914 (TNA, CO 904/94).
49 CI Monaghan, Nov. 1914 (TNA, CO 904/95).   50 *NS*, 26 Aug. 1916.
51 CI Monaghan, Sept. 1916 (TNA, CO 904/101).   52 *NS*, 16 Sept. 1916.
53 Ibid.   54 Ibid.   55 *NS*, 15 July 1916.
56 *DD*, 18 Dec. 1915.   57 *DD*, 8 July 1916.   58 *DD*, 11 Nov. 1916.
59 Hughes died in 1942, an impoverished bachelor, who had brought controversy upon himself in 1924 when he was prosecuted for possession of poteen; *AC*, 10 Jan. 1942.
60 *DD*, 22 Apr. 1916.   61 *DD*, 29 Aug., 3 Oct. 1914.
62 Kavanagh, *Green fool*, pp 58, 65; see also Peter Kavanagh, *Beyond affection: autobiography of Peter Kavanagh* (New York, 1977), p. 1.
63 *DD*, 11 July 1914, 30 Mar. 1918.   64 Kavanagh, *Green fool*, pp 63–4.
65 CI Monaghan, Sept. 1914 (TNA, CO 904/94), Nov. 1914 (TNA, CO 904/95), Dec. 1914 (TNA CO 904/95), Jan. 1915 (TNA, CO 904/96), May 1915 (TNA, CO 904/97), Nov. 1915 (TNA, CO 904/98).
66 *DD*, 8 Jan. 1916.   67 Ibid.   68 *DD*, 4 Mar. 1916.
69 *DD*, 7 Nov. 1914.   70 *DD*, 13 Jan. 1917.
71 CI Monaghan, Jan. 1915 (TNA, CO 904/96).   72 *DD*, 4 Mar. 1916.
73 Quoted in *DD*, 11 Mar. 1916.
74 CI Monaghan, Feb. 1915 (TNA, CO 904/96).   75 *DD*, 6 Nov. 1915.
76 *DD*, 29 Jan. 1916.   77 Ibid.   78 Ibid.
79 *DD*, 22 Apr. 1916.   80 Livingstone, *Monaghan story*, p. 371.
81 http://www.census.nationalarchives.ie/reels/nai000119513/ (accessed 13 Dec. 2016).
82 *NS*, 6 May 1916.   83 Quoted in *DD*, 15 Jan. 1916.
84 *NS*, 19 Sept. 1914.

CHAPTER FOUR   '*The Dublin Insurrection of 1916 came and went without a ripple*'

1 Peter Kavanagh (ed.), *Patrick Kavanagh: man and poet* (Newbridge & Maine, 1987), p. 28.
2 Proclamation of the Irish Republic 1916.   3 *DD*, 13 Nov. 1915.
4 Ibid.   5 *Cuimhneacháin Mhuineacháin*, pp 18–19.
6 Ibid.   7 My thanks to Kitty McMahon for this information.
8 *DD*, 25 Mar. 1915.
9 P.V. Hoey, 'Farney in the fight for Irish freedom' (MS copy in author's possession).
10 *DD*, 13 Nov. 1915.   11 Ibid.; CI Monaghan, Nov. 1915 (TNA, CO 904/98).
12 *DD*, 13 Nov. 1915.   13 Ibid.   14 *DD*, 18 Dec. 1915.
15 Pašeta, *Before the revolution*, p. 1.   16 *DD*, 14 Sept. 1918.
17 *DD*, 8 Jan. 1916.   18 See Dooley, *Bernard O'Rourke*, pp 29–46.
19 CI Monaghan, Jan. 1915 (TNA, CO 904/96); *DD*, 27 Feb., 13 Mar., 27 Mar., 8 May 1915.
20 *DD*, 27 Feb. 1915.   21 *DD*, 27 Mar. 1915.
22 *DD*, 3 Apr. 1915.   23 Charlie Duffy (MCM, Marron papers).
24 *DD*, 3 Apr. 1915.

25 Ibid., Feb. 1916; see also Ernest Blythe to Fr Laurence Marron, 26 Jan. 1966 (MCM, Marron papers).
26 CI Monaghan, Nov. 1914 (TNA, CO 904/95).
27 Antoinette Quinn, *Patrick Kavanagh: a biography* (Dublin, 2001), p. 27.
28 Frank Burke (BMH, WS 105), p. 2.
29 My thanks to Brian Crowley of the OPW for alerting me to this fact.
30 Francis Tummons (MCM, Marron papers). 31 *NS*, 12 Nov. 2015.
32 *DD*, 27 Nov. 1915. 33 Ibid. 34 Ibid.
35 *DD*, 13 Nov., 4 Dec., 11 Dec. 1915. 36 *DD*, 8 Jan. 1916.
37 *DD*, 25 Mar. 1916.
38 Editor of *DD*; quoted in McGarry, *O'Duffy*, p. 21.
39 Thomas Conlon to B.J. Browne, 27 Oct. 1926 (TNA, CO 762/7/5, Irish Grants Committee, Lieutenant Bernard J. Browne, County Monaghan, No. 40).
40 On the MacMahons, see Hugh MacMahon, *A fist to the black-blooded: the MacMahons of Coas* (Dublin, 2015).
41 CI Monaghan, May 1916 (TNA, CO 904/100).
42 John McGahey (BMH, WS 740), p. 2.
43 Frank Marron (MCM, Marron papers); *Cuimhneacháin Mhuineacháin*, p. 29.
44 Kavanagh (ed.), *Patrick Kavanagh: man and poet*, p. 28.
45 *Chuimhneacháin Mhuineacháin*, p. 20. 46 Francis Tummons (BMH, WS 820), p. 1.
47 *DD*, 6 May 1916. 48 Ibid. 49 Ibid.
50 *NS*, 15 Dec. 1916. 51 *IT*, 10 June 1916; McRoe, 'J.C.R. Lardner', p. 229.
52 Ibid. 53 Ibid.
54 Minutes, 12 May 1916 (MCM, Monaghan County Council minute book).
55 *NS*, 6 May 1916. 56 Ibid. 57 Ibid.
58 Ibid. 59 *IT*, 18 May 1916.
60 On the impact of imprisonment see William Murphy, *Political imprisonment and the Irish, 1912–1921* (Oxford, 2014). The eight suspects were Proinnsias de Búrca, Willie Loughran, P.J. O'Daly, James O'Brien, Tommy Nolan, Tom Martin, Paddy Reilly and Tom Ward. De Búrca and Loughran were detained in Frongoch until December and the others released in July; Livingstone, *Monaghan story*, p. 373.
61 *DD*, 23 Dec. 1916. 62 *DD*, 10 Mar. 1917.

CHAPTER FIVE '*The Sinn Féin party is gaining strength in all parts*', 1917–18

1 CI Monaghan, June 1917 (TNA, CO 904/103). 2 *DD*, 13 May 1916.
3 *DD*, 14 Oct. 1916. 4 *DD*, 17 Apr. 1917.
5 Tom Garvin, *The evolution of Irish nationalist politics* (Dublin, 2005), p. 98.
6 For a fuller discussion, see Dooley, *Inniskeen*, pp 38–46.
7 Clare O'Rourke to Fr Stephen, 18 May 1916 (UCDA, O'Rourke papers, P117/26).
8 Ibid., n.d., P117/27. 9 *DD*, 17 June 1916.
10 *Dundalk Examiner*, 3 June 1916. 11 Ibid.
12 Clare O'Rourke to Fr Stephen, 18 May 1916 (UCDA, O'Rourke papers, P117/26); *DD*, 20 May 1916.
13 *Dundalk Examiner*, 3 June 1916. 14 *DD*, 3 June 1916.
15 *DD*, 7 Apr. 1917; *Cuimhneacháin Mhuineacháin*, p. 32. 16 *DD*, 12 Apr. 1917.
17 *DD*, 21 Apr. 1917. 18 *DD*, 9 June 1917.
19 *DD*, 28 Oct. 1916; CI Monaghan, Sept. 1919 (TNA, CO 904/110).

20 Jackson, *Home rule*, p. 172.
21 *DD*, 10 June 1916.
22 *NS*, 17 June 1916.
23 *Ulster and home rule: no partition of Ulster* (1920) (PRONI, D1545/8).
24 'Report of Major Saunderson', 1917 (PRONI, J.M. Wilson papers, D989/A/8/7/1).
25 Ibid.; Somerset Saunderson to William Martin, 10 July 1916, quoted in *NS*, 22 July 1916.
26 Carson to William Martin, 17 July 1916, quoted in *NS*, 22 July 1916.
27 Hugh de Fellenberg Montgomery to Edward Carson, 11 June 1916 (PRONI, Montgomery papers, D627/429/30).
28 Ibid., 20 July 1918.
29 Edith Wheeler to Lady Londonderry, 8 July 1916 (PRONI, Theresa Lady Londonderry papers, D2846/1/8/37).
30 *NS*, 20 July 1918.
31 Quoted in Patrick Buckland, *James Craig* (Dublin, 1980), p. 34.
32 Jackson, *Home rule*, p. 171; Laffan, *Resurrection of Ireland*, p. 61.
33 Jackson, *Home rule*, p. 185.
34 *Boston Post*, 2 Apr. 1919.
35 McGarry, *O'Duffy*, pp 1–5.
36 James Murnane & Peadar Murnane, *At the ford of the birches: the history of Ballybay, its people and vicinity* (Monaghan, 1999), p. 436.
37 McGarry, *O'Duffy*, p. 7.
38 Long, 'Eoin O'Duffy', *DIB*.
39 *DD*, 26 Feb. 1916.
40 Ibid.
41 *NS*, 11 May 1912.
42 *DD*, 25 Mar. 1916.
43 Cormac Moore, 'Luke O'Toole: servant of the GAA' in Gearóid Ó Tuathaigh (ed.), *The GAA and revolution in Ireland, 1913–23* (Cork, 2015), p. 54.
44 Quoted in McGarry, *O'Duffy*, p. 26.
45 McAnallen, 'Role of Owen O'Duffy', 711.
46 McGarry, *O'Duffy*, p. 27.
47 *DD*, 20 Feb. 1915; quoted in McGarry, *O'Duffy*, p. 14.
48 CI Monaghan, June 1917 (TNA, CO 904/103).
49 Francis Tummons (BMH, WS 820), p. 8.
50 CI Monaghan, June 1918 (TNA, CO 904/106); *DD*, 8 June 1918.
51 Laffan, *Resurrection of Ireland*, pp 142–3.
52 CI Monaghan, June 1918 (TNA, CO 904/106).
53 Andrew McGuire & David Hassan, 'Cultural nationalism, Gaelic Sunday and the Gaelic Athletic Association in early twentieth century Ireland', *International Journal of the History of Sport*, 29:6 (2012), 917–19; http://www.gaa.ie/the-gaa/history/1884–1945 (accessed 15 May 2016).
54 CI Monaghan, Feb. 1917 (TNA, CO 904/102).
55 CI Monaghan, Aug. 1918 (TNA, CO 904/106).
56 Ibid.
57 Owen O'Duffy to 'Whom it may concern, 30 Oct. 1940; IRA military pension application of Anne Jane McEntee (nee Farmer)', http://mspcsearch.militaryarchives.ie/docs/files//PDF_Pensions/R4/MSP34REF47635McENTEEANNEJANE/WMSP34REF47635McENTEEANNEJANE.pdf (accessed 8 Dec. 2016).
58 My thanks to Maeve Mullan for this information; see http://mspcsearch.militaryarchives.ie/docs/files//PDF_Membership/9/MA-MSPC-CMB-58.pdf (accessed 18 Dec. 2016).
59 Ibid., Sept. 1918 (TNA, CO904/107).
60 McGarry, *O'Duffy*, p. 26.
61 CI Monaghan, Sept. 1917 (TNA, CO 904/104).
62 Ibid.
63 CI Monaghan, Nov. 1917 (TNA, CO 904/104).
64 *DD*, 8 Sept. 1917.
65 Quoted in *DD*, 13 Oct. 1917.
66 D.C. Rushe to Shane Leslie, 30 Apr. 1918 (Clogher Historical Society, DCR 18/19).

67 NS, 25 May 1918.   68 DD, 9 Dec. 1916.
69 Minutes, 15 Apr. 1918 (MCM, Monaghan County Council minute book).
70 Oliver Rafferty, Catholicism in Ulster, 1603–1983: an interpretative history (London, 1994), pp 193–4.
71 DD, 3 Nov. 1917.   72 CI Monaghan, Apr. 1918 (TNA, CO 904/105).
73 Ibid.   74 Ibid.
75 'Solemn covenant to resist conscription', signed at Castleblayney, 21 Apr. 1918 (NLI, MS 3,310).
76 Charles Townshend, Political violence in Ireland (Oxford, 1983), p. 280.
77 CI Monaghan, Sept. 1917 (TNA, CO 904/104), Dec. 1918 (TNA, CO 904/107).
78 Laffan, Resurrection of Ireland, p. 187.
79 Ó Dúfaigh, 'Patrick McKenna', p. 185.
80 McCluskey, Tyrone, pp 45–6; also Patrick McCartan (BMH, WS 766), p. 32.
81 DD, 3 Nov. 1917; see also Fr Eugene Coyle (BMH, WS 325), pp 7–8.
82 James McKenna (MCM, Marron papers).
83 Charlie Duffy (MCM, Marron papers).   84 Ibid., 28 July 1917.
85 Emigration statistics of Ireland, 1914 [Cd 7313], lxix, 1001.
86 Emigration statistics of Ireland, 1915 [Cd 7883], lxxx, 319.   87 NS, 11 May 1912.
88 Patrick Long, 'Eoin O'Duffy', DIB.
89 CI Monaghan, Jan. 1918 (TNA, CO 904/105).   90 Ibid.
91 CI Monaghan, Mar. 1919 (TNA, CO 904/108).
92 Ibid., Jan. 1918 & Mar. 1918 (TNA, CO 904/105); Mar. 1919 (TNA, CO 904/108), May 1919 & June 1919 (TNA, CO 904/109); Oct. 1919 (TNA, CO 904/110).
93 DD, 3 Feb. 1917.
94 CI Monaghan, Apr. 1915 (TNA, CO 904/96); DD, 5 Feb. 1916.
95 DD, 5 June 1916.
96 CI Monaghan, Sept. 1916 (TNA, CO 904/101), ibid., Mar. 1917 (TNA, CO 904/102).
97 CI Monaghan, Sept. 1917 (TNA, CO 904/104); Kavanagh, Green fool, pp 104–5.
98 DD, 9 Sept. 1916.
99 See Terence Dooley & Tony McCarthy, 'The 1923 Land Act: some new perspectives' in Mel Farrell et al. (eds), A formative decade: Ireland in the 1920s (Dublin, 2015), pp 132–56.
100 Terence Dooley, 'IRA veterans and land division in independent Ireland, 1923–48' in Fearghal McGarry (ed.), Republicanism in modern Ireland (Dublin, 2003), pp 86–107; Townshend, Political violence in Ireland, p. 339.
101 DD, 13 Jan. 1917.
102 The term 'grazier', as is generally understood, was defined by Monaghan County Council as referring to holders of over fifty acres; Minutes, 8 Jan. 1917 (MCM, Monaghan County Council minute book).
103 DD, 24 Feb. 1917.   104 Ibid., 3 June 1916.
105 CI Monaghan, June 1917 (TNA, CO 904/103).
106 Minute book of Killanny AOH (NAI, LOU 5/1).
107 CI Monaghan, June 1917 (TNA, CO 904/103).
108 McGarry, O'Duffy, p. 41; see also chapter 6.   109 DD, 15 Sept. 1917.
110 DD, 14 Sept. 1918.
111 http://www.rte.ie/archives/exhibitions/920-first-dail-eireann-1919/139408-an-chead-dail-1919/ (accessed 8 Apr. 2016); see also De Blaghd, Slán le hUltaibh.
112 Kavanagh, Green fool, pp 105–6; see also DD, 12 Dec. 1918.
113 Tom Carragher (MCM, Marron papers); DD, 21 Dec., 4 Jan 1918.
114 CI Monaghan, Dec. 1918 (TNA, CO 904/107).

115 http://www.ark.ac.uk/elections/h1918.htm (accessed 19 Dec. 2016); on AOH, see chapter 9.
116 *DD*, 4 Jan. 1919.
117 *DD*, 13, 27 Oct. 1917.
118 *DD*, 7 Sept. 1918, 4 Jan. 1919.
119 Tom Carragher (MCM, Marron papers).
120 McGarry, *O'Duffy*, p. 23.
121 *DD*, 7 Sept. 1918, 4 Jan. 1919.
122 'Life of Thomas Toal'.
123 Ó Dúfaigh, 'Patrick McKenna', p. 202.

CHAPTER SIX *'Private vengeance exacted its toll over cover of civil turmoil', 1919–21*

1 *DD*, 31 Dec. 1921.
2 Ibid.
3 Peter Hart, *The IRA at war, 1916–1923* (Oxford, 2003), p. 39.
4 CI Monaghan, Jan. 1919 (TNA, CO 904/108).
5 CI Monaghan, Feb. 1919 (ibid.).
6 CI Monaghan, Dec. 1918 (TNA, Co 904/107).
7 Laffan, *Resurrection of Ireland*, p. 251.
8 Report of the district inspector of Carrickmacross, 12 June 1920 (TNA, CO 904/12/347).
9 Lists of subscriptions collected by Bernard O'Rourke for Dáil Éireann loan in south Monaghan, 1919–20 (UCDA, O'Rourke papers, P117/67).
10 McCluskey, *Tyrone*, p. 79.
11 Bernard O'Rourke to Clare O'Rourke, 25 Oct. 1920 (UCDA, O'Rourke papers, P117/65).
12 CI Monaghan, Mar. 1919 (TNA, CO 904/108).
13 *DD*, 3 Jan. 1920.
14 *DD*, 17 Jan. 1920.
15 *DD*, 8 May 1920.
16 Quoted in *DD*, 15 May 1920.
17 *DD*, 19 June 1920.
18 James McKenna (MCM, Marron papers).
19 *DD*, 19 June 1920.
20 Untitled newspaper clipping (NLI, O'Duffy papers, MS 48,280/2).
21 *DD*, 15 May 1920.
22 Untitled newspaper clipping (NLI, O'Duffy papers, MS 48,280/2).
23 *DD*, 19 June 1920.
24 http://mspcsearch.militaryarchives.ie/docs/files//PDF_Membership/8/RO%2060%20–%20611/MA-MSPC-RO-449.pdf (accessed 14 Dec. 2016).
25 McAnallen, 'Role of Owen O'Duffy', p. 719.
26 O'Duffy, 'Days', p. 176.
27 Pension application on behalf of Andrew Sherry made by Mrs Sarah Sherry, Glaslough, 31 July 1924 (IMA, Military Service Pension Applications, 3D294); Pension application on behalf of James Marron, Carrickmacross, 5 Dec. 1933 (IMA, Military Service Pension Applications, DP3019).
28 See chapter 5.
29 They are the subject of Hugh MacMahon, *A fist to the black-blooded: the MacMahons of Coas* (n.p., 2015); also Murnane, *Ford of the birches*, p. 436; Brian MacMahon (MCM, Marron papers); http://www.theeasterrising.eu/150CumannNamBan/CumannnamBan.htm (accessed 25 May 2016).
30 Brian MacMahon (MCM, Marron papers)
31 James Hackett (BMH, WS 228), p. 115.
32 *DD*, 3 Jan. 1920.
33 Jail diary of Owen O'Duffy (NLI, O'Duffy papers, MS 48,280/1).
34 P.V. Hoey (BMH, WS 530), p. 4.
35 On his men's attitudes towards Hogan see chapter 9.
36 *DD*, 27 Mar. 1920.
37 Quoted in Michael Hopkinson, *Green against green: the Irish Civil War* (Dublin, 1988), p. 45.
38 This will become possible in the future as a result of a proposed prosopographical database in collaboration between the author and Monaghan County Museum.

39 Jim Sullivan (BMH, WS 518), p. 4. 40 Pat McDonnell (MCM, Marron papers).
41 Brian MacMahon (MCM, Marron papers). 42 McGarry, *O'Duffy*, p. 44.
43 Francis Tummons (BMH, WS 820), p. 2.
44 James Mulligan (MCM, Marron papers). 45 *NS*, 2 July 2015.
46 Thomas Brennan to Dear Sister [Ellie], 3 Dec. 1921; to mother and sister, 22 Sept. 1921 (MCM, Thomas Brennan papers, uncatalogued).
47 *DD*, 21 Jan. 1922. 48 Patrick Woods (MCM, Marron papers).
49 Seamus McKenna (MCM, Marron papers).
50 Phil Marron to 'My Dear Mother', 9 Apr. 1920 (MCM, Marron papers).
51 *DD*, 23 July 1921. 52 James McKenna (MCM, Marron papers).
53 Thomas Donnelly (BMH, WS 519), p. 3.
54 K. Gilsenan (MCM, Marron papers).
55 Ó Dúfaigh, 'Patrick McKenna', p. 177.
56 Joe McCarville (MCM, Marron papers).
57 James McKenna (MCM, Marron papers).
58 P.V. Hoey (BMH, WS 530), p. 5; Thomas Donnelly (BMH, WS 519), p. 3; Francis Tummon (BMH, WS 820), pp 21–2.
59 O'Malley, *On another man's wound*, p. 126.
60 Joost Augusteijn, *From public defiance to guerrilla warfare: the experience of ordinary volunteers in the Irish War of Independence, 1916–1921* (Dublin, 1996), p. 142.
61 Capt [?O'Connor] to Col. O'Higgins, quartermaster, Collins Barracks, 1 Feb. 1923 (in private possession). The three young men executed – James Melia, Joseph Ferguson and Thomas Lennon – all from Dundalk, had been found guilty of possession of arms. Melia and Lennon had hijacked Bernard O'Rourke's car on 7 January; *IT*, 23 Jan. 1923. My thanks to Donal Hall for this information.
62 Joe McCarville (MCM, Marron papers).
63 James Mulligan (MCM, Marron papers).
64 Eoin O'Duffy to secretary, Military Service Pensions Board, 4 Aug. 1942 (MCM, Marron papers).
65 James Mulligan (MCM, Marron papers).
66 *AC*, 22 Dec. 1967. 67 MacMahon, *A fist to the black-blooded*, p. 127.
68 See, for example, CI Monaghan, Aug. 1919 (TNA, CO 904/109).
69 Quoted in Fitzpatrick, *Politics & Irish life*, p. 10. 70 *DD*, 6 Sept. 1919.
71 Weekly summaries of outrages against police and returns of recruitment and retirement, 17 Apr., 23 May, 27 June, 8 Aug., 3 Oct. 1920 (TNA, CO 904/149).
72 Laffan, *Resurrection of Ireland*, p. 275.
73 Quoted in Augusteijn, *From public defiance*, p. 207.
74 CI Monaghan, Dec. 1919 (TNA, CO 904/110).
75 *DD*, 21 Feb. 1921; Jim Sullivan (BMH, WS 518), pp 5–6.
76 *DD*, 21 Feb. 1920.
77 Ibid.; statements of James McKenna and Paddy Mohan (MCM, Marron papers).
78 McGarry, *O'Duffy*, p. 42. 79 John McGahey (BMH, WS 740), p. 5.
80 Ibid. 81 Joseph E. McKenna (BMH, WS 575), p. 2.
82 Eugene Sherry (BMH, WS 576), p. 2.
83 *DD*, 2 Apr. 1921; McGarry, *O'Duffy*, p. 54.
84 John McGahey (BMH, WS 740), p. 7.
85 McGarry, *O'Duffy*, p 54. 86 *NS*, 17 July 1920.
87 *NS*, 24 Sept. 1920.
88 Letter signed 'Drum Town Guard' to editor *NS*, 20 Sept. 1920; *NS*, 24 Sept. 1920.
89 *NS*, 1 Oct. 1920.

90 *NS*, 15, 22 Oct. 1920; *DD*, 23 Oct. 1920; James Sullivan (BMH, WS 518), p. 8; Joseph McKenna (BMH, WS 575), p. 3.
91 Statements of Brian MacMahon, Paddy McMahon (MCM, Marron papers).
92 Peter Woods (MCM, Marron papers).
93 Buckland, *Irish unionism ii*, p. 161.
94 Conn Ward (MCM, Marron papers); see also O'Duffy, ch. 5, p. 3.
95 McGarry, *O'Duffy*, p. 58. 96 *DD*, 3 Jan. 1920.
97 Peadar Ó Casaide (ed.), 'Some snippets from a notebook kept by Wm Daly, UDC, publican, Main Street, entry for 17 June 1921', *Macalla*, 3:4 (Winter, 1978), 22.
98 Ibid., pp 22–3. 99 *DD*, 19 Feb. 1921.
100 John McGahey (MCM, Marron papers); Murnane, *Ford of the birches*, p. 425; *NS*, 7 Jan. 1921.
101 Court of inquiry in lieu of inquest – Constable Sidney George (TNA, WO 35/147B/11).
102 Philip Marron (BMH, WS 657), p. 16; *NS*, 28 Jan. 1921.
103 *DD*, 12 Feb. 1921. 104 Ibid.
105 David Nesbitt, *Full circle: a story of Ballybay Presbyterians* (Ballybay, 1999), p. 125.
106 Quoted in ibid.
107 Copy of RIC report, Co. Monaghan, 1921 (PRONI, Madden papers, D3465/J/37/ 139/3).
108 Ó Casaide (ed.), 'Some snippets from a notebook kept by Wm Daly', 30.
109 Ibid., 30–1.
110 Tom Carragher (BMH, WS 681), pp 4–5; *DD*, 2 July 1921; *Armagh Guardian*, 8 July 1921.
111 Phil Marron to Mrs Marron n.d. (MCM, Marron papers).
112 Patrick McMeel (BMH, WS 520), p. 4.
113 CI Monaghan, Aug. 1919 (TNA, CO 904/109). 114 *DD*, 20 Mar. 1920.
115 McPhillips, 'AOH in County Monaghan', p. 106.
116 Copy of RIC report, Co. Monaghan, 1921 (PRONI, Madden papers, D3465/J/37/139/3).
117 *NS*, 11, 18 Mar., 15 Apr. 1921; *AC*, 23 Apr. 1921. 118 *DD*, 22 June 1918.
119 McPhillips, 'AOH in County Monaghan', pp 19, 22, 90. 120 Ibid., p. 90.
121 Jim Sullivan (MCM, Marron papers). 122 *AC*, 23 Apr. 1921.
123 *DD*, 16 Apr. 1921; *AC*, 23 Apr. 1921.
124 Quoted in Éamon Phoenix, *Northern nationalism: nationalist politics, partition and the Catholic minority in Northern Ireland* (Belfast, 1994), p. 118.
125 *NS*, 6 Oct. 1933. 126 Quoted in McGarry, *O'Duffy*, p. 67.
127 *DD*, 2 July 1921. 128 Joseph E. McKenna (BMH, WS 575), p. 5.
129 Patrick McGrory (MCM, Marron papers). 130 *DD*, 31 Dec. 1921.
131 John McGonnell (BMH, WS 574), pp 6–7.
132 John McGahey (BMH, WS 740), pp 12–13. 133 Ibid.
134 Copy of RIC report, Co. Monaghan, 1921 (PRONI, Madden papers, D3465/J/37/139/3).
135 John McGahey (MCM, Marron papers).
136 CI Monaghan, Mar. 1921 (TNA, CO 904/114).
137 *DD*, 2 Apr. 1921. 138 Ibid.
139 Anne Dolan, '"Spies and informers beware ..."' in Diarmaid Ferriter and Susannah Riordan (eds), *Years of turbulence: the Irish revolution and its aftermath* (Dublin, 2015), p. 162.
140 Patrick Corrigan (MCM, Marron papers).
141 *DD*, 23 Apr., 16 July, 15 Oct. 1921. 142 *DD*, 15 Oct. 1921.
143 Ibid., 16 Apr. 1921. 144 CI Monaghan, Apr. 1921 (TNA, CO 904/115).
145 See, for example, Peter Hart, *The IRA and its enemies: violence and community in Cork, 1916–1923* (Oxford, 1998); John Borgonovo, *Spies, informers and the 'Anti-Sinn Féin society': the intelligence war in Cork city, 1920–1921* (Dublin, 2007).

146 *DD*, 12 Jan. 1912.
147 *DD*, 18 Mar. 1916.
148 *DD*, 14 July 1920.
149 Hart, *The IRA at war*, pp 78–80.
150 Court of inquiry in lieu of inquest – Hugh Duffy, Rockcorry (TNA, WO 35/149A/61); *AC*, 4 June 1921.
151 Ibid.
152 Copy of RIC report, Co. Monaghan, 1921 (PRONI, Madden papers, D3465/J/37/139/3); CI Monaghan, Apr. 1921 (TNA, CO 904/115).
153 Jim Sullivan (MCM, Marron papers).
154 Court of inquiry in lieu of inquest – Kate Carroll Aghanameena, County Monaghan (TNA, WO 35/147B/5). In earlier work, I mistakenly identified Carroll as a Protestant as stated in newspaper reports of the time; Terence Dooley, 'Monaghan Protestants in a time of crisis' in R.V. Comerford et al. (eds), *Religion, conflict and coexistence in Ireland* (Dublin, 1990), pp 240–1; *DD* of 23 Apr. 1921. My thanks to Daithí Ó Corráin for correcting this error.
155 General orders, new series 1920, no. No.12, 9 Nov. 1920 (UCDA, Mulcahy papers, P7/A/45).
156 *DD*, 19 June 1920.
157 CI Monaghan, Apr. 1921 (TNA, CO 904/115); *NS*, 21 Apr. 1921.
158 McGarry, *O'Duffy*, pp 65–6; see also Marie Coleman, 'Violence against women during the Irish War of Independence, 1919–21' in Ferriter & Riordan (eds), *Years of turbulence*, p. 139.
159 *DD*, 23 Apr. 1921.
160 McGarry, *O'Duffy*, p. 64.
161 *NS*, 8 Apr. 1921.
162 Quoted in Joseph McKenna, *Guerrilla warfare in the Irish War of Independence* (Jefferson NC, 2011), p. 116.
163 Ibid., p. 69.
164 See T.K. Wilson, *Frontiers of violence: conflict and identity in Ulster and Upper Silesia, 1918–1922* (Oxford, 2010).
165 McCluskey, *Tyrone*, p. 102.
166 John McGahey (BMH, WS 740), pp 7–8.
167 Francis Tummons (BMH, WS 820), p. 45.
168 Seamus McKenna (MCM, Marron papers); *NS*, 25 Feb. 1921.
169 *NS*, 25 Feb. 1921.
170 Report of Monaghan Brigade IRA to GHQ, Feb. 1921 (UCDA, Mulcahy papers, P7/A/39).
171 Seamus McKenna (MCM, Marron papers); *Belfast Telegraph*, 23 Mar. 1921.
172 *NS*, 8 Apr. 1921.
173 *DD*, 26 Mar. 1921.
174 Copy of RIC report, County Monaghan, 1921 (PRONI, Madden papers, D3465/J/37/139/3).
175 *DD*, 2 Apr. 1921.
176 Ibid.
177 Application by Patrick McKenna, 27 Nov. 1923 (IMA, Military Service Pensions, 1D235).
178 Report of Monaghan Brigade IRA to GHQ, Mar. 1921 (UCDA, Mulcahy papers, P7/A/39).
179 *NS*, 8 Apr. 1921.
180 Report of Monaghan Brigade IRA to GHQ, Mar. 1921 (UCDA, Mulcahy papers, P7/A/39).
181 Owen O'Duffy to Minister of Defence, 24 Nov. 1921 (NLI, O'Duffy papers, MS 48,281/2).
182 Ibid.
183 McGarry, *O'Duffy*, p. 55.
184 Michael Farrell, *Northern Ireland: the Orange State* (London, 1976), p. 29; Laffan, *Partition of Ireland*, p. 76.
185 CI Monaghan, July 1920 (TNA, CO 904/112).

186 Minute book of First Monaghan Presbyterian Church, 7 Oct. 1920 (Presbyterian Church Records, Monaghan town).
187 Brown, *Shepherding the Monaghan flock*, p. 117. 188 *DD*, 31 July 1920.
189 Dáil Éireann, minutes of proceedings, 1919–21, p. 191.
190 Minutes of 2nd Session of Dáil Éireann, 6 Aug. 1920, p. 191.
191 Ibid., pp 192–3. 192 Farrell, *Northern Ireland*, p. 32.
193 *NS*, 21 Aug. 1920. 194 CI Monaghan, Aug. 1920 (TNA, CO 904/112).
195 *NS*, 21, 28 Aug. 1920.
196 Letter from DC Rushe to Shane Leslie, 14 Sept. 1920 (NLI, Leslie papers, MS 22,837).
197 *NS*, 24 Sept. 1920. 198 CI Monaghan, Apr. 1921 (TNA, CO 904/115).
199 Report of Monaghan Brigade IRA to GHQ, Apr. 1921 (UCDA, Mulcahy papers, P7/A/39).
200 Notebook Scotstown SF Club: entry for 11 Sept. 1921 (MCM, Brennan papers, uncatalogued).
201 Report of Monaghan Brigade IRA to GHQ, Apr. 1921 (UCDA, Mulcahy papers, P7/A/39).
202 Seamus McKenna (MCM, Marron papers).
203 John McGahey (BMH, WS 740), pp 15–16. 204 *NS*, 27 Jan. 1922.
205 *NS*, 28 Aug. 1920. 206 Ibid.; *DD*, 28 Jan.1922.
207 *NS*, 27 Jan. 1922. 208 O'Hegarty, *Victory of Sinn Féin*, p. 36.
209 McCluskey, *Tyrone*, p. 87. 210 Farrell, *Northern Ireland*, p. 39.
211 *NS*, 14 Dec. 1918, 31 Jan. 1920.
212 *NS*, 13 Mar. 1920. 213 *NS*, 13, 20 May 1920.
214 *DD*, 17 July 1920. 215 Ibid. 216 Ibid.
217 *DD*, 13 Aug. 1921. 218 *DD*, 16 Dec. 1921.
219 *DD*, 6, 13, 20 Aug. 1921. 220 *DD*, 15 Oct. 1921.
221 Orders from 5th Northern Division, 12 July 1921 (MCM, Thomas Brennan papers, uncatalogued).
222 CI Monaghan, Sept. 1921 (TNA, CO 904/116). 223 *NS*, 25 June 1921.
224 Farrell, *Northern Ireland*, p. 41.
225 Ó Dúfaigh, 'Patrick McKenna', p. 206. 226 *NS*, 28 Oct. 1921.
227 Quoted in Farrell, *Northern Ireland*, p. 81.
228 O'Duffy to Collins, 14 Oct. 1921 (UCDA, Mulcahy papers, P7/A/26).

CHAPTER SEVEN *'The best interests of the country demand ratification of the Treaty': 1922–3*

1 *DD*, 7 Jan. 1922. 2 Peter Woods (MCM, Marron papers).
3 Tom Armstrong to Fr Marron, 14 Feb. 1967 (MCM, Marron papers).
4 Jackson, *Ireland*, p. 272. 5 *DD*, 7 Jan. 1922. 6 Ibid.
7 Ibid. 8 Ibid.
9 Peadar Ó Casaide (ed.), 'Some snippets from a notebook kept by Wm Daly UDC', *Macalla*, 14:1 (Spring, 1979), 26.
10 *DD*, 4 Feb. 1922. 11 Ibid.
12 *Dáil debates*, 3 Jan. 1922, vol. 10, 192. 13 Ibid., 194.
14 Quoted in McGarry, *O'Duffy*, p. 93.
15 Handwritten note by Seán MacEntee, n.d. (UCDA, MacEntee papers, P67/60).
16 *NS*, 13 Jan. 1922; *DD*, 7 Jan. 1922. 17 *DD*, 24 Dec. 1921.
18 Michael Gallagher, 'The pact general election of 1922', *IHS*, 22:84 (1979), 412.
19 Ibid., p. 414. 20 McAnallen, 'Role of Owen O'Duffy', 716.

21 *NS*, 20 Jan. 1922.
22 Collins to Churchill, 11 Feb. 1922 (NAI, Gov & Cab Files, S8 037).
23 McGarry, *O'Duffy*, p. 99.   24 Laffan, *Partition of Ireland*, p. 92.
25 Paul Bew, *Ireland: the politics of enmity, 1789–2006* (Oxford, 2007), p. 424.
26 Ibid., pp 426–7.   27 Ibid., p. 427.
28 Leon Ó Broin, *Michael Collins* (Dublin, 1980), p. 182.
29 Buckland, *Irish unionism ii*, p. 153.   30 McAnallen, 'Role of Owen O'Duffy', 716.
31 *NS*, 17 Feb. 1922.
32 James Craig to David Lloyd George, 8 Feb. 1922, quoted in McGarry, *O'Duffy*, p. 371.
33 Quoted in Buckland, *James Craig*, pp 75–6.
34 Findings of Military Court of Enquiry into the circumstances surrounding the death of Acting Divisional CMDT Matt Fitzpatrick (NLI, O'Duffy papers, MS 48,281/3); *NS*, 17 Feb. 1922; *Belfast Newsletter*, 11 Apr. 1922.
35 Collins quoted in Pearse Lawlor, *1920–1922: the outrages. The IRA and the Ulster Special Constabulary in the border campaign* (Cork, 2011), pp 233, 235–56.
36 McGarry, *O'Duffy*, p. 100.
37 Basil Brooke to Home Office, 31 Mar. 1922 (PRONI, HA 5/913).
38 Churchill to Irish Provisional Government, *c*.15 Feb. 1922 (NAI, Gov. and Cabinet Files, S8 037); *NS*, 17 Feb. 1922.
39 Churchill to Michael Collins and Arthur Griffith, 17 Feb. 1922 (NAI, Gov. and Cabinet Files, S8 037).
40 *NS*, 17 Feb. 1922.   41 McGarry, *O'Duffy*, p. 100.   42 *AC*, 11 Mar. 1922.
43 *NS*, 24 Feb. 1922.   44 *NS*, 10, 17 Mar. 1922.   45 *NS*, 24 Mar. 1922.
46 Ibid.   47 Ibid.   48 *NS*, 31 Mar. 1922.
49 Alan Parkinson, *Belfast's unholy war: the troubles of the 1920s* (Dublin, 2004), p. 237.
50 Bew, *Politics of enmity*, p. 430.   51 McGarry, *O'Duffy*, p. 102.
52 Farrell, *Northern Ireland*, pp 52–3.   53 *NS*, 14 Apr. 1922.
54 Ó Casaide (ed.), 'Snippets from a notebook', p. 26; *DD*, 4 Feb. 1922.
55 Livingstone, *Monaghan story*, p. 392.
56 C.S. Andrews, *Dublin made me: an autobiography* (Dublin, 2001 [1979]), p. 263.
57 Ibid.
58 Livingstone, *Monaghan story*, pp 392–3; Rory O'Connor, who led the takeover of the Four Courts in April 1922, once said there was no need to worry about money because there was plenty of it in banks and post offices; O'Hegarty, *The victory of Sinn Féin*, p. 84.
59 *NS*, 3 June 1922.
60 Livingstone, *Monaghan story*, p. 393.
61 Michael O'Hanlon, Adjutant 4th Northern Division to chief-of-staff [Frank Aiken], 13 Mar. 1924 & 3 June 1924 (UCDA, Moss Twomey papers, P69/35 (91, 111)). I would like to express my gratitude to Dr Donal Hall for this reference.
62 *AC*, 9 Sept. 1922.   63 Ó Dúfaigh, 'Patrick McKenna', p. 206.
64 *AC*, 9 Sept. 1922.   65 Ibid.
66 Matthew Lewis, *Frank Aiken's war: the Irish revolution, 1916–23* (Dublin, 2014), p. 179.
67 Ibid., p. 180.   68 MacMahon, *A fist to the black-blooded*, pp 124–5.
69 Seán Woods to Richard Mulcahy, 29 Sept. 1922 (UCDA, Mulcahy papers, P7/B/287).
70 McAnallen, 'Role of Owen O'Duffy', p. 718.
71 Memo by Ernest Blythe, 9 Aug. 1922 (UCDA, Blythe papers, P24/70/1).
72 *DD*, 25 Mar. 1922.
73 Darach MacDonald, 'Clones: what partition did to life in one border town', *IT*, 5–6 Nov. 1985.
74 *NS*, 6 Oct. 1922.   75 *NS*, 7 Feb. 1923.   76 *NS*, 14 May 1921.

77 Ibid., 15 Oct. 1920.
78 Aiken McClelland, 'Orangeism in Co. Monaghan', *Clogher Record*, 9:3 (1978), 400.
79 *The Weekely Bulletin*, 17 July 1923 (PRONI, Madden papers, D3465/J/37/143); *NS*, 13 July 1923.
80 *NS*, 13 July 1923; Report on 12 July celebration at Clones by H. McCartan for Executive Council, 17 July 1923 (NAI, Gov. and Cabinet Files, S 1955).
81 *NS*, 9 Dec. 1921.   82 *NS*, 20 July 1923.
83 Brown, *Shepherding the Monaghan flock*, p. 117.   84 *NS*, 22 May 1925.
85 Ibid.   86 *DD*, 6 May 1922.

CHAPTER EIGHT *'Is everything we love gone forever': the Big House, 1912–23*

1 Gill Lucas Scudamore to Sybil, n.d. (Lucas Scudamore papers, Kentchurch Court).
2 Terence Dooley, *The decline of the big house in Ireland* (Dublin, 2001), pp 171–207.
3 *DD*, Apr. 1912.   4 *DD*, 6 July 1912.
5 Anita Leslie, *The gilt and the gingerbread: an autobiography* (London, 1931), p. 11.
6 Anita Leslie, *Lady Randolph Churchill: the story of Jennie Jerome* (New York, 1969), pp 374–5.
7 Bowman, *Carson's army*, pp 168–9.
8 Sir John Leslie to Shane Leslie, 27 Oct. 1916 (PRONI, Leslie papers, MIC606/3).
9 War diary of Captain Anketell Moutray, 25 Apr., 1 May 1916 (PRONI, Moutray papers, D2023/7/2/30).
10 *NS*, 24 June 1916.   11 Seymour Leslie, *The Jerome connexion* (London, 1964), p. 89.
12 Leslie, *The gilt & the gingerbread*, p. 11.
13 Author in conversation with present owner, Johnny Madden.
14 Robert Devine to the author, 8 Feb. 2016.
15 Robert Devine to the author, 8 Dec. 2015.
16 'Gola House', http://archiseek.com/2012/gola-house-co-monaghan/ (accessed 18 Apr. 2016).
17 Notebook Scotstown SF Club: entry for 11 Sept. 1921 (MCM, Brennan papers, uncatalogued).
18 Ibid.   19 *Weekly Irish Times*, 24 June 1922.   20 *AC*, 2 Feb. 1924.
21 Robert Devine to the author, 8 Feb. 2016.   22 Ibid.
23 *AC*, 23 Apr. 1921.   24 *DD*, 4 July 1921.   25 *NS*, 18 Jan. 1912.
26 Ibid.   27 *NS*, 3 June 1921; *DD*, 4 June 1921.
28 *NS*, 11 Mar. 1922.   29 *NS*, 9, 16 July 1921.
30 CI Monaghan, Feb. 1919 (TNA, CO 904/108).   31 Ibid.
32 CI Monaghan, May 1919 (TNA, CO 904/109).
33 McGarry, *O'Duffy*, pp 53–4.   34 O'Duffy, 'Reminiscences'.
35 *DD*, 11 Mar. 1922.   36 *NS*, 12 Jan. 1923.
37 *NS*, 16 Feb., 2 Mar. 1923.   38 *DD*, 11 Mar. 1922.
39 Unless otherwise stated the documentary evidence in this sections is taken from the uncatalogued Lucas Scudamore archive in Kentchurch Court, Herefordshire.
40 Untitled newspaper clipping.
41 *NS*, 21 Feb. 1920.
42 Ibid.; *AC*, 31 Aug. 1935; Jack Lucas Scudmore to Sybil, 17 Mar. 1920.
43 *Ulster Herald*, 21 Feb. 1920; *NS*, 21 Feb. 1920.   44 *NS*, 21 Feb. 1920.
45 Miss Murray-Ker to Mrs Lucas Scudamore [hereafter Sybil], 17 Feb. 1920.
46 Mary Crawshay to Sybil, n.d.   47 Julia, Lady Dartrey to Sybil, 20 Feb. 1920.

48 J.J. Turley to Sybil, 24 Feb. 1920; also, Monaghan Girl Guides to Sybil, 28 Feb. 1920.
49 M. Cassidy to Sybil, 16 Dec. 1920. 50 Jack Lucas Scudmore to Sybil, 17 Mar. 1920.
51 Gill Lucas Scudamore to Sybil, n.d. 52 Ibid.
53 T.F. Crozier to Sybil (?) Jan. 1921. 54 Poppy Geddes to Sybil, 15 May 1920.
55 Clontibret Select Vestry to Sybil, 12 Jan. 1923.
56 M. Cassidy to Sybil, 10 Aug. 1921. 57 Ibid.
58 M. Cassidy to Sybil, 16 Jan. 1921.
59 Newspapers clippings, untitled and undated (Lucas Scudamore archive, Kentchurch Court, Herefordshire).
60 Morgan to Sybil, 6 Sept. 1920. 61 Morgan to Sybil, 9 Feb., 21 Feb. 1921.
62 S. Simpson to Sybil, 19 Mar. 1921. 63 M. Cassidy to Sybil, 21 Dec. 1921.
64 S. Simpson to Sybil, 19 Mar. 1921. 65 Morgan to Sybil, 7 Sept. 1922
66 Morgan to Sybil, 2 Nov. 1922. 67 *Cork Examiner*, 31 Aug. 1922.
68 *NS*, 11 Sept. 1922. 69 Morgan to Sybil, 1 Aug. 1923.
70 Ibid.
71 *Irish Independent*, 3 Jan. 1924; *Donegal News*, 5 Jan. 1924; *Fermanagh Herald*, 9 Feb. 1924.
72 Crozier to Sybil, (?) Jan. 1921. 73 Ibid.
74 Crozier to Sybil, 18 Jan. 1921. 75 Ibid.
76 Crozier to Sybil, 19 Apr. 1921. 77 Ibid.
78 Crozier to Sybil, 7 June 1921. 79 Crozier to Sybil, 7 July 1921.
80 Crozier to Sybil, 1 Mar. 1922. 81 Report of M.T. Henchey, 30 June 1931.
82 Crozier to Jack Lucas Scudamore, 13 Apr. 1932.
83 Shane Leslie to Jack Lucas Scudamore, 27 Sept. 1961.
84 Shane Leslie to Jack Lucas Scudamore, 14 Oct. 1962.
85 Brian McMahon to Fr Marron, 27 Jan. 1966 (MCM, Marron papers).
86 See Dooley, *The decline of the Big House*.
87 See also, J.S. Donnelly Jr, 'Big House burnings in County Cork during the Irish revolution, 1920–21', *Eire-Ireland*, 47:3&4 (Fall/Winter 2012), 141–97; Ciarán J. Reilly, 'The burning of country houses in Co. Offaly during the revolutionary period, 1920–3' in Terence Dooley and Christopher Ridgway (eds), *The Irish country house: its past, present and future* (Dublin, 2011), pp 110–33.
88 Olwen Purdue, *The Big House in the north of Ireland: land, power and social elites, 1878–1960* (Dublin, 2009), pp 145–51.
89 Terence Dooley, 'National patrimony and political perceptions of the Irish country house in post-independence Ireland' in Terence Dooley (ed.), *Ireland's polemical past: views of Irish history in honour of R.V. Comerford* (Dublin, 2010), pp 192–212.

CHAPTER NINE *Revolution?*

1 Patrick Butler (BMH, WS 1,187), pp 1–11.
2 Edward Glendon (BMH, WS 1,127), pp 1–2.
3 Matt Smith (MCM, Marron papers). 4 O'Duffy, 'Reminiscences', chapter 5, p. 3.
5 Johnnie McKenna (MCM, Marron papers).
6 It is described in some detail in several of the BMH and Marron statements and in O'Duffy's papers in the NLI.
7 Private possession.
8 http://www.tipperarystar.ie/news/local/tipperary-freedom-fighters-1-2264882 (accessed 28 May 2013).
9 Quoted in *AC*, 24 Feb. 1924. 10 Quoted in McGarry, *O'Duffy*, p. 44.

11 Ibid. 12 O'Hegarty, *The victory of Sinn Féin*, p. 46.
13 *DD*, 21 Jan. 1922.
14 McGarry, *O'Duffy*, p. 75 and quoting John M. Regan, *The Irish counter-revolution, 1921–1936* (Dublin, 1999), p. 247.
15 *DD*, Feb. 1920.
16 Quoted in J.J. Lee, *Ireland, 1912–1985: politics and society* (Cambridge, 1989), p. 105.
17 Regan, *Irish counter-revolution*, p. 245.
18 Mel Farrell, 'Cumann na nGaedheal: a new "national party"' in Mel Farrell et al. (eds), *A formative decade: Ireland in the 1920s* (Sallins, 2015), p. 37.
19 *AC*, 24 Feb. 1934. 20 *The Argus*, 4 Sept. 1954.
21 'Life of Thomas Toal'. 22 McGarry, *O'Duffy*, p. 75.
23 Brian Walker (ed.), *Parliamentary election results in Ireland, 1918–92* (Dublin & Belfast, 1992), pp 189, 196, 203.
24 Ted Nealon, *Tales from the Dáil bar* (Dublin, 2008), p. 55.
25 Edward Kelly (MCM, Marron papers). 26 Ibid.
27 Quoted in MacMahon, *A fist to the black-blooded*, p. 121.
28 Tom Carragher (MCM, Marron papers).
29 Kavanagh, *Green fool*, pp 104–9.
30 Lenten pastoral, 1924 (Clogher Diocesan Archives, McKenna papers).
31 Brian MacMahon (MCM, Marron papers); my thanks to Dr Tom Nelson for his insights on this.
32 O'Duffy, 'Reminiscences'.
33 Hogan to O'Duffy, 11 Feb. 1929 (NLI, O'Duffy papers, MS 48,283/4).
34 *An tÓglach*, 12 Jan. 1924. 35 *Irish Independent*, 30 July 1927.
36 http://www.tipperarystar.ie/news/local/tipperary-freedom-fighters-1-2264882 (accessed 28 May 2013).
37 Andrews, *Dublin made me*, p. 263.
38 Hogan to O'Duffy, 11 Feb. 1929 (NLI, O'Duffy papers, MS 48,283/4).
39 Reference for Dan Hogan 'to my many friends in USA' (NLI, O'Duffy papers, MS 48,283/4).
40 Military service pension application, Dan Hogan, Collins Barracks, Dublin, 2 Jan. 1925 (IMA, Military Service Pensions, W24D67); also http://mspcsearch.militaryarchives.ie/detail.aspx (accessed 19 Dec. 2016).
41 C.T. Rice to Fr Laurence Marron, 6 May 1968 (MCM, Marron papers).
42 Betty Hogan to Marron, 28 Apr. 1968 (MCM, Marron papers).
43 Jackson, *Ireland*, p. 239.
44 '2,117 Protestants from Free State living in Co. Fermanagh since 1920', dated 15 May 1925 (NLI, Boundary Commission papers, Pos 6515).
45 *IT*, 8 Aug. 2016. 46 Ibid. 47 *IT*, 21 Jan. 2016.
48 *IT*, 31 Mar. 2015.
49 Quoted in Frank McNally, 'An Irishman's diary'; *IT*, 23 Jan. 2016.

Select bibliography

PRIMARY SOURCES

A. MANUSCRIPTS

Armagh
Cardinal Tomás Ó Fiaich Memorial Library & Archive
Fr Louis O'Kane papers.
Minute books of Ulster GAA Council.

Belfast
Public Records Office of Northern Ireland
Crawford papers.
Dartrey papers.
Department of Home Affairs HA/5 series.
Department of Home Affairs secret HA/32/1/2815 series.
Irish (Carson) papers.
Leslie papers.
Madden papers.
Monaghan UVF papers.
Moutray papers.
Ulster Unionist Council papers.
J.M. Wilson papers.

Dublin
Irish Valuation Office
Valuation lists for County Monaghan.

Military Archives
Bureau of Military History witness statements.
Department of Military Statistics Eastern Command 5th Northern Division intelligence communications reports (CW/OPS/07 series).
Military service pension collection.
5th Northern Division reports, 1921–2.

National Archives of Ireland
Finance compensation (post-truce) files.
Minute book of Killanny AOH.
Northeast Boundary Bureau records.
Rebellion papers relating to County Monaghan.

National Library of Ireland
Michael Collins papers.
Bulmer Hobson papers.

Select bibliography

Irish Boundary Commission papers.
Shane Leslie papers.
Maurice Moore papers.
Owen O'Duffy papers.
Solemn Covenant to resist conscription, County Monaghan.

Trinity College, Dublin
John Dillon papers.

University College Dublin Archives
Frank Aiken papers.
Ernest Blythe papers.
Michael Collins papers.
Fianna Fáil papers.
Seán MacEntee papers.
Richard Mulcahy papers.
Ernie O'Malley papers & notebooks.
Bernard O'Rourke papers.
Moss Twomey papers.

London
National Archives
Cabinet papers.
Colonial Office papers.
Home Office papers.
Irish Grants Committee files.
War Office papers.

Monaghan
Clogher Diocesan Archives
Patrick McKenna papers.

Clogher Historical Society
Denis Carolan Rushe papers.
Fr Lorcan Ó Ciaráin papers.

First Presbyterian Church
First Presbyterian Church Monaghan minute books.

Monaghan County Museum
Thomas Brennan papers.
Clones Urban District Council minute books.
Fr Laurence Marron papers.
Monaghan County Council minute books.
Thomas Toal papers.

B. OFFICIAL RECORDS

Agricultural statistics of Ireland [Cd 7429], HC 1914, xcviii.
Table showing by poor law union, the number of holdings, their size in statute acres, the number of holdings owned and tenanted, and the division of land in the year, 1913; Cd. 7429, 1914, xcviii.
Table showing number of holdings owned and tenanted, and the division of land in the year, 1913; Cd. 7429, 1914, xcviii.
Census of Ireland, 1901–11.
Dáil Éireann. Parliamentary debates.
Hansard House of Commons parliamentary debates.
Report of the 1911 census, Province of Ulster, County Monaghan (London, 1911).

C. NEWSPAPERS AND PERIODICALS

Anglo-Celt
An tÓglach
Argus
Armagh Guardian
Belfast Newsletter
Belfast Telegraph
Cork Examiner
Donegal News
Dundalk Democrat
Dundalk Examiner
Fermanagh Herald
Freeman's Journal
Irish Independent
Irish Times
London Morning Post
Monaghan People
Northern Standard
People's Advocate
Thom's Irish almanac and official directory
Ulster Herald
Weekly Irish Times

D. PRINTED PRIMARY MATERIAL

Andrews, C.S., *Dublin made me* (Dublin, 2001 ed.).
Cumann Seanchais Mhuineacháin, *Cuimhneachain Mhuineacháin* (Monaghan, 1967).
De Blaghd, Earnán, *Slán le hUltaibh* (Dublin, 1971 ed.).
Hand, G.J. (ed.), *Report of the Irish Boundary Commission, 1925* (Shannon, 1965).
Hobson, Bulmer, *A short history of the Irish Volunteers* (Dublin, 1918).
Kavanagh, Patrick, *The green fool* (London, 1938).
Kavanagh, Peter, *Beyond affection: autobiography of Peter Kavanagh* (New York, 1977).
— (ed.), *Patrick Kavanagh: man and poet* (Newbridge and Maine, 1987).
Leslie, Seymour, *Of Glaslough in the kingdom of Oriel and of the noted men who have dwelt there* (Glaslough, 1913).
Martin, F.X., 'The McCartan Documents', *Clogher Record*, 6:1 (1966), 5–65.
Mac Giolla Choille, Breandán (ed.), *Intelligence notes, 1913–16* (Dublin, 1966).
O'Farrelly, Agnes (ed.), *Leabhar an tAthar Eoghan: the O'Growney memorial volume* (Dublin, 1904).
O'Hegarty, P.S., *The victory of Sinn Féin* (Dublin, 1988 ed., 1st ed. 1924).

O'Malley, Ernie, *On another man's wound* (Dublin, 1979 ed.).
O'Neill, Thomas (ed.), *Private sessions of second Dáil minutes of proceedings 18 August 1921 to 14 September 1921 and report of debates 14 December 1921 to 6 January 1922* (Dublin, 1972).
Orange Institution of Ireland, *The laws and ordinances of the Orange Institution of Ireland* (Belfast, 1924).
Pearse, P.H., *Collected works of Padraic H. Pearse* (Dublin, 1916).
Rossmore, Lord, *Things I can tell* (London, 1912).
Rushe, Denis Carolan, *Historical sketches of Monaghan, from the earliest records to the Fenian movement* (Dublin, 1895).
Swann, William (ed.), *Co. Monaghan year book and directory* (Monaghan, 1912).
Taylor, J.W. (ed.), *The Rossmore incident* (Dublin, 1884).
Vaughan, W.E. & E.J. Fitzpatrick (eds), *Irish historical statistics: population, 1821–1970* (Dublin, 1978).
Walker, Brian (ed.), *Parliamentary election results in Ireland, 1918–92* (Dublin & Belfast, 1992).

SELECT SECONDARY SOURCES

E. PUBLISHED WORKS

Augusteijn, Joost, *From public defiance to guerrilla warfare: the experience of ordinary Volunteers in the Irish War of Independence, 1916–21* (Dublin, 1996).
Bew, Paul, *Ireland: the politics of enmity, 1789–2006* (Oxford, 2007).
Borgonovo, John, *Spies, informers and the 'Anti-Sinn Féin society': the intelligence war in Cork city, 1920–1921* (Dublin, 2007).
Bowman, Timothy, 'The UVF and the formation of the 36th (Ulster) Division', *IHS*, 32:128 (2001), 498–518.
—, *Carson's army, the Ulster Volunteer Force, 1910–22* (Manchester, 2007).
Brown, L.T., *Shepherding the Monaghan flock: the story of First Monaghan Presbyterian Church* (Monaghan, n.d.).
Buckland, Patrick, *Irish unionism, 1885–1923: a documentary history* (Belfast, 1973).
—, *Irish unionism ii: Ulster unionism and the origins of Northern Ireland, 1885–1922* (Dublin, 1973).
—, *James Craig* (Dublin, 1980).
Callan, Patrick, 'Recruiting for the British army in Ireland during the First World War', *Irish Sword*, 17 (1987–8), 42–56.
Campbell, Fergus, *Land and revolution: nationalist politics in the west of Ireland, 1891–1921* (Oxford, 2005).
Coleman, Marie, *County Longford and the Irish revolution, 1910–1923* (Dublin, 2003).
—, 'Violence against women during the Irish War of Independence, 1919–21' in Ferriter & Riordan (eds), *Years of turbulence*, pp 137–56.
Comerford, R.V., *Ireland* (London and New York, 2003).
Cullen, Kevin, *Book of honour for Co. Monaghan: remembering Monaghan's war dead, 1914–18* (n.p., 2010)

Dolan, Anne, *Commemorating the Irish Civil War, history and memory, 1923–2000* (Cambridge, 2003).
—, '"Spies and informers beware ..."' in Ferriter & Riordan (eds), *Years of turbulence*, pp 157–72.
Donnelly, James, 'Big House burnings in County Cork during the Irish revolution, 1920–21', *Eire-Ireland*, 47:3&4 (2012), 141–97.
Dooley, Terence, 'The organization of unionist opposition to home rule in counties Monaghan, Cavan and Donegal, 1885–1914', *Clogher Record*, 16:1 (1997), 46–70.
—, *The plight of Monaghan Protestants, 1912–1926* (Dublin, 2000).
—, *The decline of the Big House in Ireland* (Dublin, 2001).
—, 'IRA veterans and land division in independent Ireland, 1923–48' in Fearghal McGarry (ed.), *Republicanism in modern Ireland* (Dublin, 2003), pp 86–107.
—, *Inniskeen, 1912–1918: the political conversion of Bernard O'Rourke* (Dublin, 2004).
Duffy, P.J., 'The territorial organization of Gaelic landownership and its transformation in Co. Monaghan, 1591–1640', *Irish Geography* (1981), 57–83.
—, *Landscapes of south Ulster: a parish atlas of the diocese of Clogher* (Belfast, 1993).
Fanning, Ronan, 'Anglo-Irish relations: partition and the British dimension in historical perspective', *Irish Studies in International Affairs*, 2:1 (1985), 1–20.
—, *Fatal path: British government and Irish revolution, 1910–1922* (London, 2013).
Farrell, Mel, Ciara Meehan & Jason Knirick (eds), *A formative decade: Ireland in the 1920s* (Dublin, 2015).
Farrell, Michael, *Northern Ireland: the Orange State* (London, 1976).
Ferriter, Diarmaid, *A nation and not a rabble: the Irish revolution, 1913–1923* (London, 2015).
— & Susannah Riordan (eds), *Years of turbulence: the Irish revolution and its aftermath* (Dublin, 2015).
Fitzpatrick, David, *Politics and Irish life, 1913–1921: provincial experiences of war and revolution* (Cork, 1998 [1977]).
—, *Descendancy: Irish Protestant histories since 1795* (Cambridge, 2014).
Foster, R.F., *Vivid faces: the revolutionary generation in Ireland* (London, 2015).
Gallagher, Michael, 'The pact general election of 1922', *IHS*, 22:84 (1979), 404–21.
Garvin, Tom, *The evolution of Irish nationalist politics* (Dublin, 2005).
Hall, Donal, *World War 1 and nationalist politics in County Louth, 1914–1918* (Dublin, 2004).
Hamell, P.J., *Maynooth students and ordinations, 1795–1895* (Maynooth, 1982).
Hanley, Brian, *The IRA, 1926–1936* (Dublin, 2002).
Hart, Peter, *The IRA and its enemies: violence and community in Cork, 1916–1923* (Oxford, 1998).
—, *The IRA at war, 1916–1923* (Oxford, 2003).
Hopkinson, Michael, *Green against green: the Irish Civil War* (Dublin, 1988).
—, *The Irish War of Independence* (Dublin, 2002).
Jackson, Alvin, *Ireland, 1798–1998: politics and war* (Oxford, 1999).
—, *Home rule: an Irish history, 1800–2000* (London, 2004).
Jefferies, Henry A. (ed.), *History of the diocese of Clogher* (Dublin, 2005).
Johnson, D.S., 'The Belfast boycott, 1920–22' in J.M. Goldstrom & L.A. Clarkson (eds), *Irish population, economy and society* (Oxford, 1981), pp 287–309.

Jones, David Seth, *Graziers, land reform and political conflict in Ireland* (Washington, 1995).
Kavanagh, Peter, *Beyond affection: autobiography of Peter Kavanagh* (New York, 1977).
— (ed.), *Patrick Kavanagh: man and poet* (Newbridge and Maine, 1987).
Kennedy, Liam, *Unhappy the land: the most oppressed people ever, the Irish?* (Sallins, 2016).
Kostick, Conor, *Revolution in Ireland: popular militancy, 1917–1923* (London, 1996).
Kotsonouris, Mary, *Retreat from revolution: the Dáil courts, 1920–24* (Dublin, 1994).
Laffan, Michael, *The partition of Ireland, 1911–1925* (Dundalk, 1983).
—, *The resurrection of Ireland: the Sinn Féin party, 1916–23* (Cambridge, 2005).
Lawlor, Pearse, *1920–1922: the outrages. The IRA and the Ulster Special Constabulary in the border campaign* (Cork, 2011).
Lee, J.J., *Ireland, 1912–85: politics and society* (Cambridge, 1989).
Leslie, Anita, *The gilt and the gingerbread: an autobiography* (London, 1931).
—, *Lady Randolph Churchill: the story of Jennie Jerome* (New York, 1969).
Leslie, Seymour, *The Jerome connexion* (London, 1964).
Lewis, Matthew, *Frank Aiken's war: the Irish revolution, 1916–23* (Dublin, 2014).
Livingstone, Peadar, *The Monaghan story* (Enniskillen, 1980).
Lynch, Robert, *The northern IRA and the early years of partition, 1920–22* (Dublin, 2006).
McAnallen, Dónal, 'The radicalization of the Gaelic Athletic Association in Ulster, 1912–1923: the role of Owen O'Duffy', *International Journal of the History of Sport*, 31:7 (2014), 704–23.
McCarthy, Pat, *Waterford: the Irish revolution, 1912–23* (Dublin, 2015).
McClelland, Aiken, 'Orangeism in Co. Monaghan', *Clogher Record*, 9:3 (1978), 384–405.
McCluskey, Fergal, *Tyrone: the Irish revolution, 1912–23* (Dublin, 2014).
McDowell, R.B., *The Irish Convention, 1917–18* (London, 1970).
McGarry, Fearghal (ed.), *Republicanism in modern Ireland* (Dublin, 2003).
—, *Eoin O'Duffy: a self-made hero* (Oxford, 2005).
McGuire, Andrew & David Hassan, 'Cultural nationalism, Gaelic Sunday and the Gaelic Athletic Association in early twentieth-century Ireland', *International Journal of the History of Sport*, 29:6 (2012), 912–23.
McKenna, Joseph, *Guerrilla warfare in the Irish War of Independence* (Jefferson NC, 2011).
MacMahon, Hugh, *A fist to the black-blooded: the MacMahons of Coas* (2015).
Martin, Natasha & Stuart McConkey, *The Ulster Covenant and the people of Monaghan* (Monaghan, 2013).
Maume, Patrick, *The long gestation; Irish nationalist life, 1891–1918* (Dublin, 1999).
Miller, D.W., *Church, state and nation in Ireland, 1898–1921* (Dublin, 1973).
Mitchell, Arthur, *Revolutionary government in Ireland, Dáil Éireann, 1919–22* (Dublin, 1995).
'Monaghan, A.', 'Monaghan in 1920', *Capuchin Annual* (1970), 445–7.
Moore, Cormac, 'Luke O'Toole: servant of the GAA' in Gearóid Ó Tuathaigh (ed.), *The GAA and revolution in Ireland, 1913–23* (Cork, 2015), pp 53–70.

Murnane, James & Peadar Murnane, *At the ford of the birches: the history of Ballybay, its people and vicinity* (n.p., 1999).
Murray, Paul, *The Irish Boundary Commission and its origins, 1886–1925* (Dublin, 2011).
Murphy, William, *Political imprisonment and the Irish, 1912–1921* (Oxford, 2014).
Nealon, Ted, *Tales from the Dáil bar* (Dublin, 2008).
Nesbitt, David, *Full circle: a story of Ballybay Presbyterians* (Ballybay, 1999).
Ní Uallacháin, Pádraigín, *A hidden Ulster: people, songs and traditions of Oriel* (Dublin, 2003).
Ó Broin, Leon, *Michael Collins* (Dublin, 1980).
Ó Casaide, Peadar, 'Some snippets from a notebook kept by Wm Daly, UDC, publican, Main Street, entry for 17 June 1921', *Macalla*, 3:4 (Winter, 1978).
Ó Corráin, Daithí, '"A most public spirited and unselfish man": the career and contribution of Colonel Maurice Moore, 1854–1939', *Studia Hibernica*, 40 (2014), 71–133.
Ó Dúfaigh, Seosamh, 'Richard Owens, bishop of Clogher (1894–1909)' in H.A. Jefferies (ed.), *History of diocese of Clogher* (Dublin, 2005), pp 163–71.
—, 'Social and political comments in the Lenten pastorals of Bishop Patrick McKenna (1916–22)' in H.A. Jefferies (ed.), *History of diocese of Clogher* (Dublin, 2005), pp 172–206.
Ó Muirgheasa, Proinsias & Peadar Ó Casaide, *A man of Farney: a short history of the life of Henry Morris* (Carrickmacross, 1974).
Parkinson, Alan, *Belfast's unholy war: the troubles of the 1920s* (Dublin, 2004).
Pašeta, Senia, *Before the revolution: nationalism, social change and Ireland's Catholic elite, 1879–1922* (Cork, 2004).
— (ed.), *Uncertain futures: essays about the Irish past for Roy Foster* (Oxford, 2016).
Phoenix, Éamon, *Northern nationalism: nationalist politics, partition and the Catholic minority in Northern Ireland* (Belfast, 1994).
—, 'Partition, the Catholic Church and the diocese of Clogher, c.1912–1928' in Jefferies (ed.), *Clogher*, pp 207–22.
Privilege, John, *Michael Logue and the Catholic Church in Ireland, 1879–1925* (Manchester, 2009).
Quinn, Antoinette, *Patrick Kavanagh: a biography* (Dublin, 2001).
— (ed.), *Patrick Kavanagh: selected poems* (London, 1996).
Rafferty, Oliver, *Catholicism in Ulster: an interpretative history* (London, 1994).
Regan, John M., *The Irish counter-revolution, 1921–1936* (Dublin, 2001).
Reilly, Ciarán J., 'The burning of country houses in Co. Offaly during the revolutionary period, 1920–3' in Terence Dooley & Christopher Ridgway (eds), *The Irish country house: its past, present and future* (Dublin, 2011), pp 110–33.
Roe, Malachy, 'J.C.R. Lardner, MP, forgotten middle-Irelander', *Clogher Record*, 21:3 (2014), 225–32.
Savage, D.C., 'The origins of the Ulster Unionist Party, 1885–6', *IHS*, 12:47 (1961), 185–208.
Stewart, A.T.Q., *The Ulster crisis* (London, 1967).
Thompson, W.I., *The imagination of an insurrection: Dublin, Easter, 1916, a study of an ideological movement* (New York, 1967)

Townshend, Charles, *The British campaign in Ireland: 1919–21* (Oxford, 1975).
—, *Political violence in Ireland* (Oxford, 1983).
—, *Easter 1916: the Irish rebellion* (London, 2006).
Trevelyan, G.M., *Clio: a muse and other essays* (London, 1913).
Wheatley, Michael, *Nationalism and the Irish Party: provincial Ireland, 1910–1916* (Oxford, 2005).
Wilson, T.K., *Frontiers of violence: conflict and identity in Ulster and Upper Silesia, 1918–1922* (Oxford, 2010).

F. THESES AND UNPUBLISHED WORK

Dooley, Terence, 'Protestant politics and society in County Monaghan, 1911–26' (MA, St Patrick's College, Maynooth, 1986).
Duffy, P.J., 'Population and landholding in County Monaghan: a study in change and continuity' (PhD, UCD, 1976).
McGimpsey, C.D., '"To raise the banner in the remote north": politics in County Monaghan, 1868–1883' (PhD, University of Edinburgh, 1982).
Mc Phillips, Seamus, 'The Ancient Order of Hibernians in County Monaghan with particular reference to the parish of Aghabog from 1900 to 1933 (MA, Maynooth University, 1999).

G. INTERNET RESOURCES

Ulster Covenant online, PRONI: http://www.proni.go.uk/.

Index

Aghabog, 6, 12, 17, 69, 88, 91
Aghalurcher, 49
agrarian issues, 2, 11, 27, 38, 48, 68–9, 74, 78, 115; conacre, 42, 69, 116, 119; grazier, 8, 11–12, 120
Aiken, Frank, 103, 106–8
America, 25, 45, 67, 130
Armstrong, Tom, 124
An tÓglach, 130
Analore, 109
Ancient Order of Hibernians (AOH), 15; Aghabog, 69, 88; Aghabog Ladies Auxiliary, 88; and the IV, 27–8; Carrickmacross, 51; Corduff, 13; demonstrations, 74; denominationally exclusive, 12; growth of, 12; Inniskeen, 48; Joseph Devlin, Ulster-based president of, 29; Killanny, 12; Monaghan branches, 9, 27–9, 48, 51, 69–71, 74, 87–9, 127; membership, 87–8; Redmondite, 127
Andrews, C.S. 'Todd', 130
Anglo-Irish Treaty, 116, 120; anti-Treaty, 102–3, 106–8, 119, 121; pro-Treaty, 101–2, 108, 109, 127, 129; and Unionist grievances, 132
Anglo-Irish truce, 73, 76, 98–9, 108, 118, 120, 125, 129
Annaveagh, 49
Annyalla, 79, 85, 125, 129
Antrim, county, 20
aristocracy, 15, 24, 33–4, 36, 111, 122, 129, 132
Armagh, county, 1, 12, 20–1, 24, 35–6, 42, 51, 69, 87, 108, 110, 123
Armstrong, Revd William, 25, 101, 124
Army Comrades Association (the Blueshirts), 131
Ashbourne, Co. Meath, 55
Ashe, Thomas, 55, 65

Asquith, Herbert (MP), 20, 29–31, 59; Liberal government, 20, 22, 31
Aughnacloy, 103–5
Aughnamullen, 33, 49–50, 68, 112
Augusteijn, Joost, 80

B Specials: *see* Ulster Special Constabulary
Bachelor's Walk, Dublin, 30
Balbriggggan, 86
Ballinasloe, 130
Ballybay House, 10, 114
Ballyhaise, 99
Ballykinlar, 77, 79
Ballyleck, 25, 37, 113
Ballytrain, 69, 73, 79, 82, 87, 90–1
Bangor, 24
Barry, Kevin, 89
Bawn, 107
Beech Hill, 25
Belfast, 8, 18, 21–2, 70, 74, 78, 87, 89, 95–9, 103–5, 109–10, 119, 123, 127; boycott, 95–6, 103, 119, 127; Corporation, 95; jail, 70, 74, 78, 89, 104
Belfast Newsletter, 22, 56
Belgium, 34, 45–6, 50
Belleek, 103, 127
Berkhampstead, 39
Bew, Paul, 103
Big Houses, 15, 27, 75, 78, 111–23, 125
Black and Tans (*see* RIC), 85–7, 89, 102
Black, J.T., 37; Sarah, 113; William, 113–14
Bloody Sunday, 85, 92, 99
Blythe, Ernest, 70–2, 74, 76, 95, 101–2, 108–9
boards of poor law guardians, 9, 89, 111
Bolshevist, 43, 118
Bonar Law, Andrew, 30

161

Bowman, Timothy, 35
Bragan, 76, 79, 87
Breen, Dan, 72, 123
Brennan, Michael, 78; Thomas, 79
Britain, 3, 9, 18, 31, 45–6, 65, 78
British army: anti-conscription, 63, 65–6; anti-recruitment, 34, 38, 49, 51, 53–4; Bedfordshire Regiment, 39; 6th Connaught Rangers, 40; Highland Light Infantry, 36; recruitment, 33–5, 37–8, 46, 49, 52; Protestant military, 35; Royal Irish Fusiliers, 15, 24, 36, 40; Royal Scots, 36, 40; Royal Scottish Fusiliers, 36; troops, 22, 32, 54, 101; evacuation of, 101
British Empire, 8, 10, 14, 16, 19, 31, 33, 36, 38, 60–1, 78, 112, 127
Brooke, Basil, 104
Broomfield, 40, 77
Brown, L.T., 110; Matt, 115
Browne, Bernard J., 52–3; Margaret, 123
Brownlow, earl of, 39; estate, 33, 68; Mrs, 19, 33
Burke, Brian, 50; John Jr, 39; John Sr, 39; Private Joseph, 39
Burns, Revd Robert, 98
Byrne, Captain Francis, 107–8

Campbell, J.H., 44; T.J., 71; Thomas, 51
Carna, 81
Carnagh railway station, 87
Carragher, Thomas (of Annyalla), 125, 129; Tom (of Dongahmoyne), 70–1, 106, 121, 129
Carrickatee, 70, 99
Carrickmacross, 6, 9–10, 12, 17, 19, 27, 31, 35, 40–1, 43, 45–56, 58–9, 61, 63–4, 66, 68, 70, 72, 74, 76, 79, 82, 85–7, 90, 95, 99, 101–2, 104, 106–7, 128; board of poor law guardians, 43, 55, 59, 72; Golf Club, 50; Harriers Club, 10; Lawn Tennis Club, 10
Carroll, Kate, 91–2
Carson, Sir Edward, 20–1, 29–30, 34, 57, 60–1, 98; James, 86

Casey, James, 40
Cassel, Sir Ernest, 16, 113
Cassidy, Mrs Phil, 118
Castleblayney, 6, 14, 17, 20–1, 33, 40–1, 61, 63, 82, 84–7, 94, 116, 125; board of poor law guardians, 40
Castleshane, 16, 37, 111, 116, 118–22
Cavan, county, 1, 6, 21, 29, 35, 61, 60, 78, 82, 87, 106; UU, 97–9; town, 123 (*see* elections)
Ceannt, Áine, 77
Celtic People, 26
Chamberlain, Austen, 104
Childers, Erskine, 30
Christian Brothers, 77, 123
Church of Ireland, 1–2, 23, 61, 94
Churchill, Winston (MP), 97, 103–4
Civil War, 69, 77, 80, 101–10, 118, 125, 128, 130–1
Clare, county, 38, 58, 78
Clarke, Kathleen, 77; Thomas, 67; William, 39
Clones, 3, 6, 10, 15–17, 21, 23, 28, 35, 39–40, 61–4, 67–9, 73, 76, 79, 81, 87, 91–2, 94–5, 103–9, 123–5; Golf Club, 10, 23
Clontibret, 21, 67, 118–19
Coas, 53, 79
Cobh, Co. Cork, 130
Coleman, John, 75
Collins–Craig pact, 105
Collins, Michael, 63–4, 77, 80, 85, 99, 100–6, 108, 131
Comerford, R.V., 10
congestion (uneconomic farms), 8, 11, 43, 113, 121
Conlon, Thomas, 52–3
Connolly, James, 43–4, 53, 56, 81, 127
Conservative Party, 5, 30, 104
Coolfore, 99
Coote, William (MP), 104
Cootehill, Co. Cavan, 6, 64, 78, 84
Corbrack House, 39
Corcaghan, 84, 86, 94
Corduff, 11, 13, 50, 74, 79
Corravaccan, 34, 38

Corrigan, Paddy, 77, 90, 99, 106
Corvoy, 90
Cosgrave, W.T., 127
Coyle, Fr Eugene, 66, 67, 77, 86, 102
Craig, James, 24, 61, 97, 103–5.
Craigavon, 18
Crawford, Colonel F.H., 24
Crawfords, merchants, Monaghan town, 68
cricket, 13
Croke Park, 85
Crozier, T.F., 120–1
Cullen, Kevin, 36
cultural nationalism, 13
Cumann na mBan, 53, 64, 77, 79, 81
Cumann na nGaedheal, 109, 121, 126–7
Curragh, 29, 79; Mutiny, 29, 47
Curzon, Lord, 65

Dáil Éireann, 72, 74–5, 81, 94–6, 99, 102, 127–8; loan, 74
Daly, Michael, 27, 86–7, 101; Tom, 128; William, 85–6, 101
Dartrey, Castle, 3, 10, 15–16, 17, 21, 24–7, 39, 116–17; countess of, 3, 25, 37, 116–17; earl of, 17, 21, 27, 37, 111, 117
Davagh, 89
Davis, Henry, 39
Dawson, Richard (earl of Dartrey), 21, 27, 37, 111
de Búrca, Proinnsias (sometimes Frank Burke), 49
de Valera, Éamon, 64–5, 131
Defence of the Realm Act (DORA), 56, 66
Department of Defence, 77, 130
Derry, 20, 80, 94, 103; gaol, 103
Derrykerrib, 79
Devlin, Joseph, 29, 88; Joe Devlinities, 87
Dillon, James, 128; John, 11, 128
Dolan, Anne, 90
Donagh, 17, 67
Donaghadee, 24
Donaghmoyne, 11, 14, 106, 121, 129; House, 121

Donegal, 21, 35, 60–1, 67, 97
Donnelly, Eugene, 46–7, 51–2, 54, 59; Patrick, 69, 79
Dromore, 103
Drum, 21, 35, 70, 83–4, 92, 98, 133
Drumcatton, 67
Drumgara, 84
Dublin, 18–20, 25, 27, 29–31, 39, 43, 45, 47, 50, 54–6, 58, 63, 65, 68, 85–6, 89, 95, 110, 112, 123, 127, 130–2; Castle, 30, 47, 89
Duffy, Charlie, 48; Margaret, 91; Peter, 67; Sergeant John, 46–7
Duffy's Cross, 91
Dundalk Democrat, 4–6, 10, 12–14, 20, 24, 28, 30, 32, 35, 40, 42, 44, 48, 51, 54, 56, 58, 69–70, 72, 75, 85, 89–90, 93, 98, 108, 111, 116
Dundalk, Co. Louth, 41, 50, 106–8, 111, 119, 123, 127; jail, 107, 119
Dunmadigan, 89
Dunn, Charles, 40; Private James, 39; William, 39
Dunsterville, J.W.E, 47

Eakin, Isabella, 17
Easter Rising 1916 (also insurrection and Dublin Rising, 1916 rebellion), 15, 29, 32, 39–41, 43, 45, 47, 49–51, 53–9, 61–2, 66–7, 70–3, 77, 87, 112, 123, 128, 133; centenary celebration, 133; golden jubilee, 128; Proclamation, 55–7, 126
elections: Monaghan by-election 1883, 3, 19; North Monaghan by-election 1907, 9; East Cavan by-election 1918, 63, 69–72, 87, 89; general election 1880, 2–3; general election 1885, 3; general election 1886, 6; general election 1892, 6; general election 1895, 6; general election 1910, 13, 17, 23, 41, 64, 69, 128; general election 1918, 23; general election 1921, 76, 97, 109; general election 1922, 102, 108–9; general election 1923, 109; general election 1925, 110, 127; local

government 1899, 6; local government 1920, 73–5
Elphinstone, John, 17
Ematris, 17 (*see* Irish Volunteers)
Emerson, Charles, 78–80, 126
emigration, 67
Emyvale, 82, 89
England, 11, 28, 33, 44; at war, 54–5, 57; army of, 86; troops of, 101; re-location to, 112, 122; landlords of, 116; landowners of, 120
Enniskillen, Co. Fermanagh, 103–4, 123
Ensor, E.N., 38
Essexford, 1, 128
Europe, 10, 28, 31–2, 34, war in, 45–6; 54, 57–8, 72; post-war, 92; aristocracy in, 132
ex-soldier(s), 85, 90–1

famine, 1–4, 6, 67, 111, 117
Farmers Party, 109
Farney, 1, 13–14, 30, 33, 40, 46, 49, 59, 64, 91
Farnham, Lord, 98
Farrell, Mel, 126
Feeha, 81
Feely, Patrick, 61
Fenians, 44–5, 49–50, 80; fenianism, 3
Fennell, Alexander, 47, 59
Fermanagh, county, 1, 19, 21, 62, 67, 73, 76, 93, 99, 104–5, 108, 110, 132; Wattlebridge, 103–4
Fianna Fáil, 121, 128
Findlater, William, 2
Fine Gael, 128, 130, 133
Finnegan, Edward, 40; Rose, 81
First World War: Compulsory Tillage Order during, 69; effects of, 41; end of, 72, 116; fatalities, 107; Loos, 40; Military Service Act, 65; outbreak of, 28, 111–12; toll on gentry, 111–12; veteran, 52, 86; shell shock, 40; watershed in Irish history, 32–3;
Fitzgerald, Brigid, 81
FitzGerald, Desmond, 130
Fitzpatrick, David, 38

Fitzpatrick, John James, 104
Fitzpatrick, Matt, 73, 81, 104, 106, 124
Fitzsimons, Jimmy, 106
Flanders, 66, 76
Fleming, William, 84
Franchise and Retribution Acts, 1884–5, 5
French, J.D.P. (Lord Lieutenant), 35
Frongoch, 63

Gaelic Athletic Association (GAA), 13–15, 26–7, 40, 45, 62–4, 76–8, 98, 103, 105, 123–4, 131; Monaghan County Board, 62; Protestants, 13–14; Ulster Council of, 27, 62, 64
Gaelic League, 13–15, 26, 62, 67, 74, 98; Protestants, 14
Gaelic revival, 77
Galbraith, William, 17
Gallipoli, 39, 48, 66, 76
Galway, 57, 86
Garda Síochána, 109, 120, 126, 131
Geddes, Poppy, 118
gentry, 2, 9–10, 15, 21–4, 33–4, 36–7, 111–12, 117–18, 121–2, 129, 132
German Plot, 63, 71
Germany, 31–2, 40, 54
Gibbs, Joseph, 90
Gillanders, Thomas, 79, 107
Gillespie, John, 14
Givan, John, 2
Given, T.F., 39
Glaslough, 1, 3, 10, 16, 21–2, 24–5, 36, 39, 61, 67, 96, 104–5, 112–13, 122
Glenburne House, 116
Glendon, Edward, 123
Glentoran FC, 105
Gola House, 37, 113–15
Gosselin, Sir Nicholas, 112
Government of Ireland (Amendment) Bill, 1914, 30
Government of Ireland Act, 1920, 97
Grangemockler, Co. Tipperary, 62, 85, 123
Gray, John, 6
Greacon, Robert, 10, 91

Index

Great Northern Railway (GNR), 62, 123–4, 126
Greenan's Cross, 62, 67
Greenmount, 25
Griffith, Arthur, 26, 49, 63–4, 69

Habsburg, 32
Hall, Donal, 36; Dr J.C., 60
Hanna, Thomas, 17
Healy, Timothy, 3, 19
Henchy, M.T., 121
Hilton Park, 6, 16, 21, 25, 37, 76, 113, 122
Hoey, P.V., 46, 70, 78
Hogan, Betty, 130; Dan, 62, 64, 70, 73, 76, 78, 80–2, 85, 90, 92, 94, 99, 101, 103–8, 123–6, 128, 130–1; Michael, 85; Patrick, 128; Thomas, 123
home rule, 3–5, 7–10, 13–15, 17–33, 40, 45–50, 54, 56, 58–61, 65, 66, 72, 97, 111–12, 115, 127–9, 131; second bill, 5, 14–15; third bill, 9, 18, 20–1, 28–30, 45, 47, 50, 60; crises (1885), 18 (1893), 14–15, 18 (1912), 4, 8–9, 13, 17–18, 20, 47, 111, 115
Hope Castle, 10, 25, 85; estate, 17
House of Lords: ix, 17–18, 20–1, 30, 65; veto, 17–18, 20
Howell, J.G., 17
Howth, gun-running, 30
Hughes, Private Thomas, 40–1
Hunter, Hugh, 14

illicit distillation, 80
Inniskeen, 4, 9, 13, 40–1, 47–51, 54, 59, 67–8, 70, 74–5, 96, 106, 127
Irish Boundary Commission, 14, 103
Irish Citizen Army, 43, 45, 53, 112
Irish Convention 1917–18, 61
Irish Farmers' Union, 79
Irish Free State (IFS), 102–4, 106, 109, 122, 127–8, 131; Government, 128; Protestants, 132; Provisional government, 99, 104, 108; Senate, 127
Irish Grants Committee, 52, 131

Irish Land Commission, 47, 68, 115, 121, 129
Irish National Teachers' Organisation, 43
Irish National Volunteers (INV), 9, 33–4, 41
Irish Parliamentary Party (IPP), 8, 27, 30, 47, 57–8, 61, 66–7, 69, 71–2, 87; Irish Party, 59, 65, 69–70
Irish Republic, 45, 59, 74, 97, 129
Irish Republican Army (IRA), 27, 48, 59, 71, 73, 75–99, 101, 103–8, 112–13, 115–16, 121, 123–6, 128–9, 131–2; Active Service Unit (ASU), 103, 119, Slieve Beagh, 79; anti-Treaty, 103; Monaghan brigade, 73; 1st brigade, 76; 2nd brigade, fatalities, 87; 4th Northern division, 107; 5th Northern division, 76, 99, 104, 107, 124; informer (spies), 48, 89, 90–2, 131; safe houses, 80–1, 106; veterans 78, 101, 126
Irish Republican Brotherhood (IRB), 45, 50, 53, 63, 67; military council, 53
Irish Socialist Republican Party, 43
Irish Transport and General Workers' Union (ITGWU), 43, 68
Irish Volunteer (IV), 26–8, 30, 33–4, 38, 45–7, 49, 51–3, 63, 65, 67, 77; Ematris company, 27, 34
Irish Volunteer Dependents Fund, 77

Jackson, Alvin, 12, 59, 61, 101, 132; H.W., 6; Noble, 35; Thomas, 35

Kavanagh, Patrick, 41, 70, 129
Keenan, Laurence, 47–8
Keenogue, 47–8, 58
Kelly, Edward (Eddie), 9–10, 13, 28, 43, 55, 58–9, 65, 69, 75, 127–8; Michael, 84, 94
Kennedy, Private James, 39
Kentchurch Court, Wales, 111, 118
Kerley, P.J., 47
Kerr, Henry, 90

Killanny, 5, 9, 12–13, 42, 50, 68–9, 74, 79, 81, 107
Killevan, 12, 94
Killybressal, 83
Killybrone, 71
Killygoan, 39
Kiltybegs, 115
Kingscourt, Co. Cavan, 106
Knight, Michael E., 10, 17–18, 23, 25, 35, 37, 39, 61, 71, 75–6, 98, 109–10, 125
Knockatallan, 79

Lacey, Dinny, 123
Land League, 3, 7, 14, 26, 46, 115
land question (*see also* agrarianism), 11, 68–9, 78, 115, 126; intimidation, 20, 46, 48, 53, 70, 74, 95; Land Act, 1903 (Wyndham), 11, 16, 42, 111, 114, 122 (1923), 69, 121; land hunger, 38; landlords, 1–3, 7, 16, 24–5, 33, 47, 54, 116, 119, 121; purchased holdings, 8, 23, 47, 80, 111, 113, 114; redistribution of land, 11, 69, 78, 114, 121, 129; tenants, 2, 68, 111, 114, 116 (evicted), 9; unpurchased estates/landholdings, 9, 68, 116; untenanted lands, 69, 119, 121, 122
Land War, 1, 3, 4, 6–7, 16, 47, 55, 57, 111, 123
Lansdowne, Lord, 60
Laragh, 62, 77
Lardner, James C.R. (MP), 9–10, 17, 27, 54, 64
Larkin, James (Jim), 12, 43
Larmer, Patrick, 87–90
Larne, Co. Antrim, 24–5, 27, 30
Latton, 11, 99
Laverty, Charles, 33, 41, 116, 121, 128
Leitrim, 12
Lennon, Thomas, 51
Leslie, Anita, 113; Lady Constance, 16; F.K., 37; family, 1, 3, 15–16, 112; H.C.E., 115; Henry, 116; Colonel John, 21, 37; Sir John, 6, 16, 24, 36, 38, 111–12; Leonie, 25, 112, 121; Norman, 36–7, 112; Robert, 6;

Seymour, 112; Sir Shane, 16, 36, 61, 65, 121
Lewis, Matthew, 107
Lisdoonan, 77
Lisnaskea, 103
Livingstone, Peadar, 10, 14, 106
Lloyd George, David, 29, 59–61
Local Government (Ireland) Act (1898), 6
lockout 1913, 43
Logue, Cardinal Michael, 12, 29, 42, 65
Londonderry, Lady, 60
Long, Patrick, 62
Longford, 12
Lough Bawn House, 99, 125
Lough Egish, 53, 99
Lough Fea, 10, 95, 122
Loughran, Willie, 63
Louis de Montfort, 104
Louth, 1, 35–6, 40, 70, 111
loyalism, 21, 84–56, 108, 119; Loyal Orange Lodge (LOL), 35
Lucas Scudamore, Colonel Edward, 7, 16, 37–8, 111, 116–19, 121–2; Gill, 118; Jack, 116–18, 120–1; Sybil, 116–21
Lucas, Edward, 6, 117
Lusitania, 40
Lynch, Liam, 103

McAnallen, Dónal, 76, 103, 108
McArdle, Hugh, 88
McCabe, Michael, 48; P.J., 59
McCaldin's bakery, Monaghan town, 95, 96
McCartan, Patrick, 69
McCarville, Joe, 80–1; Patrick, 79, 102, 107–9, 126
McCaul, Dr Bernard, 10, 46
McCluskey, Patrick, 83
McDonnell, Pat, 79
McEneaney, Michael, 87; Thomas, 87
MacEntee, Seán, 64, 70–1, 74, 76, 95, 102, 123
McGahey, John, 27, 53, 82–4, 89–90, 93, 96, 132

Index

McGahon, Thomas, 4, 20, 24, 32–3, 48, 54, 57–8, 67, 71, 73, 75, 78, 89, 93, 111, 126,
McGarry, Fearghal, 11, 63, 82, 92, 94, 125–7
McGee, Thomas, 76
McGimpsey, Christopher, 1, 2
McGinn, Mary, 43
McGrane, Eileen, 102
McGrory, Patrick, 89
McHugh, Thomas, 108
McKean, John, 64, 68
McKearney, Private Thomas, 40
McKenna, Felix, 67; Joseph, 33, 89; Patrick (bishop of Clogher), 12, 14, 29, 62, 65, 67, 72, 74, 80, 86, 95, 99, 107, 129; Dr Peter, 10, 46; Seamus, 79
McKeown, Canon Patrick, 12, 107
MacMahon, Brian, 77, 81, 108, 121, 128, 130; Peadar, 53, 77, 130; Sorcha, 53, 77
McMahon, Owen, 105
McNamee, Fr James, 95
MacNeill, Eoin, 27, 53
McNello, Dan, 48, 70
McPhillips, Fr James, 66–7, 77, 84; Francis, 87–90; Patrick, 78
MacSwiney, Terence, 89
McWilliam, Herbert, 23
Madden, family, 3, 6, 15–17, 21, 23–6, 34, 37, 75–6, 86, 98, 111–13, 122; Gerald, 21–3, 37, 111; Colonel J.C.W., 6, 21, 23–5, 75, 76, 86, 98, 111–13; John, 16
Magee, Phil, 75
Magheracloone, 5, 23, 28, 33, 40, 50
Magheross, 40
Maguire, Fr Bernard, 33, 49, 51–2, 66–8, 74, 115; Fr Thomas, 28, 88
Malone, Michael, 86
Markievicz, Constance, 112
Marron, Bernard, 84; James, 77; Fr Laurence, 101, 130–1; Phillip, 86–7
Martin, Thomas, 43; William, 23, 60, 109, 116

Meath, 1, 12, 55, 86
Meegan, James, 47–8
Meenan, Fr John, 31, 50
Mellows, Liam, 57
Methodists, 1, 39
Mills, Jim, 133
Monaghan, asylum, 40, 96; County Council, 1, 3, 6, 9, 11, 23, 27, 37, 55, 60, 62, 65, 69, 75, 86, 94, 101, 118, 127–8; Soldiers and Sailors Help Society, 37; town, 3, 4, 6, 13, 15–17, 21, 25, 27, 34–5, 39, 48–9, 54, 68, 71, 77, 84, 95–7, 105–6, 116; War Pensions Committee, 117
Monanton, 86
Montgomery, Hugh de Fellenberg, 60
Morgan, George, 117, 119
Morris, Henry, 14
Mount Louise, 22
Mountjoy Prison, 65, 125
Moutray, Anketell, 104, 112
Muckno, 17, 49
Mulcahy, Richard, 92, 99, 131
Mulhern, Edward (bishop of Dromore), 65
Mullan, Alice, 64, 81; William, 35
Mulligan, James, 79, 81; Fr Phillip, 114
Murray-Kers, 1, 3, 25, 37, 117
Murray, John, 114

National army, 77, 103, 106–8, 119, 126
National Insurance Act, 1911, 12
National League, 46
nationalism, 6, 13, 24, 26, 30, 36, 77, 90, 113
nationalist, 3–14, 16–21, 23–32, 34, 36–38, 40–1, 44–6, 50–2, 54–8, 61, 64–6, 69, 71, 74–5, 77, 80, 84, 88, 90, 92–7, 99, 103–5, 108, 110–13, 117, 123, 126, 128
Newbliss, 1, 3, 13, 15, 21, 25, 33, 35, 39, 43, 62–4, 69, 81, 91, 97, 117
Newtownards, 104
Newtownbutler, 103–5, 108
Nixon, Samuel, 75
Nolan, Mary, 64

North Monaghan Unionist Association (NMUA), 60, 109, 113
Northern Ireland, 95, 97, 99, 103–6, 108, 122

O'Brien, William, 11
Ó Ciaráin, Fr Lorcan, 14, 26–7, 34, 38, 49, 67, 70
O'Connell, J.J. 'Ginger', 26
O'Connor, Revd Daniel, 11, 54, 66
O'Curry, Eugene, 26
O'Daly, Fr James, 67, 72, 77; P.J., 79, 106, 126
O'Donovan, John, 26
O'Donovan Rossa, Jeremiah, 50
O'Duffy, Frank, 77, 80, 126; Owen, 13–15, 27, 61–4, 67, 70, 73–82, 87–8, 90–4, 96, 99–103, 105–9, 115, 123–7, 130–1
O'Growney, Fr Eugene, 26
O'Hanlon, J.F., 69
O'Hegarty, P.S., 97, 125
O'Higgins, Kevin, 126, 128
O'Leary, John, 107
O'Malley, Ernie, 10, 80, 106
O'Rahilly, Michael ('The O'Rahilly'), 52
O'Reilly, Peter, 83
O'Rourke & Co., Dundalk, 127
O'Rourke Bros (Millers), Inniskeen, 127
O'Rourke, Bernard, 9–10, 13, 47–52, 58–9, 65, 69–70, 74–6, 101–2, 106, 127; Clare, 58
O'Rourke, Coniffe & Co., Dublin, 127
O'Toole, J.F., 51; Luke, 63
Orange Hall, 20, 25, 35; Braddox, 95; Glaslough, 105; Lough Fea, 95; Madden and Johnston Memorial, 34
Orange Order, 3, 12, 15; band, 20; lodges: Grand Orange Lodge (County Monaghan), 10, 15, 19, 21, 23, 29, 35, 56, 65, 109, 112
orangeism, 62, 109, 113; 12 July celebrations, 15, 20, 25, 66, 84, 98, 109, 133

Pain, General Hacket, 24
Parliament Act, 1911, 18, 20

Parnell, Charles Stewart, 8, 45
partition, 21, 29–31, 35, 40, 47, 49, 59–61, 72, 97, 102, 108, 129
Pašeta, Senia, 47
Pattons, merchants, Monaghan town, 68
patriotism, 37, 44, 59, 78, 124
Pearse, Patrick, 28, 49–51, 53, 71, 127
Pennant, Charles, 37
Perkins, Constable Walter, 86
Petrie, George, 26
Pettigo, Co. Donegal, 67
Phelan, Edward, 45–7
Poplar Vale, 21–2, 25
Presbyterian, 1–3, 10, 15, 70, 86, 88, 110, 120, 129; First Monaghan Church, 95; clergy, 23
Protestant Defence Association, County Monaghan, 84
Purdue, Olwen, 122

Quigley, James, 55
Quinn, John, 46–7, 51–2, 54, 59

Raeburn, Emily, 17
Ranch War, 11
Rebellion, 1641, 1; 1798, 1, 44, 54; 1848, 54; 1867, 54
Redmond, John, 8–9, 11, 20, 29–30, 32–4, 40, 43–5, 47, 49, 55, 58–9, 88; Redmondite, 4, 33, 41, 43, 47, 51, 69, 72, 126–7
Regan, John, 126
Representation of the People Act, 1918, 70
Richardson, Colonel, 37; Major E.J., 7, 21, 37
Rockcorry, 3, 14, 16, 26–7, 34–5, 38–9, 53, 61, 68, 70, 82, 86, 89, 91
Roden, Lord, 111
Roe, Peter, 59
Rokeby Hall, 111
Roslea, Co. Fermanagh, 19, 73, 91, 93–4, 103–4, 124
Ross, George, 23; James, 46; Private Joseph, 46
Rossmore, 3, 10

Rossmore, Lord, 3, 6–7, 15–16, 111
Royal Irish Constabulary (RIC), 14–15, 24, 28, 47, 49, 51, 55, 58, 68, 72, 80–2, 92–3, 102; killed; 87; police, 33–6, 46–9, 58, 64, 66, 69, 71–2, 79, 81–2, 84–90, 92–3, 95, 99, 101, 105, 109, 112, 114–15; Auxiliaries, 85–7; Black and Tans (*see* RIC), 85–7, 89, 102
Rushe, Denis Carolan, 6, 9, 15, 23, 27, 64–5, 94–5, 111

Saunderson, Major Somerset, 60
Scotch Corner, 1
Scotshouse, 1, 26, 49
sectarianism, 2–4, 6–7, 11, 17, 20–2, 28, 31, 53, 57, 91–9, 104, 110, 119, 123–4; anti-Treaty, 119; casualties, 94; killings, 93; strife, 99; tensions, 95, 97, 119
Selborne, Lord, 60
Shannon, G.H., 47
Shanroe, 21
Shantonagh House, 115
Sheehy Skeffington, Hannah, 74
Shercock, Co. Cavan, 87
Sherry, Andrew, 76; Eugene, 83
Shevlin, Brian, 10; Jack, 10; James, 43, 74, 78; Joe, 79
Shirley, 10–1, 68, 122
Sinn Féin (SF), 13–14, 26, 33–4, 38, 49, 52–4, 56, 58–72, 73–7, 80, 85–9, 94–7, 101, 104, 108, 114–15, 118, 123, 125, 127–9; anti-Treaty, 108; clubs, 64, 66, 74; comhairle ceanntair: north Monaghan, 66, 85; south Monaghan, 101; police, 71
1641 rebellion, 1
Smith, Matt, 124
Smithboro, 7–8, 21, 26, 82, 84, 94, 108
Snowdon, Lord, 121
socialism: *see* socialist, 12, 112
socialists, 3, 12, 17, 43–4, 52, 55, 68, 87, 112, 129; revolutionaries, 87, 129
Solemn League Women's Declaration, 1912, 19–20, 132
Soloheadbeg, Co. Tipperary, 72
Somerville, John, 86

Somme, battle of, 86
Sproule, Alex, 35
St Enda's School, Rathfarnham, 50
St Louis Convent, Carrickmacross, 50
St Macartan's College (seminary), 26, 49, 77
St Patrick's College Maynooth (Maynooth seminary), 8, 26, 49, 67
Stack, Revd C.M., 23
Steenson, Samuel, 38
Stratton, Robert, 17
Swann, William, 29, 44

Tanderageebrock, 35
Tarry Flynn (1948), 129
Tennison, William, 6, 99, 125
Thompson, James, 42
Threemilehouse, 79
Thurles, Co. Tipperary, 86
Tipperary, county, 62, 72, 85–6, 123–4
Toal, James, 7; Thomas, 3, 7–11, 15, 17, 23, 26–7, 55, 58, 61–2, 64–5, 72, 75, 86, 94–5, 101, 110, 127
Totten, Robert, 24
Tottenham, H.I., 6
Treacy, Seán, 123
Treanor, Arthur, 69, 89
Tullyvaragh, 90
Tummons, Francis, 50, 54, 62, 79, 93
Ture, 81
Turley, John, 71
Turner, Victor, 133
Tyacke, Ernest Phillip (CI), 15, 20–1, 23–4, 26, 28–9, 31, 33–4, 37–8, 42–3, 49, 63–4, 66, 68–9, 73, 82, 90–1, 95, 99
Tydavnet, 63, 66, 82, 84, 91, 94
Tyholland, 99
Tyrone, 1, 21, 23, 35, 67, 74, 76, 92, 94, 97, 100, 103–5, 110; Caledon, 104–5

Ulster Day, 19, 21
Ulster Division, 34, 37, 39
Ulster Solemn League and Covenant, 18–21, 23, 29–30, 33–4, 57, 60, 66, 97–8, 132–3

Ulster Special Constabulary (USC), 85, 91–4, 102–5, 108
Ulster Unionist Council (UUC), 18, 30, 60–1, 97–9, 104
Ulster Volunteer Force (UVF), 21–8, 34–5, 37–8, 47, 50, 76, 82, 85, 97, 112–13, 125; indemnity fund, 25; nursing corps, 25
Ulster, 1–3, 13, 18–21, 24–5, 27–31, 32, 34–5, 37–40, 43, 46–7, 50, 57, 60, 62, 64, 66, 72–4, 76, 85, 95, 97–8, 103–4, 107, 127, 132–3
unionism, 3, 5–6, 8, 10, 15, 17–22, 25–9, 31, 33, 35–8, 40–1, 44, 46–7, 50, 55–7, 60–1, 64–6, 68, 70–3, 75, 82, 84–5, 92–9, 104–5, 107, 109–10, 113, 116, 125, 129, 132; Carsonites, 27–8; Unionist club, 15, 21, 28
United Irish League (UIL), 8–9, 11, 13, 15, 25, 27–8, 33, 47–8, 51, 64, 67, 74, 78, 89, 113
United Irishmen, 26, 80
Urban District Council (UDC): Monaghan, 40
Vogan, James, 24, 113

Wallace, Jack, 39; Lance-Corporal Mark, 39

War of Independence, 41, 57, 70, 72–3, 76–7, 79, 82, 84, 86–7, 90, 92, 95, 99, 101–2, 121, 124–5, 127
Ward, Dr Conn, 27, 76, 79, 85, 98, 106, 126, 130
Warterloo, 35
Watson, Revd T.S., 40
Westenra, Peter, 6
Westmeath, county., 12
Wheatley, Michael, 12
Wheeler, Edith, 60
Whelan, Patrick, 13, 15, 27, 33, 62, 67
Whinnery, Gibson, 119
Willis, T.H., 40
Wilson, J.M., 38–9; Revd W.M., 39; Sir Henry, 38
Wilson, Woodrow (president of US), 74
Women's Unionist Association (affiliated with Women's Unionist Council), 25
Woodenbridge, Co. Wicklow, 33
Woods, Brigid, 79; Cassie, 79; John, 79; Mary, 79; Michael, 79; Patrick, 79; Peter, 79, 85, 101
Wright, John, 83
Wyndham, Lady Edith, 116
Wyse-Power, Mrs, 74

Ypres, battle of, 48